# PHILOSOPHICAL UNDERSTANDING

# AND RELIGIOUS TRUTH

# PHILOSOPHICAL
# UNDERSTANDING
# AND
# RELIGIOUS TRUTH

ERICH FRANK

**OXFORD UNIVERSITY PRESS**
LONDON    NEW YORK    TORONTO

# THE MARY FLEXNER LECTURES

SINCE 1931 THE LECTURES HAVE BEEN PUBLISHED AS THE BRYN MAWR
SERIES BY THE OXFORD UNIVERSITY PRESS

| | | |
|---|---|---|
| 1929 | JAMES H. BREASTED | Lectures embodied in *The Dawn of Conscience,* published 1933 |
| 1930 | ALFRED NORTH WHITEHEAD | Lectures included as Chapters 1, 2, 3, 7, and 8 in *Adventures of Ideas,* published 1933 |
| 1931 | PAUL HAZARD | *Quatre Etudes: Baudelaire; Romantiques; Sur un Cycle poétique; L'Homme de sentiment,* published 1940 |
| 1932 | KIRSOPP LAKE | *Paul, his Heritage and Legacy,* published 1934 |
| 1933 | RALPH VAUGHAN WILLIAMS | *National Music,* published 1934 |
| 1935 | I. A. RICHARDS | *The Philosophy of Rhetoric,* published 1936 |
| 1937 | ERWIN PANOFSKY | *Studies in Iconology,* published 1939 |
| 1943 | ERICH FRANK | *Philosophical Understanding and Religious Truth,* published 1945 |

# THE MARY FLEXNER LECTURESHIP

*The Mary Flexner Lectureship was established February 17, 1928, at Bryn Mawr College, by Bernard Flexner, in honour of his sister, Mary Flexner, a graduate of the College. An adequate endowment was provided by the gift, the income to be used annually or at longer intervals at the discretion of the Directors of the College as an honorarium to be given to an American or foreign scholar, highly distinguished in the field of the 'Humanities,' using the term 'Humanities' in its broadest connotation. The lecturers have taken up residence at Bryn Mawr for a six weeks' period and besides delivering the series of public lectures have taught graduate and undergraduate students. The object of the Mary Flexner Lectureship is to bring to the College scholars of distinction, who will be a stimulus to the faculty and students, and who will contribute to the maintenance of those ideals and standards of scholarship which will bring increasing honour to the College. The gift provides that the Mary Flexner Lectures shall be published. The present volume is the eighth in the series to be published.*

# Preface

THIS BOOK, though concerned with the problem of religion, is a philosophical study. It addresses itself to the philosophical understanding rather than to religious sentiment. The only faith that a present-day philosopher may presuppose in his readers is faith in a truth arrived at through reason and rational arguments. This truth, however, in the eyes of modern man is opposed to religion; in fact it seems to have blocked the road to the understanding of religion. In this situation, only reason can remove the obstacles which it has thrown in its own way, thus clearing the path to religious truth. For the medieval thinker, philosophy meant 'Faith Seeking Understanding'; for the modern, on the contrary, it is Understanding that finds itself in search of a faith. By scrutinizing objectively its own presuppositions, philosophy once more may hope to find access to religious truth.

The invitation to give The Mary Flexner Lectures at Bryn Mawr in 1943 provided me with a welcome opportunity to formulate my thoughts on the relations between philosophy and religion in our time. The response of the faculty and the student body encouraged me in my hope that a discussion of this problem might contribute toward a clarification of our present difficulties.

In revising the lectures for publication I have made a number of changes primarily for the sake of achieving unity and a more tightly knit arrangement. Certain problems which in the spoken lectures could be touched upon only in a rather general way have been dealt with more fully in a series of notes in which I have elaborated the philosophical arguments and given evidence for the historical foundation of my ideas. (See Comment on the Notes, p. ix.)

I cannot adequately express my indebtedness to Professor and Mrs. Ludwig Edelstein. Mrs. Edelstein translated my manuscript from the German with the greatest care; and she and Professor Edelstein gave most generously of their time and advice, both in regard to the form and matter of the book.

I am grateful to Mrs. Philip Haring for her painstaking work on the manuscript. Her suggestions have enabled me to eliminate many obscurities. I have greatly profited from the acute and sensitive comments of my friend Mrs. James H. Woods. I wish to thank also Dr. Howard E. Roman and Miss Margaret Nicholson for their help in smoothing out a number of uneven passages in the text. Professor Arthur C. Sprague, Professor and Mrs. Paul Weiss, and Dr. Leo Roberts have kindly helped me at various points.

E. F.

*Cambridge, Massachusetts*
*September* 1944

# Contents

# Comment on the Notes

THE NOTES follow the chapters to which they belong. The following notes deal with special and integral topics in detail:

Other topics dealt with in the notes are listed under the entry 'Notes' in the General Index.

The translations of Greek and Latin authors are generally based on the Loeb Classical Library. In addition, I consulted B. Jowett's and F. M. Cornford's translations of Plato, *The Works of Aristotle,* translated under the editorship of W. D. Ross, Oxford, 1927 ff., and the *Works of Aurelius Augustine,* translated by Rev. M. Dods, Edinburgh, 1872 ff., together with the translations in the *Nicene and Post-Nicene Fathers,* edited by P. Schaff, Buffalo, 1887 ff.

The following translations and editions were also used:

St. Anselm, *Proslogium, Monologium,* etc., transl. by S. N. Deane, Chicago-London, 1903.

St. Thomas Aquinas, *The Summa Theologica,* transl. by the Fathers of the English Dominican Province, vol. 1 ff., London, 1921 ff.

St. Thomas Aquinas, *The Summa contra Gentiles,* transl. by the English Dominican Fathers, vol. 1 ff., London, 1923 ff.

Descartes, *The Meditations,* transl. by J. Veitch, Chicago, 1903.

Blaise Pascal, *Pensées,* publiés par M. Léon Brunschvicg, Paris, 1923.

—— *Pensées,* transl. by W. F. Trotter, London, 1940.

Hobbes, *Works,* collected and edited by Sir W. Molesworth, London, 1839 ff.

Shaftesbury, *Characteristics,* ed. by J. M. Robertson, New York, 1900.

Hume, *A Treatise of Human Nature,* ed. by T. H. Green and T. H. Grose, London, 1898.

Kant, *Critique of Pure Reason,* transl. by Norman Kemp Smith, London, 1929.

— *Critique of Practical Reason,* transl. by T. K. Abbot, London, 1889.

— *Kritik of Judgment,* transl. by J. H. Bernard, London, 1889.

— *Fundamental Principles of the Metaphysics of Ethics,* transl. by T. K. Abbot, London, 1926.

Hegel, *The Science of Logic,* transl. by W. H. Johnston and G. Struther, New York, 1929.

— *The Logic of Hegel,* transl. from the *Encyclopaedia* by W. Wallace, Oxford, 1892.

— *Philosophy of History,* transl. by T. Sibree, New York, 1899.

— *Philosophy of Religion,* transl. by E. B. Speirs and J. B. Sanderson, vols. I-III, London, 1895.

— *Philosophy of Fine Art,* transl. by F. P. B. Osmaston, vols. I-III, London, 1920.

— *Philosophy of Right,* transl. by S. W. Dyde, London, 1896.

Kierkegaard, *Either-Or,* vol. I, transl. by D. F. Swenson and L. M. Swenson; vol. II, by W. Lowrie, Princeton, 1944.

— *Philosophical Fragments,* transl. by D. F. Swenson, Princeton, 1936.

— *The Journals,* transl. by A. Dru, London, 1938.

Schopenhauer, *World as Will and Idea,* transl. by R. B. Haldane and J. Kemp, vols. I-III, London, 1886.

# PHILOSOPHICAL UNDERSTANDING
# AND RELIGIOUS TRUTH

# I. The Nature of Man

THE conflict between religion and philosophy is as old as philosophy itself. Even Plato speaks of it as dating back to times long past.[1] In our day this struggle has reached an intensity hardly known in any former period of history. In fact, one may well ask if, considering the discoveries of modern science and the conditions of modern life, the philosopher can still attribute any importance or any truth to the ideas of traditional religion. Is not all we know about the nature of man and the character of the world strictly opposed to the teachings of religion?

Science has searched heaven and earth in all directions, but nowhere has it encountered God or found even a trace of His works. Nature has lost its secrets; we see in it merely the rule of mathematical laws and of blind forces which seem to have no regard for the aims and interests of man. From the time Copernicus removed the earth from the center of the universe and made it revolve around the sun, like any other planet, the earth and consequently man have been deprived of their central position in the universe. All anthropomorphic concepts of psychic forces, of aims and ends through which ancient and medieval philosophers tried to explain nature, today have been radically eliminated from our picture of reality.[2] Organic life on this earth likewise progresses in accordance with clearly perceptible natural laws and man himself is no exception to this rule.[3] No longer does an absolute barrier separate him from mere animal life, and even his highest intellectual achievements appear simply as the effects of certain biological factors.[4]

'Soul,' then, to the modern, has become an empty word. To most people an ethico-religious interpretation of man would seem an anachronism. They think that all human values are determined by the chance situation in which man finds himself and to which he has to adjust his way of living,[5] so that even his moral standards are subject to change.[6] Moreover, modern psychology has dealt perhaps the hardest blow at the traditional concept of man. According to recent theories, even in his own conscious ego man is not master of himself—on the contrary, the conscious life of his soul is governed by animal instincts hidden and embedded in the unconscious. This discovery cuts at the very root of the freedom of the autonomous personality which had been the pride and dignity of man for centuries.[7]

In opposition to this autocracy of nature, philosophers have made ever-renewed attempts to establish history as a realm in which the freedom of man may be demonstrated.[8] But gradually the empirical knowledge of history has proved to be a still more dangerous enemy of the traditional concept of man than was natural science. Modern historical investigation, in increasing measure, has purified our picture of history of all traces of supernatural connotations. Everywhere it has discovered the predominance of general geographical, economic, social, and other causes that serve to explain even the most astounding human accomplishments. Thus, the study of history shows that man and human civilization are merely the products of natural and material forces.

All these factors have strengthened modern man in his conviction that he must seek future happiness in this world alone. He maintains that the true aim of human life is to bring about a constant development of man's natural and rational faculties, to contribute to the advancement of culture and civilization—which are to lead to an ever more complete rule over nature and thus to even greater happiness and general welfare. The modern individual feels sure that he can be master over his own destiny, and for this reason he is so busy in this world that he cannot concern himself with the Beyond. It would indeed seem to be true that the faith in this world, in man and his earthly life, has really brought about greater happiness, a wider range of freedom and justice. Modern man trusts in himself and is certain that the future of the race can be determined by himself.

Such convictions seem hard to reconcile with the concepts of traditional religion. Many people feel that religion constitutes an outright danger to our modern accomplishments, that it threatens progress and the freedom of science. They ask: Is religion not simply an escape from the hard facts of reality and from its urgent tasks? Does not religious faith furnish man with an excuse to accept existing conditions of political and social injustices? It is along these lines that the opposition to religion has been gaining momentum since the days of the Renaissance. Atheism is no recent phenomenon. In the beginning of the seventeenth century in Paris alone—at that time a city of not much over 300,000 inhabitants—the number of atheists was estimated by Mersenne, a close friend of Descartes, at about 50,000.[9] In the eighteenth century, the movement had reached Germany. Goethe simply admits that he no longer considers himself a Christian.[10] Even in Rome it was felt at that time that within fifty years there would be neither a pope nor a priest in the Holy City.[11] During the nineteenth century the democratic trend brought about a strengthening of religious tendencies; for in the democratic countries it was the lower middle classes, those who had had less occasion to come in contact with contemporary thought and its scepticism, who then gained political influence. But today, when modern education has infiltrated the ideas of modern science and of new practicality into the minds of common men, and when for the first time in history even powerful states have taken up an open fight against religion—today religion is in critical danger. To great numbers of people religious belief now is only a childish delusion that serves to satisfy men's emotional needs. At best it is held to be the private concern of a few individuals or of certain small groups.

The attitude of the average person towards religion is one of detached scepticism, and modern philosophy has been determined by a similar mode of thinking.[12] Both the philosophic and the ordinary points of view reflect a feeling of intellectual prowess. Descartes, flung by doubt into the abyss of desperation, found the Archimedean point in the certainty of his own Ego and in the evidence of his ideas.[13] It is precisely in his sceptical doubt that he found the proof for the sovereignty of his reason, and this proof gave him the strength to defy the world. This sovereign feeling of the intellect, which considers itself capable of understanding everything outside itself in the categories of its own thinking and acting, has remained the basic principle of modern philosophy.

It is reason that constitutes the greatness of man. Reason, that capacity of finding truth through thinking and of making this truth the aim of our actions, is the faculty that distinguishes him from all other living beings.[14] No matter how insignificant man may be as compared with the universe, he is yet a conscious, a thinking being. Even if the universe utterly destroys him, still he remains superior to that which crushes him, for he is aware of his annihilation; he knows that the universe has power over him, whereas the universe knows nothing of all this.[15]

While in his theoretical understanding man proceeds

from reality to thinking, trying thereby to find a universal truth, in his practical actions he follows the opposite way, which leads him from thought to reality, to the particular. What he has recognized as truth in his thinking becomes the ideal good he strives to attain in his particular situation in life. What we are is determined by that which we do, and what we do by that which we think. Thus, our very being is radically affected by our thought. Therefore the complex problem, 'what is man,' can best be expressed in the old threefold question: 'What can I know?' 'What ought I to do?' 'What may I believe?' [16]

It is in our thought that we seem to participate in the truth; we may doubt everything, except the truth. For proof of this we have the radical sceptic who is convinced of the truth of his own scepsis—a most impressive manifestation of the power of truth over thinking.[17] And yet, though man's sovereignty consists in his conviction that through his thought he can understand the truth, it is this very truth that humiliates him and makes him aware of his insignificance. The truth with which he is brought face to face is this: that in his own actual existence he finds himself utterly dependent, a mere plaything of the blind forces of nature, of psychological, social, and historical conditions. These factors seem to determine his thought, and thereby to make its truth questionable. Man finds himself amidst a conflict of antagonistic principles which even the philosopher can only acknowledge and analyse, but not resolve.

It is as impossible to find man's true essence only in thought, in his comprehension of the truth, as it is to take his material existence for his real being. Idealism is just as untenable a thesis as Realism. The Idealist overlooks the fact that the seemingly sovereign consciousness of thought is itself only a phenomenon within this world and dependent upon it; while on the other hand the Realist and the Materialist are wont to ignore the fact that thought constitutes the distinctive character of man. Idealism is of philosophical interest only in so far as it refutes Realism. And the latter has philosophical importance only in so far as it disproves Idealism. The fundamental fact from which all philosophy has to start in its interpretation of man is neither thought alone, nor nature alone, but the dialectical conflict of the two, their irreconcilable antinomy.[18]

Whether man comprehends himself in terms of subjective thought, or of objective nature, or of both, he remains within the limits of merely intellectual and theoretical contemplation. He is always more than he is able to comprehend of himself. While taking himself as an object, he is also the subject which apprehends and knows itself. Thus man is forever transcending himself. Concentration on pure theory leads him to forget his real self, his own origin. Man is not merely intellect; he is also will, love, desire, feeling; he is not only soul, but also body. In the self-detached contemplation of the intellect, however, man is deceived by the illusion that, elevated above reality, he can look upon himself and thus can understand himself as he really is.[19] Actually he is not merely an observer; he is not remote from the world or from himself, and particularly in the act of understanding he remains within the world. He is not separated from his fellow-men and from their claims upon him. This limitation the philosopher is prone to forget in his detached contemplation, thus deceiving himself about his own nature and his actual situation in the world. The true essence of man, the ultimate source from which his thought and his will have originated, he cannot grasp by a merely theoretical or intellectual vision. The root of his existence lies deeper than his thought can penetrate.

Man remains a mystery to himself.[20] The task of the

philosopher, therefore, cannot be confined to establishing a purely theoretical, logically faultless system. He must never neglect the fact that even in his highest speculative flight he is still a human being, a particular and concrete individual, who even in his truth remains determined by the conditions of his existence. Only by taking this fact into account can the philosopher approach that philosophical ideal, according to which his life actualizes his thought.

But how should the philosopher grasp this other element in human nature, which lies beyond the reach of the intellect, except again through his own thinking? [21] It is often said today that all wisdom consists in our recognizing clearly and courageously the actual situation in which we find ourselves, and in acting accordingly. In such statements what is meant by the word 'situation' is the particular set of circumstances that determine our life, in so far as they either restrict our actions, or, on the contrary, give them free play. 'Situation' in this sense signifies the whole of the specific and ever-changing conditions in which we live, the particular people and their interests upon which we depend.[22] Yet, it is not these particular situations of the individual with which I am concerned, but rather the general situation in which man, *qua* human being, finds himself. What I want to define is this finitude from which man cannot escape, and which his intellect must recognize as actually existent, that limitation which in fact reveals the true nature of man. I mean the inevitability of death, of struggle, of suffering, and of history.[23] For it is here, where man arrives at the ultimate limits of his sovereignty, that he begins to recognize what he really is, his actual existence.

We know that we have to die; we understand death as a biological phenomenon. Man has learned that whatever comes into existence, must perish. Birth and death, to him, are natural processes. He tells himself: in infinite time, in infinite space, out of infinite matter an organic cell has been formed; this cell will last a while, and then it will perish; and this cell am I.[24] It is a fact just like other facts, that the individual must die. Man may try to find consolation about his own end and that of his friends by considering the unending life of nature of which he himself is part; or else he may strive beyond the limits of his own individual existence, to secure the permanence of certain values for which he lives. Yet, in experiencing the death of his closest relative or friend he sees at once the flimsiness of all these arguments; for he cannot follow him whom he loves. Something has gone for ever. Suddenly man feels his own insignificance and loneliness amidst a great empty space. The truth of the whole intellectual aspect of life becomes questionable in the face of death. Essential to him can be only that which retains its value even in the face of death, while that which does not stand this ultimate test reveals itself in its utter delusiveness.

Death is not merely the physical end of our life: it also has bearing on our moral existence. When in the ultimate moments of our life our moral decisions are put to the test, it is death which we may have to choose for their sake. Death is the final touchstone of the sincerity of our moral actions; it reveals the true nature of man, who sometimes only by perishing can save his real self. In such situations the human self understands its own significance even beyond the limits of its temporal existence, it has a glimpse of that which in the language of religion is called immortality. At the same time we recognize that this life is something irrevocable, that none of our deeds here can be undone, and this is precisely what gives it another dimension, that of depth. It is not the mere fact, then, that life comes to an end, not even the dread of non-existence, which fills us with the horror of death; it is rather the crucial question with which death confronts us, whether we have made use of all the opportunities that life has offered us, or whether we have wasted our existence. Death makes us feel that we are centered not in ourselves, but that we are dependent upon something beyond ourselves.

It is in experiencing moral failure that we encounter another limit of human existence. Modern man is characterized primarily by his belief in his own free personality and in his moral perfectibility. Moral failure is viewed as a consequence of certain shortcomings, be it of human reason, or of human will; these insufficiencies, however, are held to be of an accidental rather than of an essential nature, and consequently it is believed that they can easily be remedied through an intensification of our rational efforts, or through a greater moderation of our passions. Modern man has been convinced that progress gradually would overcome all limitations of his knowledge as well as of his moral sense.[25]

But such an assumption seems hard to reconcile with the facts of experience. No matter how noble our conscious motives may be, in reality our deeds are bound to have consequences of which we had not thought at all, but for which we feel nevertheless responsible. Our actions may easily lead to results quite contrary to our original intentions. Every step we take necessarily causes suffering, sorrow, and disappointment for others. The opportunities of life are limited, and whatever we own we are bound to have taken away from others. In pursuing our own moral aims we cannot help trespassing upon others. We may avoid this or that particular fault, but we cannot live and act without becoming guilty. For even our not acting is an omission which may have consequences just as grave for others. Ordinarily we try to draw a veil over these facts, and are satisfied with the feeling that our conscience is clear.[26]

And yet, it is not always our conscious motives which really determine our actions. Modern philosophers and psychologists have persistently shown to what an extent the human ego is capable of deceiving itself about its own real motives, how powerless it is in view of its own unconscious instincts.[27] Still, we feel responsible even for that which lies dormant in the unconscious part of our soul. Furthermore, man is as he is and never changes. He may think that he could start a new life any time he wishes to, but after some experience he will find that in spite of all his good intentions his actions and his character have not changed. We feel responsible, however, not only for that which we do, but also for that which we are.[28] Complacency never ceases to tempt us with a feeling of our own moral faultlessness; but every human being reaches a point where he cannot help becoming guilty. The higher developed the moral conscience of the individual, the more seriously he takes his moral obligations, the more clearly he will understand the inevitability of guilt in the very process of perfecting himself.

There is another difficulty from which there is no escape: man has not created himself. He finds himself thrown into this world. 'He is caught in a temporal web.' In his origin and in his upbringing he is conditioned by the particular historical situation into which he is born. This factor constitutes man's unalterable fate by which his free will is impaired, and which he must acknowledge and take upon himself in order to become a truly mature person. Man is born as a link in the chain of generations; he does not lead an independent existence in empty space. For one thing he is a social being, related to his fellow-men. The Cartesian concept of an ego that understands itself as essentially different from its object finds its limitations in practical life, where the object opposing the ego is no longer an unconscious object of nature, but another conscious ego. Just as speaking has its counterpart in listening, so our conscious thinking and acting are fundamentally correlated to the thought and action of other individuals.[29]

Furthermore, are our natural faculties, our intellectual ideas, and our moral standards at all times the same? Certainly, man's interpretation of himself has changed with history, and even the most obvious achievements of reason were not independent of the particular historical moment in which they were attained. The rational supposition of a truth that, once established by reason, remains one and the same at all times and for all men, is contrary to the facts: *veritas temporis filia*—truth is the daughter of time.[30]

Man's sovereignty, thus, in thought and action is limited by the historicity of his existence. No one can start fresh. What happened before him, he cannot undo; on the contrary, he has to reckon with the consequences of what previous generations have done. Or again, if his view is directed towards the future and he inaugurates something new, the results of his willed actions are beyond his own reach, they depend on forces outside of himself. Everywhere the supposed sovereignty of man's will and reason collides with the exigencies of history.

Life means struggle. Every living being has a will to live, to expand, and this can be done only at the expense of another's existence. Thus the fact that man lives within the limits of history and society implies that conflict is unavoidable. It is the greatest triumph of civilization that in human society the struggle for existence has been reduced to a minimum—that, based on the principle of sensible mutual co-operation, it has taken on more civilized forms. From a purely intellectual point of view it seems impossible to understand why we should not be able to settle all our difficulties with our fellow-men in a reasonable way, why men should not be persuaded to live together in peace and to work together towards a steady advancement of justice, freedom, and human welfare. By the good manners of civilized life and by the carefully balanced objectivity with which we have been indoctrinated, we are only too apt to be deceived about the true nature of man. For this reason we are prone to believe that justice and order, as they can be attained within the narrow limits of communities or states, could easily be extended over the whole world. In fact, however, civilized society is constantly threatened by the blind instincts of man, which drive mankind to ever-renewed battle, just as the individual is always endangered by the unknown forces of his unconscious self. Besides, we must not forget that law and order are based on force and power, that the establishment of any social order is preceded by strife, and that in many cases it results from the oppression and exploitation of others. The philosophical dream of a legal system that once and for all would do away with the necessity of forceful action has not yet been confirmed by the experience of history. Moral reason demands of the individual that he should overcome his selfishness and live for the common good, that he should be intent on the universal; but any such attempt finds its limits in the inborn nature of human will. The individual, in the inmost core of his existence, offers stern resistance to the demands of abstract reason. He wants to be what he is and wishes to express his individuality in his life. It is the peculiar character of man, his innate obstinacy and the inconsistency of his reactions, which make conflict in practical life unavoidable.

What is true of practical life is valid even for theoretical thinking. Truth cannot be found solely through the logical harmony of our own thought. We must contend with the truths of others, which in themselves may be equally logical and harmonious and yet are contrary to what we think to be true. The final antinomy that appears in all philosophical discussions results from the contradictory character of our fundamental rational principles. This dialectical character of philosophical thought cannot be explained simply by the subjective limitations of our intellect, but must have its origin in the nature of reality itself, which everywhere manifests a tension of opposing forces. Therefore, even philosophizing means strife.[31]

In all these situations, in the inevitability of death, of failure and suffering, of history, and of conflict, man finds himself at the ultimate limits of his sovereignty. In becoming aware of the limitations even of his purely theoretical and intellectual understanding, he recognizes the true nature of his existence, which everywhere impinges upon impassable boundaries. Our theoretical reasoning makes us see beyond these narrow limits of our subjective self. It allows us to contemplate as though we had part in the truth of the gods, and, freed of all fetters, could look at ourselves from above. Yet, this very process involves the danger that we deceive ourselves about the final and serious character of these boundaries which we can actually never cross. They are like a wall against which we are butting all the time only to be thrown back again. It is in such ultimate moments as I have tried to outline here, that we discover reality as it is.

Certainly, these limits are only negations, yet, as the old saying goes: *negatio est determinatio* [32]—these limits determine our existence in its very essence. As long as man interprets himself merely in terms of objective nature and shapes his life and his world according to this concept, he estranges himself from his real self, and his soul becomes empty. For the merely theoretical aspect of the world blinds him to the fundamental facts of his existence and gives him the illusion of a sovereignty and a truth which actually he does not own. If, on the other hand, man recognizes the definite limitations of his autonomy and his truth—if he accepts these limitations as part of his own existence—in constantly contending with them he grows and matures, and thus becomes a true personality. In this way he understands the full import of the fact that we are dependent on an objective power by which our whole existence is determined.

This, however, is the truth with which religion also is concerned. It is in those situations where he experiences the inevitability of death, of suffering, of struggle, and of guilt—not in his merely theoretical contemplation—that the philosopher, like the religious person, grasps the fundamental problems of life. And here our discussion returns to the point from which it started. It began with the conflict between the theories of modern science and the concepts of traditional religion, a conflict which results in the fact that modern man feels more and more inclined to regard the teachings of religion as mere delusions. Yet, if man of today with all the veracity and sincerity which he has been taught by modern science tries to understand himself as he really is, he discovers that his sovereignty and his truth have final limitations which make even the concepts of religion appear to him in a new light.

Is it possible, in view of these facts, that religious concepts have not yet lost all their meaning? Does the attitude of the modern intellect tend to blind the man of today to the seriousness and irrevocability of his limitations? That power upon which we feel dependent in our thinking and being is objective and present in a sense quite other that is true of the objects we understand through empirical methods. Of this power we become aware only in practical life, where we experience it as the limit to which our whole existence is related, and through which we are what we are.

This spontaneous feeling, however, that our existence has its center not in itself, is precisely what in religion is called faith. It is in this feeling that the true nature of man reveals itself, for it is his principal characteristic that in his being, in his thought, and in his volition he is related to something other than himself, to a truth that transcends him. Even faith is experience, not the experience of an external object, but the experience that in his own existence, in his own consciousness and truth, man is dependent upon an objective force. 'Faith is the evidence of things not seen.' [33] It is only in the experience of faith that God is felt to be present as the power which determines our being and thinking. The concepts of faith, to modern man, become understandable again in their real meaning and in their truth only when he encounters the limits of his factual existence and realizes that even the scope of his theories is definitely limited. This does not impair the truth of scientific discoveries, as far as they concern the rational explanation of phenomena. On the contrary, it is precisely against the background of this truth, that the actual situation of modern man stands out and becomes discernible for him.

It is obvious that religious documents necessarily reflect also the intellectual background of the time and sphere in which they were written. But such connotations are of no consequence for the understanding of the quintessence of their truth. It is not the aim of religion to prove scientific propositions, but only to reveal religious truths. These revelations, therefore, for the modern philosopher become truly understandable only if he shows regard for their essence rather than for their accidental connotations. Interpreted in this way, they will divulge to him their full philosophical meaning, which remains valid even for the modern intellect. And this, in my opinion, is the task which religion imposes upon the philosopher.

NOTES

*Special topics dealt with in the Notes of this and succeeding chapters are listed in the General Index under the entry* Notes.

GOD was the centre of all thought for medieval philosophers, who were accustomed to begin with the problem of His existence. Wherever God recedes from the consciousness of man, however, nothing higher remains than man himself. His thinking and being now become the chief subject of philosophy. Descartes begins his *Meditations* with the question of his own existence, and since then the nature of man has been the chief problem of modern philosophy. While in medieval times philosophy was in the service of theology, now the proper study of the philosopher has become man. And the discoveries of biology, psychology, and sociology in our time have even strengthened this tendency towards 'anthropology' (see below, note 16. Cf. K. Goldstein, *Human Nature in the Light of Psycho-pathology*, Cambridge, Mass., 1940.) R. Niebuhr's *The Nature and Destiny of Man, a Christian Interpretation* (New York, 1941-3), Jacques Maritain's *Humanisme Integral* (Paris, 1936), and other similar publications show how today theologians also try to take their starting point from the nature of man. (Cf. Christopher Dawson, *Christianity*, New York, 1911. W. M. Horton, *Contemporary English Theology, an American Interpretation*, New York, 1936, and *Contemporary Continental Theology, an Interpretation for Anglo-Saxons*, New York, 1938, pp. 48 f. and 85 ff.)

1. To be sure, Plato, in the passage referred to, does not speak explicitly of the quarrel between philosophy and religion, but of the 'ancient feud between philosophy and poetry.' (*Republic*, x, 607B; cf. J. Adams in his edition, vol. II, 1902, p. 417.) To the Greeks, however, poets like Homer and Orpheus were also prophets of their religion, and thus in the *Republic* (cf. II, pp. 379A ff.), Plato means also the popular theology when he uses the word 'poetry.' Homer and Hesiod were called 'theologians' by Aristotle (e.g. *Metaphysics* III, 4, p. 1000 a 9. Cf. W. Jaeger, *Humanism and Theology*, Milwaukee, 1943, pp. 46 f. and 82 f.)

2. Natural science of the sixteenth century still worked with the traditional ideas of psychic forces in natural events. Before Galileo

founded modern mathematical physics, such psychic forces provided the only reasonable explanation for the mathematically exact movements of the heavenly bodies. It was with Galileo and Descartes that the battle began against these ideas of a bygone time. Cf. note 39 to ch. III.

3. For instance, Mendel's two laws of heredity, which have been shown to hold also for man.

4. J. B. Bury, 'Darwin and History' (in *Selected Essays*, Cambridge, 1930, p. 33): 'A historian may be a theist but so far as his work is concerned this particular belief is otiose.' Cf. note 12.

5. J. Dewey, *Influence of Darwin on Philosophy*, New York, 1910, p. 44: 'Life is a process of experimented adjustment in a precarious world. Problems are solved when they arise, namely in action, in the adjustment of behaviour.'

6. J. Dewey, *Experience and Nature*, Chicago, 1925, ch. x, esp. p. 399: 'Values are as unstable as the forms of clouds. The things that possess them, are exposed to all the contingencies of existence, and they are indifferent to our likings and tastes.' In general cf. R. B. Perry, *General Theory of Value*, New York, 1926; W. Koehler, *The Place of Values in a World of Facts*, New York, 1938.

7. Cf. S. Freud, *Introductory Lectures on Psychoanalysis*, translated by J. Rivière, London, 1922, p. 240. 'Humanity has in the course of time had to endure from the hands of science two great outrages upon its naïve self-love. The first was when it realized that our earth was not the center of the universe, but only a tiny speck in the world-system . . . That is associated in our minds with the name of *Copernicus* . . . The second was when biological research robbed man of his peculiar privilege of having been specially created, and relegated him to a descent from the animal world, implying an iradicable animal nature in him; this transvaluation has been accomplished in our time upon the instigation of *Charles Darwin*, Wallace, and their predecessors . . . But man's craving for grandiosity is now suffering the third and most bitter blow from the present-day psychological research which is endeavouring to prove to the "ego" of each one of us that he is not even master in his own house but that he must remain content with the veriest scraps of information about what is going on unconsciously in his own mind.' Cf. note 27.

8. R. G. Collingwood, *Human Nature and Human History*, London, 1937, and *Speculum Mentis*, Oxford, 1924, ch. VI: 'Historical thought is the discovery of individuality, and individuality is freedom.' It was Hegel who formulated this concept of history. Cf. his *Philosophy of History*, Introduction *passim.;* P. Tillich, *The Interpretation of History*, New York, 1936.

9. Cf. Marin Mersenne, *Quaestiones celeberrimae in Genesin* . .

*In hoc volumine athei et deistae impugnantur et expugnantur . . .* Paris, 1623. The pertinent passage is quoted by F. C. Bouillier, *Philosophie Cartesienne,* Paris, 1868, vol. I, p. 27. On the reliability of Mersenne's figures, cf. E. M. Robertson, *A History of Free Thought,* London, 1936, vol. II, p. 534. 'Even taking the term "atheist" in the loosest sense . . . the statement was never credited by any contemporary, or by its author; but neither did anyone doubt that there was an unprecedented amount of unbelief.' Cf. also Fortunate Strowski, *De Montaigne à Pascal,* Paris, 1907, pp. 138 ff.

10. Goethe in his letter to J. K. Lavater of 29 July 1782: 'I [am] to be sure no anti-Christian, nor an un-Christian, but I am certainly a decided non-Christian.' Kant, in his letter to Lavater of 28 April 1775, expresses himself more cautiously, but he too hardly looked upon himself as a true Christian. (Cf. K. Vorlaender, *Kant,* 1924, vol. II, p. 173; and Robertson, op. cit., vol. II, ch. XVIII.)

11. J. Winckelmann's letter from Rome of 26 February 1768.

12. Lord Acton (*Selections from the Correspondence of the First Lord Acton,* ed. by J. N. Figgis and R. V. Lawrence, vol. II, London, 1917 ff.), letter of 19 July 1891: 'For 200 years, from the time of Hobbes, unbelief has been making its way . . . Unbelief came to be founded on science . . . about one half of the classic writing, of the creative thinking of the world, was done by unbelievers. The influences that reigned were in great measure atheistic. No mind could be reared except by aid of Grote, Mill, Austin, Darwin, Lewis, Huxley, Tyndall—to take England only.' Cf. note 3 to ch. II.

13. Descartes, *Meditations,* I, 16, p. 27: 'I will suppose, then, not that Deity who is sovereignly good and the fountain of truth, but some *malicious demon who is at once exceedingly potent and deceitful, has employed all his artifice to deceive me* . . . I will continue resolutely fixed in the belief, and shall at least do what is in my power and guard with settled purpose against being imposed upon by this deceiver.' II, 1, p. 29: '[This meditation] has filled my mind with so many doubts that it is no longer in my power to forget them . . . and, just as if I had fallen all of a sudden into very deep water, I am so greatly disconcerted as to be unable either to plant my feet on the bottom or sustain myself by swimming on the surface.' Through the power of his thinking Descartes managed to banish this bugbear which appeared to him in his doubt, and with this effort to overcome scepticism modern rational philosophy begins. Still, at the bottom of modern philosophy, this phantom of doubt kept lurking and came to unrestrained sway in the thought of Schopenhauer and Nietzsche. Nietzsche says: 'We moderns are all opponents of Descartes and defend ourselves against the dogmatic frivolity of his doubt. We must doubt better than Descartes did. We find the reverse, the countermovement against the absolute author-

ity of the goddess "Reason" everywhere that there are deeper people.' (*Works*, xiv, 5.) Thus for Nietzsche that malicious demon of Descartes becomes the primary cause of the world under the name of Dionysus.

14. This traditional definition of man comes from Aristotle: 'Man is the only animal that possesses reason [*logos*]' (*Politics*, i, 2, 1253a10; cf. vii, 13, 1332b4.). It has found its classical expression in Thomas Aquinas, *Summa Contra Gentiles*, iii, 39; *In lib.* i, *Metaph. Arist.*, lect. i, 2 and 3; cf. W. Jaeger, *op. cit.*, p. 16 f.

15. Pascal, *Pensées* (ed. Léon Brunschvicg, Nr. 347), whose formulation I follow here.

16. Kant's *Logic* (transl. by Richardson, London, 1819, p. 30): 'The first question is answered by *metaphysics*, the second by *ethics*, the third by *religion*, and the fourth [viz. 'what is man?'] by *anthropology*. But they at bottom might all be considered as pertaining to anthropology; because the three first questions refer to the last one.' (Cf. *Critique of Pure Reason*, 2nd ed., p. 833.)

17. This thought has been expressed in an impressive manner by St. Augustine: *De Vera Religione*, 39, 73 ff. (Migne, xxxiv, 154): 'Everyone who knows that he is in doubt about something knows the truth, and in regard to this that he knows he is certain. Therefore he is certain about a truth.' (Transl. in E. Przywara and C. C. Martindale, *An Augustine. Synthesis*, New York, 1936, p. 6.) Cf. Augustine's deeply penetrating analysis in *De Vera Religione*, 49, 94: 'Every spectator [*speculator*] admits that he wishes to arrive at the truth in being vigilantly on guard against getting caught in any delusions; therefore he takes pains to see and recognize and judge more sharply and vigorously than others. So we look most diligently at a juggler, who promises us tricks and we watch him cautiously . . . and if we are deluded we are delighted by the skill of him who deluded us. But if anyone of the audience catches him, the former thinks he has earned greater praise than the juggler and precisely for no other reason than because he could not be deceived by him. Therefore the victor's prize belongs to the truth and the knowledge, skill, and in short to the comprehension of truth at which no one arrives who seeks the truth outside of himself.' These are indeed the motives of the sceptic; he sees the world as the work of a juggler or wicked genius, and tries to excell others in penetrating his deceptions. Cf. note 13.

18. This idea forms the basis of Plato's dialectic, a method which he used with the greatest mastery, above all in his *Parmenides*. In modern philosophy the understanding of dialectic was lost, to be regained only by Kant in his *Critique of Pure Reason* (Cf. 'The Antinomy of Pure Reason'). This rediscovery signifies Kant's greatest contribution to philosophy but he is himself conscious of having

understood anew a thought of Plato's. (Op. cit., 2nd ed., pp. 9, 370-75, 530, where he clearly alludes to Zeno, who develops the dialectical method in Plato's *Parmenides*.)

19. In this sense Plato (in *The Sophistes*, p. 216) makes fun of those philosophers who believe that they, like 'the gods, can look down on human life from above.'

20. In spite of the fact that Socrates devoted his whole life to the task of acquiring a knowledge of man's nature and of understanding himself, he had to admit that he remained an unfathomable mystery to himself, as Plato so impressively shows us in the *Phaedrus*, p. 229 A. (Cf. S. Kierkegaard's striking interpretation in *Philosophical Fragments*, transl. by D. F. Swenson, Princeton, 1936, p. 22.) This thought of the unfathomableness of the human soul has been expressed by Augustine again and again; e.g. 'Thou seekest the depth of the sea, what is deeper than the human consciousness.' (*In Psalm.* LXXVI, 18, transl. by E. Przywara and C. C. Martindale, op. cit. p. 421.) In his *Confessions*, he makes himself and the inner life of his soul the principal object of his study: 'Mihi quaestio factus sum': I became a great problem to myself. (Cf. E. Frank, *Saint Augustine and Greek Thought*, Cambridge, Mass., 1943, pp. 10 ff.)

21. In order to make clear this other element Plato gave his philosophy the strange form of Socratic Dialogues, a form which at first sight seems unfit for a merely logical and objective chain of reasoning. But if Platonic philosophy implies that the real life of the man who philosophizes is an essential presupposition for his recognition of the truth—then there is no more perfect way of expressing this theory than by making evident the ideal of such a philosophical existence through the concrete example of a philosopher like Socrates. With him every word is really true, since it refers to the historical situation of one particular moment and to the friendly or hostile contact with other people. (Cf. E. Frank, *American Journal of Philology*, 1940, p. 41.) Yet such a merely poetical description, which shows the philosopher in the particular circumstances of his actual existence, in his attitude towards life and death—such a literary representation would no longer satisfy the philosophical need as we understand it today; it may symbolize in a poetical metaphor the necessary limitation of philosophical reasoning, but it could not clearly define what constitutes that limitation.

22. J. Dewey, *Logic, The Theory of Inquiry* (New York, 1938, pp. 66 ff.): 'What is designated by the word "situation" is *not* a single object or event or set of objects and events . . . We live and act in connection with the existent environment . . . The pervasively qualitative . . . constitutes in each situation an *individual* situation, indivisible and induplicable.' To Dewey, 'situation' is a qualified existential whole which is unique.

23. For the absolute situation of man, Jaspers coined the expression 'limitative situation' (border situation), which reminds one of Kant's term of 'limitative conception,' and is indeed its very existential counterpart. In certain points I here follow Jaspers's excellent analysis. (Cf. K. Jaspers, *Psychologie der Weltanschauung*, Berlin, 1919, pp. 202 ff.; *Philosophie*, vol. ii, Berlin, 1932, pp. 201 ff.) The idea of Jaspers's has been taken over by M. Heidegger, *Sein und Zeit*, Halle, 1927, p. 307; cf. also Gabriel Marcel, *Du Refus à l'Invocation*, Paris, 1940, p. 284.

24. Cf. Tolstoy (*Anna Karenina*, part viii, ch. 8, transl. by N. H. Dole, New York, 1880), who expresses this experience of modern man as follows: 'Ever since that moment when, as he sat beside his dying brother, he had examined the problem of life and death, in the light of the new convictions, as he called them, which from the age of 20 to 34 years had taken the place of his childhood beliefs, he was terrified not only at death, but at life. Our organism and its destruction, the indestructability of matter, the laws of the conservation and development of forces were words which were substituted for the terms of his early faith. These words, and the scientific theories connected with them, were doubtless interesting from an intellectual point of view, but they stood for nothing in the face of real life. And he suddenly felt in the position of a man who in cold weather had exchanged his warm coat for a muslin garment, and who for the first time should indubitably, not with his reason, but with his whole being, become persuaded that he was absolutely naked, and inevitably destined to perish miserably . . . More than by anything else, he was surprised and puzzled by the fact that the men of his class, who for the most part had, like himself, substituted science for religion, seemed to experience not the least mental suffering, but to live entirely satisfied and content. Thus in addition to the main question there were others which tormented him: Were these men sincere? Were they not hypocrites?'

The strong influence which Schopenhauer's philosophy exercised on Tolstoy is unmistakable in his whole approach to these problems.

25. On the idea of progress, see ch. v, note 11.

26. Schopenhauer is perhaps the first philosopher who, free of the prejudices and conventions of modern man, again devoted serious thought to these problems: 'Since we are what we ought not to be, we also necessarily do what we ought not to do. Therefore we need a complete transformation of our mind and nature. That is the new birth. Although the guilt lies in action, *operari*, yet the root of the guilt lies in our *essentia* and *existentia*, for out of these the *operari* necessarily proceeds. Accordingly our one true sin is really original sin.' (*World as Will and Idea*, Book ii, ch. 48, vol. iii, p. 421.) When Kierkegaard, shortly before his death in 1854, became acquainted

with Schopenhauer's work he was surprised to see how close to his own ideas Schopenhauer had come, whose point of view was so much the opposite of his own Christian convictions: 'I am astonished to find an author who, in spite of complete disagreement, touches me at so many points.' (*The Journals of Søren Kierkegaard*, pp. 502 ff.) If one intends to grasp the historical origin of certain philosophical trends of thought which are characteristic of the present time, he will have to turn not only to Kierkegaard and his philosophical teachers (Hegel and Schelling) but also to Schopenhauer. Wiser and gentler than Schopenhauer's criticism is that which St. Augustine makes of the belief that it is possible for man to be without sin: 'No great error is made . . . when a man indulges such an opinion, carried away by a certain benevolent feeling . . . but whoever thinks so much of *another* should not deem *himself* to be so pure a being unless he has really and clearly discovered all this of himself . . .' (*Letter and Spirit*, ch. 3, p. 159.)

27. Freud, *Introductory Lectures on Psychoanalysis* (tr. by J. Rivière, London, 1922, p. 279): 'The poet [Sophocles in *Oedipus*] says: "In vain do you deny that you are accountable, in vain do you proclaim how you have striven against these evil designs. You are guilty, nevertheless; for you could not stifle them; they still survive unconsciously in you." And psychological truth is contained in this; even though man has repressed his evil desires into his unconsciousness and would then gladly say to himself that he is no longer answerable to them, he is yet compelled to feel his responsibility in the form of a sense of guilt for which he can discern no foundation.' Freud himself reminds us (ibid. 122) of Plato's famous statement (*Republic*, IX, pp. 571 ff.): 'That the lawless desires are innate in everyone and that the good are those who content themselves with dreaming of what others, the wicked, actually do'; and Freud adds the following words, which the modern philosopher should take to heart: 'It is no part of our intention to deny the nobility in human nature . . . we dwell upon the evil in human beings with a greater emphasis only because others deny it, thereby making the mental life of mankind not indeed better but incomprehensible.' It is worth noting that two thinkers as atheistic as Schopenhauer and Freud are led by facts to attitudes that harmonize with the ideas of Christianity and of all deeper philosophy. The psychoanalysts do not deny that Schopenhauer in his analyses preceded them in their method of explaining the origin of psychic disturbances by pointing to the suppression of painful images and ideas in the consciousness. (Cf. A. Hitschmann, *Imago*, II, 1913, pp. 169 ff.) One need only quote such passages as the following (*World as Will and Idea*, Book 1, #36, Eng. transl., vol. I, p. 250): 'Lasting pain . . . exists only in thought and therefore lies in the *memory*. If now

such a sorrow, such painful knowledge or reflection, is so bitter that it becomes altogether unbearable, and the individual is prostrated under it, then, terrified nature seizes upon *madness* as the last resource of life; the mind so fearfully tortured at once destroys the threat of its memory, fills up the gaps with fictions, and thus seeks refuge in madness from the mental suffering that exceeds its strength, just as we cut off a mortified limb and replace it with a wooden one . . . A faint analogy of this kind of transition from pain to madness is to be found in the way in which all of us often seek, as it were mechanically, to drive away a painful thought that suddenly occurs to us by some loud exclamation or quick movement— to turn ourselves from it to distract our minds by force.' The modern tendency to explain phenomena of the psychic life through unconscious processes goes back to romanticism (cf. Freud, op. cit. 137, on Schubert), and was then developed by Kierkegaard and Nietzsche in their masterful analyses.

28. Cf. Schopenhauer in note 26 and op. cit. Book I, #23 (Eng. transl., p. 147): 'Hence arises the strange fact that everyone believes himself *a priori* to be perfectly free, even in his individual actions, and thinks that at every moment he can commence another manner of life, which just means that he can become another person. But *a posteriori*, through experience, he finds to his astonishment that he is not free, but subjected to necessity; that in spite of all his resolutions and reflections he does not change his conduct and that from the beginning of his life to the end of it, he must carry out the very character which he himself condemns, and as it were play the part he has undertaken to the end.' And ibid. #55 (p. 393): '*Velle non discitur*. We only become conscious of the inflexibility of another person's character through experience, and till then we childishly believe that it is possible, by means of rational ideas, by prayers and entreaties, by example and noblemindedness, even to persuade anyone to leave his own way . . . So is it also with ourselves. We must learn from experience what we desire and what we can do. Till then we know it not, we are without character, and must often be driven back to our own way by hard blows from without.' It is this insight that Heraclitus had already formulated in the famous words: 'Man's character is his fate' (Fr. 121) and to which Plato gave expression in his philosophical myths.

29. This process of consciousness was first analysed by Hegel, who therewith laid the basis for a new understanding of social phenomena. Yet his analyses in the *Phenomenology of Mind* are so difficult to understand that his influence on later philosophers remained rather limited. Cf. note 53 to ch. VI.

30. Cf. ch. V. Concerning the saying *veritas filia temporis,* see F.

Saxl in *Philosophy and History: Essays Presented to E. Cassirer,* Oxford, 1936, pp. 197 ff.

31. Cf. note 18.

32. Spinoza, *Ethics,* I, prop. VIII, sch. 1; and *Epistula* 50 (opera IV, p. 240, 13). Cf. H. A. Wolfson (*The Philosophy of Spinoza,* Cambridge, Mass., 1934, vol. I, p. 134), who traces the history of this formulation as far as Aristotle (*De Interpretatione* 10, *Metaph.* v. 22, p. 1022b22).

33. Hebrews 11. 1: 'Now faith is the substance of things hoped for, the evidence of things not seen.' Cf. note 45 to ch. II.

# II. The Existence of God

To speak of God may seem rather bold in a philosopher at a time when this word has lost its meaning for most people.[1] Today, moreover, it is not in good taste. So strange and inconceivable has the phenomenon of religious experience become to modern man, that he puzzles only over the origin of the idea of God. A great many diverse theories have been offered in regard to this question. Logical, psychological, sociological, historical, and other factors have been adduced as causes for man's conceiving of the idea of God. Consequently, religion in modern times has become the subject of scientific investigation. It is regarded as something that may be studied as is any other problem. Comparative religion, psychology of religion, sociology of religion, history of religion, philosophy of religion—all these various disciplines within the past century have accumulated a vast quantity of empirical facts that they have tried to integrate into their respective theories.[2] Modern man is neither willing nor able to believe. Yet, the more firmly he is convinced that belief in the existence of God belongs to a historical phase that has been superseded by modern science, the more seriously is he disquieted by the fact that at all times and even to this day there have been people who do believe with so much sincerity and personal fervor that he cannot help but be impressed by their attitude.[3]

We have seen how the modes of modern thought have deceived man in regard to the serious and definite nature of the limits which the facts of his existence seem to impose. Only if faced with death, and with the inevitability of suffering, of guilt, and of struggle, does he become aware of the narrowness and superficiality of his accustomed way of looking at the world. Only in experiencing the ultimate limitations of his existence does he discover his dependence upon an objective power beyond himself. But is not this objective power precisely that which in religious terms is called God?

Yet, what modern man experiences in those ultimate moments when his intellectual mainstays are threatened, is only a negative feeling, something merely subjective. The question arises regarding the validity of this experience.[4] For granted that man in such a situation may feel perplexed concerning the truth of his basic philosophy, and even if the answers that religion has given to the eternal questions of the origin and aim and meaning of life may then suddenly seem significant again, still such moments pass. Once they *have* passed, man is unable to retain his momentary impression. His feeling cannot stand up against the critique of his intellect. He may be even ashamed of the fact that in a weak moment he could have questioned the truth of his reason, which otherwise has been verified throughout his life.

No matter how uncomfortable the modern philosopher may feel whenever the word God is mentioned, he cannot deny the fact that the question of the existence of God, seen from a merely theoretical point of view, constitutes a fundamental problem of philosophy. Those philosophers who do not seem to understand how a concept as meaningless as that of God should be connected at all with modern philosophy, have by this selfsame attitude given a most definite, though negative answer to this question— an answer that is the ultimate presupposition of their own philosophy.

People who refuse to believe in the existence of God

are inclined to say that they would like to believe, provided such an existence could be proved as clearly as the propositions of science. It is scientific evidence that they demand of philosophy. Consequently, philosophers have been untiring in their search for such proof. There are a great many ways in which the existence of God has been demonstrated. From the oldest times, proofs, such as the cosmological, the teleological, and the ontological arguments, have been offered by philosophers in ever varying forms. All these demonstrations may seem sensible and convincing to one who believes in the existence of God. But modern man, who no longer has faith, will never be convinced of God's existence through such artificial and complicated argumentations.[5] Fundamentally, they all presuppose faith; in fact, they merely transpose the act of faith into the medium of rational thinking, and this is their true philosophical significance. If we analyse them logically, we find that through them human thought rises above this world and above itself unto God. For this reason they give to the faithful who can follow such a procedure a feeling of religious devotion.[6]

Let us consider first the simplest, the so-called cosmological proof of the existence of God, which is drawn from the character of the universe. Here the argument is based on the indisputable fact that everything in the world has its cause in some other thing through which its existence is determined. This cause, again, is the effect of another cause which precedes it, and in this way the world presents itself as an endless chain of causes, each of which in turn is merely effect. This means that each thing is conditional and therefore contingent. Thus everything in the world is relative, and nature a system of relations. But—so the metaphysician may ask—does not this endless chain of causes necessarily lead to the assumption of a primary cause which potentially contains all these effects—an all-pervad-

ing force and energy? And is not this energy which manifests itself everywhere in nature precisely that which we
call God? Can we possibly deny the existence of such a
God? [7]

Upon closer examination of this argument we find that
with such an idea of a primary cause—of an all-pervading
energy, or whatever we may call it—we transcend the world
and ourselves, and rise to the idea of a primary source of
all being and becoming in which our thought finds rest
and satisfaction. But he who does not believe in God is
precisely the one who refuses to take this step from a contingent and relative world to an unconditioned cause. The
Positivist remains in this world and is satisfied with it. He
does not see any reason why he should leave the sphere
of relative truth; why he should abandon this world, the
only thing which he really knows; or why he should not be
content with the logical principles that have been verified
by science. He does not understand why he should leap
into the unknown Absolute which is the very essence of
the cosmological argument. He believes in the truth of
this world alone, and sticks to it. The Metaphysician may
reply that under this presupposition the chain of causes
would have no end. This argument can certainly be no
serious objection for the Positivist who thinks that the
world is everything. For in his opinion, exactly what constitutes the greatness of the world is that there is nothing
beyond it—that to the thinking mind it has no bounds. [8]

Still, the Metaphysician need not yet give in; he may
try to attack the Positivist in his most vulnerable spot, his
naïve belief in scientific truth. Has modern science not
proved that nature in every move follows exact mathematical laws—that its seemingly chaotic processes actually
are subject to a most amazing mathematical order and harmony? Does this fact not force our intellect to conclude
that there must be a cause in the world which accounts

for this astounding aspect of nature? No matter how in-comprehensible this primary cause of the universe may be to us, we cannot help attributing to it some rational character, conformable and akin to human reason. This conclusion is fundamentally the same as the old argument from design.[9] The greatest philosophers, such as Plato, Kepler, Newton, and Kant,[10] were deeply impressed by the mathematical order of the world and believed they saw in it the dominance of a divine reason. And the most recent development of the natural sciences has shown not only in physics, but also in chemistry, astronomy, biology, etc. an even more admirable mathematical order than had been imagined only a short time ago. On account of these discoveries many leading scientists of our time are more inclined than were their predecessors to grant a place to purpose and to admit the possibility that the truth of religion may be reconcilable after all with that of science.[11]

Yet even those arguments will hardly suffice to convince one who does not feel a certain readiness to believe in God. Otherwise he would still refuse to draw any far-reaching conclusions from these scientific facts, which to him appear in an entirely different light. The mathemati-cal order, in his view, may be a product of the blind forces of nature. Even though he may acknowledge this order, he will claim that it is far outweighed by all the disorder, senseless destruction and inexpediency which he encoun-ters everywhere in the world.[12] Instead of understanding the primary cause of nature as something analogous to the human intellect, he demands, on the contrary, that even the human intellect and its thinking be understood in terms of the blind and unreasonable forces of nature. The fact remains that he who does not believe in God, finds senselessness, the forces of chaos, the evil and the harmful everywhere in the world. To such a philosopher, even the teleological proof of God will only be a begging of the question.[13]

The same is true of that argument which for modern man still seems the most plausible one, I mean that drawn from the beauty of the world. In view of the imposing beauty of nature—as it manifests itself even in the most insignificant plant or animal, or, most strikingly in the human soul—it seems hard for us to doubt a nobler origin of this world than blind forces.[14] Nevertheless, the greatest poets and artists of our time, whose appreciation of beauty is beyond dispute, have, in the name of artistic truth, most emphatically advocated a basically negative and sceptical view of the world and of man.

It seems that everywhere the requisite presupposition of a proof of God is the belief in His existence. Philosophical proofs of God, therefore, were meaningful in the Middle Ages when those people whom the philosophers addressed believed unreservedly in the truth of religion. But today, when the philosopher has to reckon with modern man, who does not acknowledge anything except the indisputable facts of science and their scientific cogency, these abstract demonstrations can hardly carry weight. They are an inheritance from times past.

To the Greeks, the arguments for the existence of 'god' were of truly philosophical importance. For god, in their opinion, was not a power beyond this world—he was this world. Nature itself was divine. Wherever the Greek felt the effect of a superior force in the world or in the human soul, he believed that a god was immediately present. The world was still 'full of gods.' [15] Even as rational a thinker as Aristotle, in his biological writings, looks at the most insignificant living being with religious awe, with the feeling that 'even here gods are present.' [16]

Atheism, as we understand it today, was unknown in Greek philosophy; for such radical negation of God is possible only when the world has lost its divine character, when God is comprehended as a Being beyond this world —as He was comprehended for the first time in the Jewish-Christian religion. Only where God is essentially apart from the world does restriction to this world mean a denial of everything divine. Of course, the Greek philosophers did not believe in the gods of popular religion. Those rational principles in which they saw the true elements, the all-dominating forces of the world—be they material atoms or ideal forms or whatever—these were their gods.[17] Even materialists like Epicurus did not deny the existence of gods; nor did they refuse to pay reverence to them. What they disavowed was only the assumption that these atomistic, material gods paid any attention to man or had any part in the mechanical process of nature.[18] An atheist, in the opinion of the Greeks, was someone who did not believe in those gods who were sanctioned by the state, and it is for this reason that so many of the Greek philosophers came in conflict with the official religion of their respective cities.[19] Philosophy, to them, was a new religion, the religion of reason, by which they hoped to replace the naïve popular beliefs, and which at the end of antiquity actually brought about the collapse of paganism.[20] In this spirit Socrates proposed the first proof of God in the form of the teleological argument. Not because of his denial of the existence of any god, but, on the contrary, because of his monotheistic belief in a moral and intelligent primary cause was he accused of being an atheist. And it was the same consideration that led the Greeks to believe that even the first Christians were atheists.[21] With the Greek philosophers, then, the traditional arguments for the existence of God served primarily to prove the true nature, the essence of their gods rather than their existence. The ancients speculated *de natura deorum,* about the nature of the gods.[22]

On the other hand, for the medieval Christian philosophers whose belief in God was unshakable, the Greek
proofs of God assumed an entirely different function,
though they retained their logical cogency. To them, the
nature of God—the truth that He, the creator of heaven
and earth, is beyond this world and beyond man—was no
problem. Through faith and through the Revelation the
nature of God was known to them once and for all. They
were far from believing that reason alone could discover
God's true nature. For reason, they thought, is capable of
understanding God only to that extent to which the Greek
philosophers had comprehended Him, that is only in so
far as He manifests himself in this world.[23] In the view
of the Christians, the issue was just the opposite of the
one that the Greek philosophers had raised: not the essence
of God was problematic, but rather the existence of such
an inconceivable Being who transcends the world as well
as man.[24]

Anselm of Canterbury, the great philosopher and theologian of the eleventh century, was the first to define the
problem thus clearly.[25] With his so-called ontological argument, philosophical thought progressed beyond the demonstrations of Socrates, Plato, and Aristotle.[26] To Anselm
the nature of God was manifest through faith, and it remained for his intellect to clarify this religious idea of
God, which he defined in the following words: 'We believe
that Thou art something than which a greater cannot be
conceived.' [27] It is evident that, for the Christian, this
formula alone can really account for the majesty of God.
Nevertheless it constitutes a simply unsurmountable difficulty for human reason. While no one will doubt the
existence of the world, and while the existence of a God
who is restricted to this world offers no problem,[28] how
can we be sure of the existence of a Being which transcends
everything we know, even our own capacity of thought?

Can he who says there is no such God except in our imagination ever be disproved?

The establishment of this ontological problem marks
the beginning of a fundamentally new phase of philosophy, which proved to be of far-reaching consequence.
Human thinking in its attempt to transcend the sphere
of objective reality discovers its own subjectivity and
anxiously struggles to ascertain the truth of its own concepts. It was Anselm who asked how human thought can
grasp a reality which lies beyond its own thinking—in
other words, how it can reach God. This question causes
him to give expression in a most stirring way to his feeling
of being far removed from God: 'If Thou art everywhere,
why do I not see Thee present? What shall this man do,
an exile far from Thee . . . I strove toward God, and I
stumbled but on myself . . . How could I measure my
own thought against that highness?' In this despair, he
finds the solution of his problem in that definition of
God's nature which, to him, is only the summary of the
content of his faith and of the Revelation: 'I wish to
understand that Thou exist as we believe Thee to exist,
and that Thou exist as that which we believe Thee to be.
Now we believe that Thou art something than which a
greater cannot be thought.' [29] This definition, as Anselm
himself admits, is open to attack; for the atheist may object: such a God actually does not exist; He is merely an
idea of our imagination. Yet, Anselm replies, in this case,
what the atheist thinks would not be all that which according to my definition he should think, namely something
than which a greater cannot be thought. For such an imaginary idea of God evidently is something than which a
greater can be thought, namely the truly existing God.[30]

The logical stringency of this argument was questioned,
however, even by Anselm's own contemporaries.[31] Later
on, Kant in his *Critique* formulated this difficulty in the

following way: [32] Does my imagining a hundred guilders prove by any means their actual existence? Does the fact that I imagine a hundred guilders in any way increase my actual fortune? Can all the effort of my thinking bring about the existence of what I think? But this argumentation misses the point of Anselm's argument.[33] It disregards the fact that the definition of God, as a Being than which a greater cannot be thought, implies the warning that we should not understand this Being as something finite, something known, like a hundred guilders; for in this thought, thinking transcends itself, it reaches out beyond every possible object that it may find; it neutralizes itself, as it were. Anselm's definition of God actually does not express anything other than the act of faith in which the Christian rises beyond this world and beyond himself.[34] Logically it is stringent only for him who like Anselm wishes to understand his own faith through his intellect and who never forgets that faith is the necessary presupposition for the cogency of this proof of God.[35]

In medieval thought, then, the arguments for the existence of God owed their validity to the fact that here the philosopher was still one of the faithful. Modern philosophy, however, starting with Descartes, no longer rests upon faith, but on the contrary is based upon doubt, upon the desperate idea that at the bottom of existence there may be no God, but rather a wicked genius, the relentless forces of nature or the blind instincts of life by which man is deceived. Only in the evidence of his sovereign and conscious thought and reason does Descartes find the means for combatting the danger of despair. The modern philosopher seeks in his Ego, in his Reason, that *pou sto,* that basis which the earlier philosopher found in his faith in God. If Descartes, then, by making use of Anselm's argument and by interpreting it in an entirely different spirit —that is, without the presupposition of faith—tries to prove the existence of God through a purely logical argument, he is bound to fail. For thus he makes the existence of God depend upon his own sovereign thinking. To him, the existence of God serves as a means by which to assure the reality of his own ego and to make his system logically complete. But such a God is merely the product of human reasoning, a metaphysical phantom.

This criticism holds good for all the attempts of modern metaphysicians to prove the existence of God through logical arguments alone and without the presupposition of faith; it is unavoidable that at some point reason will discover the illusory character of all its purely speculative proofs of God. Their authority has been shaken once and for all by Kant's critical analysis. Kant thought, however, that he could replace these speculative proofs of God by another rational proposition, the so-called moral argument. He tried to show that our moral will presupposes the existence of God as a guarantor of morals and of social order. This idea has a certain plausibility for modern man, who has supplanted the concepts of traditional religion by his belief in ethics and in the moral nature of man.[36] But actually this argumentation is not essentially different from that of Descartes, except that here the existence of God is based on the sovereignty of our moral will rather than on that of our logical reasoning; God is postulated in order to assure man of the truth of his ethical consciousness and of his moral dignity. No doubt, innumerable people have had—and do have even today—this moral belief in God as their only true religion. But can such a belief be based on rational arguments? The supposedly indestructible moral nature of man proves to be extremely vulnerable when confronted with the necessities of practical life. On the other hand, if we maintain the postulate of ethical autonomy, we find that moral independence may be used as an argument against the existence of God rather than for it. For the modern nihilist may say in heroic defiance: 'If I only see what is good, I shall act accordingly, no matter what the ultimate principle of the world may be. Whether it is nothingness, or whether it is evil, whether it may crush myself and my own will and thus forever destroy my own goodness and that of every-one else—all I can say is this; so much the worse for the ultimate principle. I shall not acknowledge it, even though its power may be unlimited. I shall persist in utter meta-physical defiance, infinitely lonely, supported only by my moral insight. I shall offer absolute resistance to the ulti-mate principle and shall despise it.' [37] Why should such a sovereign personality need an overlord? Why should he not give himself his own law and follow it in his actions, just because this law is his own, the expression of his own noble nature for which otherwise he could have no re-spect?

Thus the modern philosopher can never cogently prove the existence of a God beyond this world, either through logical or through moral arguments, to him who has no faith. How should he be able to do so, since human reason, in his opinion, is only the formal faculty of clarifying a given and clearly perceptible content and of reducing it to general abstract ideas? In science, our thinking is based on sense-perception and verifies its concepts by this means. But if human reason tries to transcend the limits of the perceptible world or of mathematics—as it must do in philosophy—its thinking is bound to get entangled in con-tradictions. While the metaphysician, starting from certain facts, may feel sure that he can prove through logically cogent arguments the truth of certain principles which transcend the objects of sense-perception, the Positivist, starting from the same facts, will feel equally sure that with the same logical stringency he can prove just the opposite, namely that all such metaphysical concepts have no meaning whatever. Every philosophical thesis can easily be disproved by its opposite.[38] If philosophers, nevertheless, stubbornly stick to their theses and refuse to yield to logical arguments, then a pre-logical presupposition, some pre-rational belief, must unknowingly be shaping their thought. The Positivist is right in saying that it is not merely the logic of the theoretical arguments which directs the argumentation of the metaphysician, but rather a certain preconceived conviction which has been borne out throughout his life. Yet the same is true of the Positivist himself; for it cannot be merely on the strength of the logic of his argument that he offers theories far transcending the mere facts of science. Instead, it must be an irrational belief, this selfsame belief in the perceptible world and in natural life which, to him, is the ultimate truth upon which he has decided to stake his whole existence once and for all.

Human reason, then, as modern scepticism has shown, does not rest upon itself. Rational conclusions are dependent on certain premises which reason itself is unable to prove because they are rooted in a deeper stratum of the human mind. They spring from a more or less unconscious belief or instinct, the justification of which is one of the principal tasks of the philosopher. Even in the exact sciences, a certain belief plays its part, in so far as their truths are based on ultimate axioms which we accept as true without being able to prove them. In practical life, we can rely even less on reason alone. Here we cannot always afford a sceptical attitude, as we may do in questions of theoretical science, which do not demand an immediate decision. In most practical questions, we cannot wait until our reason has clarified the theoretical aspects. Life is a constant struggle with the unknown, and even our rational arguments are based on a vague belief, on a trust or instinct or feeling of which we can give no further account.

Or, to quote Pascal's classical formulation of this fundamental epistemological fact: 'The heart has its reasons
which Reason does not know.' [39]

If it is thus evident that we can neither act nor live on
the basis of rational thinking alone, but that everywhere
we are guided by a certain belief—are not philosophers like
Pascal or William James right in demanding that even
regarding the question of the existence of God we should
renounce merely rational certainty and should follow our
subjective feeling or belief? [40] What is true of all other
important decisions and of every critical situation in life
is likewise valid concerning this issue: we cannot wait
until our reason has carefully weighed all the pros and
cons, the less so since the existence of God can never be
proved by reason alone. In the meantime we waste our
life in indecision. Pascal says, let us take the risk, therefore, let us boldly dare to believe, even though merely on
the strength of a vague probability.[41]

In a similar way Kierkegaard has tried to appeal to
modern man. He starts from the presupposition that the
existence of God cannot be proved by the intellect, to
which it remains an eternal paradox that God's existence
is based entirely on our belief, on our free decision, which
is not supported by any external evidence. God is the unknown, the stumbling-block which reason encounters
everywhere. Therefore, Kierkegaard admonishes us, we
should make up our minds to accept God as true, even
though this may mean a 'leap' into the dark. According to
Kierkegaard, the true nature of belief is that it offers no
certainty; otherwise, belief would not be what it is, a free
decision.[42]

I do not deny that all these philosophers, as compared
with their opponents, are right in so far as they have recognized the fact that the existence of God cannot be proved
to the modern sceptic who no longer believes in God. It is

their merit to have pointed out that that God whose existence we want to prove is not the god of nature or of metaphysics; for such a God would be no more than an entity
of the actual world, or an ideal energy which pervades the
universe. To prove the existence of such a God would be
no harder for the modern philosopher than it was for the
Greek. Such a naturalistic concept of God is certainly
easier to reconcile with the most recent views of science,
for it reflects the tendency of this-worldliness and cheer-
ful acceptance of life by which modern man hopes to do
justice to all the values in this world and to the manifold
riches of life. Even where he still believes in God and
holds a positive view of religion, he refuses to renounce
the supremacy and variety of this world. He seeks the
divine everywhere, in the phenomena of nature and above
all in the noblest pursuits of man, in ethics, science, philosophy, and art. This pantheistic feeling has found its
philosophical expression in the various systems of Anglo-
Saxon Realism and of German Idealism, which no modern
philosopher will regard without esteem. But in opposition
to all these modern tendencies, Kierkegaard has brought
back to the mind of present-day philosophers the fact that
in view of the negative forces in the world and in man, a
God of *this* world cannot be God for us and that what we
do call God, we can find only in our faith, not in any
theoretical philosophical system.

Yet, the merely subjective consciousness of those who
have faith is not sufficient foundation upon which to base
the existence of God. The principle of voluntary belief,
this 'I believe,' hardly differs from the principle of the
sovereign 'I think' or 'I will,' which it was to replace. One
may object that Pascal and Kierkegaard only appeared in
the guise of a sceptic, because they were convinced that
they could not impress modern man unless they tried to
meet him on his own ground. But if they took advantage

of the scepticism of modern man and tried to convince him that, in a question where mathematical certainty is unattainable, he should dare 'the leap' into belief and should make his decision in favor of its truth—does this not mean that with such a deliberate decision and conscious incurring of a risk the modern feeling of sovereignty has broken even into the sphere of faith? Is such a willed act of belief still faith at all? Does this sceptical attitude not, on the contrary, threaten belief in its vital nerve? No wonder that the naïve student of the great modern Christian apologists, of Pascal, Kierkegaard, and even of Dostoevski at times becomes doubtful about how far they themselves still had faith. It is true that in order to maintain faith in spite of all possible obstacles, and in order actually to realize faith amidst the manifold conditions of life, a strong will and a firm determination are needed. Yet, faith itself cannot be enforced by any willed effort or intentional decision. No objective truth can ever be founded on the merely subjective truthfulness of the believer. The unconditional sincerity of faith, whatever its object, is that which makes man worthy of himself. One may even say that that truth in which man believes and on which he builds his whole life is his God. Yet, if we believe in such a personal God not because He is the truth, but assume His truth only because we believe in Him, then there are as many gods and as many truths and values as there are beliefs. In that case, pluralism is the inescapable consequence, and it remains for the individual and his subjective liking to choose his own truth and his own God.[43] If he does so to the best of his knowledge, and if he sincerely believes in this truth and lives accordingly, he has done everything that can possibly be done. Such an attitude certainly deserves our respect. But still, this subjective concept of belief is a contradiction in itself. A belief that believes only in itself is no longer a belief.

For true belief transcends itself; it is belief in something —in a truth which is not determined by faith, but which, on the contrary, determines faith.

The spontaneous feeling of the proximity or presence of God, however, is not real faith either. 'Faith is the evidence of things not seen.' [44] We need only remember the words of Anselm which I quoted before and which express his disturbing experience of remoteness from God. Similar sentences are easy to find in other Christian thinkers from St. Augustine to Dostoevski. To believe in the immediate presence of their gods is characteristic of the religious feeling of primitive peoples. Even for the Greeks, god was near, he was the god of this or that particular city; he was there in his temple-statue; at least he was present in the universe. The Christian philosopher, in seeking God, however, always encounters only himself and feels as though he were continually repulsed by God. In this experience of remoteness from God, in being thrown back upon himself, lies the origin of the revolt against God— man's attempt to find his centre in himself.

At the bottom of faith, there is doubt, fear lest it be our own arbitrariness from which God ensues. This doubt is far from being the comparatively harmless distrust of the sceptic; it is absolute doubt, it is despair which shakes man in his entirety. This is not only denial of God; this is defiance against Him. However, it is precisely in this desperate struggle against God that man experiences what God really is. He finds he cannot escape Him. In his frustration he recognizes God as a 'gigantic massif with threatening precipices and heights.' He discovers that God is terrifying, that He is a hidden God, that 'what can be comprehended is not yet God.'

Thus it may be permissible to make the paradoxical statement that the real proof of God is the agonized attempt to deny God. It has often been remarked that atheism is but a kind of negative theology. The atheist may feel the inadequacy of all human concepts of God compared with that which God would really be, the author of all things, even of the atheist. Indeed only one who has experienced God in all His incomprehensible and inescapable greatness will understand the question of the existence of God in its true philosophical import.

What does it really mean: God exists? Existence is a category much too inferior to be applied to the greatness of God. For this reason some Christian philosophers, following Plato, even defined God as non-existence or super-existence.[45] For as the source of all reality, He is so far above the sphere of any determinate being that He cannot be called existent in a sense similar to the existence of all other beings. In their intention these philosophers were right: like all other categories, that of existence, if applied to God, can be used only in an analogical sense. Existence of God can be only an analogy of existence.[46] For the existence of God infinitely transcends our thought, our will, and even our belief. And it is precisely in this transcendence that God and His existence can be grasped by us.

## NOTES

1. The evidence for and against the existence of God is discussed from a modern, though fundamentally Hegelian, point of view by J. M. E. McTaggart in his books, *The Nature of Existence,* Cambridge, 1921, ch. 43, and *Some Dogmas of Religion,* London, 1906. A. N. Whitehead's views on this subject can be found most succinctly brought together in *Religion in the Making,* New York, 1926. Cf. G. Santayana, *The Life of Reason,* vol. III: *Reason in Religion,* New York, 1930; *Scepticism and Animal Faith,* New York, 1923; J. Dewey, *A Common Faith,* New Haven, 1934. Significant for the modern attitude towards the problem of the existence of God are Bertrand Russell's publications, the content of which is fairly expressed in their titles: *Religion and Science,* New York, 1935; *Why I Am Not a Christian,* New York, 1940; *An Outline of Intellectual Rubbish:*

*A Hilarious Catalogue of Organized and Individual Stupidity,* Kansas, 1943; cf. also Freud, *The Future of an Illusion,* London, 1928.

2. Kant tried to show in his *Critique of Pure Reason* that human reason is led to the idea of God with logical necessity; other philosophers have preferred a psychological explanation of religion, and one of the finest products of this psychological interest is William James' book, *The Varieties of Religious Experience,* New York, 1902. James seeks to analyse the peculiarity of the religious phenomenon with that combination of psychological understanding and respect which is so characteristic of his genius. Cf. also W. James Leuba, *The Psychology of Religious Mysticism,* New York, 1925; W. Sante de Sanctis, *Religious Conversion,* Eng. transl., London, 1927. A different attempt to determine the 'Sources of the Idea of God' was made by Paul Weiss (cf. *Journal of Religion,* vol. XXII, 1942, pp. 156-72, and *Science, Philosophy and Religion: Symposium,* 1940, pp. 379 ff.). There is a vast literature dealing with the history of religion, which is summarized in the following works: G. Foot Moore, *History of Religions,* 2 vols., New York, 1913 ff.; H. Pinard de la Boullay, S.J., *L'Étude comparé des religions,* 2 vols., 1929 ff.; W. Schmidt, *Handbuch der Religionsgeschichte,* 1930, and the latter's chief work: *Ursprung der Gottesidee,* Münster, 6 vols., 1928-35. In the domain of the sociology of religion the epoch-making work is Émile Durkheim, *The Elementary Forms of the Religious Life,* London, 1915. Cf. Max Weber, *The Protestant Ethic and the Spirit of Capitalism,* New York, 1920; J. Wach, *Sociology of Religion,* Chicago, 1944. The most significant work on the philosophy of religion is that of G. W. F. Hegel. E. S. Brightman, *A Philosophy of Religion,* New York, 1940, gives a good introduction to the contemporary status of the problem and the modern literature on the subject.

3. T. S. Eliot, *Essays,* New York, 1936, p. 122: 'The greater part of our reading matter is coming to be written by people who not only have no real belief [in a supernatural order] but are even ignorant of the fact that there are still people in the world so "backward" or so eccentric as to continue to believe.' Cf. Lord Acton in note 12 to ch. I.

4. Cf. D. Elton Trueblood, *The Trustworthiness of Religious Experience,* London, 1939.

5. Even religious thinkers have often emphasized this fact, e.g. Pascal, *Pensées* (ed. by Léon Brunschvicg, nr. 543): 'The metaphysical proofs of God are so remote from the reasoning of men, and so complicated, that they make little impression; and if they should be of service to some, it would be only during the moment that they see such demonstration; but an hour afterwards they fear they have been mistaken.' St. Thomas prefaces his discussion of the proofs of the existence of God (in *Summa Contra Gentiles,* I, 9)

# 46    NOTES TO CHAPTER II

with the following words: 'I speak of a twofold truth of divine things [faith and reason] . . . In support of this kind of truth [faith] certain probable arguments must be adduced for the practice and help of the faithful but not for the conviction of the opponents, because *the very insufficiency of these arguments would rather confirm them in their error if they thought that we assented to the truth of faith on account of such weak reasonings.'* (Engl. Dominicans' translation, p. 24; my italics.)

6. This is admitted even by philosophers who, like Hegel, attach great philosophical significance to proofs of the existence of God: 'The proofs of God ought to be taken in a general sense as expressing the elevation of the human spirit to God through the medium of thought.' (*Philosophy of Religion*, III, 164; I, 80. Cf. *The Logic of Hegel*, § 68, transl. by W. Wallace, p. 132.)

7. It is in a very simplified and abbreviated form that I have given the cosmological proof found first in Plato (*Laws* x, p. 894 f., *Phaedrus*, p. 245c, *Timaeus*, p. 27D f.); then in Aristotle (*Metaphysics* III, 4, 999b6; XII, 3, 1070a4; 6,1071b3 ff.; *Physics*, II, 7, 198a35, etc.). If anything is moved there must be another mover that imparts movement to it. This leads then to the acceptance of an unmoved Mover as the first cause of all change in the physical world; for there must be some stopping point, since otherwise the process would go on into infinity. Cf. Thomas Aquinas, *Summa Contra Gentiles*, I, 10, and *Summa Theologica*, I, qu. 2, art. 1. (For the history of the proofs of the existence of God, cf. C. Baeumker, *Witelo*, 1908, p. 317 f.; R. Garrigou-Lagrange, O.P., *God, His Existence and His Nature*, Engl. transl., 2 vols., London, 1936, pp. 245 ff.; E. Rolfes, *Gottesbeweise*, 1898, pp. 12 ff.)

8. Cf. Bertrand Russell, *Philosophy of Leibniz*, 1937, p. 175: 'The cosmological argument . . . has a formal vice, in that it starts from finite existence as its datum and . . . proceeds to infer an existent which is not contingent. But as the premise is contingent, the conclusion also must be contingent.' Cf. *Why I Am Not a Christian*, p. 7: 'There is no reason to suppose that the world had a beginning at all. The idea that things must have a beginning is really due to the poverty of our imagination.' Aristotle's cosmological proof has as tacit hypothesis the naïve Greek idea that this world is everything, and that therefore all movement in it finds its absolute limit and final origin in the sphere of fixed stars, or its mover—the world-soul or world-nous. (Cf. *On the Heavens*, II, 1, p. 284a5 and *Metaphysics*, XII, 7, 1072a19.) This world, on the other hand, can be thought of as infinite in itself, wherever man believes that God sends it forth from Himself, as its Creator. Pascal therefore conceives (*Pensées* nr. 72): 'the whole visible world as an infinite sphere the center of which is everywhere, the circumference nowhere.' This is the famous pas-

sage that gave Leibniz the chief instigation towards the discovery of differential calculus. The Cambridge Platonist, H. More, who was inspired by a similar idea of infinity (e.g. *Psychozoia* II, 2, 10, etc.), influenced in turn Newton's conception of mathematics and of cosmic physics. Thus in the idea of infinity the pioneers of modern science found the key with which to unlock the secrets of nature. Cf. D. Mahnke, *Unendliche Sphaere*, Halle, 1937, pp. 22 ff.

9. From Plato's *Phaedo*, 97B, and Aristotle's *Metaphysics* I, 4, p. 985a18, one might conclude that the teleological argument goes back to Anaxagoras. However, it was first given its well-known formulation by Socrates. (Xenophon, *Memorabilia*, IV, 3). The medieval and later authors are indebted chiefly to Cicero for it (*De Natura Deorum*, II, 5, 15, etc.).

10. On Kepler and Newton, see D. Mahnke, op. cit. p. 127 ff.; for Kant see the important #62 of his *Critique of Judgment*.

11. E.g. H. S. Eddington, J. S. Haldane, C. Lloyd Morgan, Max Planck, W. Heisenberg. Max Planck, *Religion und Naturwissenschaft* (7th ed., Leipzig, 1938, p. 11): 'The principle of the conservation of energy is by no means enough to enable us to compute beforehand the course of a physical event in all its details, since it leaves infinitely many possibilities open. There is yet another much more inclusive law, the so-called principle of least action. It strikes us most surprisingly that an entirely adequate formulation of this law gives every unbiased person the impression that nature is governed by a reasonable purposeful will. Thus light, for instance, takes precisely that path from among all possible paths which it can travel over in the shortest time . . . We can characterize the course of every event by means of the following statement: among all imaginable processes which transform a physical object from one definite condition to the other in a definite time—the actual process is that one for which the integral of a certain size covering this time (the so-called Lagrange function) possesses the smallest value. This principle of the least action—is the principle from which the elementary effect-quantum later received its name . . . To the causa efficiens, the cause which acts out of the present into the future, now comes the causa finalis, which reversely takes the future as its hypothesis and derives from it the course of events. In its historical development theoretical-physical research has been led to a formulation of physical causality which possesses a definitely teleological character.' This law of least action gave its discoverers, Leibniz and Maupertuis, cause for enthusiasm, since they thought they had found in it a sign of reason prevailing in nature (Cf. also P. Brunet, *Maupertuis*, Paris, 1929, ch. v, pp. 200 ff.).

12. B. Russell, *Religion and Science*, New York, 1935, ch. VIII, esp. p. 209: 'Our human world [is a world] of cruelty and injustice

and war . . . I find for my part untruth, injustice, and uncharitable-
ness and ugliness pursued not only in fact but as ideas.'

13. Russell, ibid. p. 183: 'The argument from design is the argument of the Bridgewater treatises and of popular theology generally.
Being more palpably inadequate than any of the others it has acquired a popularity which they have never deserved.'

14. Kant, *Critique of Pure Reason*, 2nd ed., p. 650: 'This world
presents to us such immeasurable variety, order, purposiveness and
beauty . . . we are brought about face to face with so many marvels
immeasurably great, that all speech loses its force, all numbers their
power to measure, and our judgment resolves itself into an amazement which is speechless.'

15. Characteristic of this idea common to all Greek philosophy is
the saying, attributed to the very first philosopher, Thales (in
Diogenes Laërtius I, 27): 'The world is animate and full of divinities.' Of Xenophanes, the founder of the Eleatic School, Aristotle
said: 'Regarding the whole universe, he stated that this unity is god.'
(*Metaphysics*, I, 5, 986b29.) The same can be said, however, of almost
every Greek philosopher. For Plato, the world and the celestial
bodies are the 'visible gods.' (*Tim.* 40D.)

16. Aristotle, *De Part. Anim.* I, 5, 645a21, a passage which refers
to Heraclitus as the authority for this conception.

17. Thus philosophers like Empedocles identify the element of
earth with Hera, the element of fire with Hephaistos. Plato identifies
the world-soul with Zeus and the planetary spheres with other
gods. (*Phaedrus* 246A; *Philebus* 30C f.; *Tim.* 40E; *Epinomis*, pp.
984 ff., etc. Cf. F. Solmsen, *Plato's Theology*, Ithaca, New York, 1942,
pp. 83 ff.) In the gods of the myth, Aristotle sees his 'prime substances.' (*Metaphysics* XII, 8, 1074b3; *On the Heavens* I, 3, 270b5; II,
1, 284a2 ff.; etc. Cf. W. Jaeger, *Aristotle,* Eng. transl., 1936, p. 140 ff.)

18. On Epicurus' conception of the gods, see Diogenes Laërtius X,
27, 123, 139; Lucretius III, 17; V, 146 ff. Yet the idea that the gods
do not care about man is interpreted already by Plato as a definite
characteristic of the atheistic teachings of his time (*Laws* X, 886C
and 887C). Epicurus' materialistic theories of the soul of gods and
men did not prevent him from stipulating in his will that the usual
sacrifices for the dead should be offered. (Diogenes Laërtius X, 18.
Cf. Plutarch, *Against Colotes* ch. XI, p. 1112 ff.; ch. VIII, p. 1111B;
and ch. XVII, p. 1117 etc.)

19. Atheism, according to ancient law, was a crime. The accusa-
tion of *asebeia* (literally: impiety or disrespect towards the gods),
which cost Socrates his life, ran as follows: 'He did not believe in
the deities in whom the State believed, but in other novel divinities.'
(Plato, *Apology*, 26d, Xenophon, *Memorabilia*, I, 1, 1, and Diog.
Laert. II, 40.) This has so little to do with what we to-day call athe-

ism that Max Müller (*Natural Religion*, London, 1889, pp. 228 ff.) suggested another term for it, namely 'adevism' (from Sanskrit: *devu*), because 'to deny the existence of Indra or Jupiter is not atheism.' Cf. J. B. Bury, *History of Freedom of Thought*, London, 1914, pp. 30 ff.; A. B. Drachmann, *Atheism in Pagan Antiquity*, Copenhagen, 1922, pp. 5 ff. The list of atheists (in Aelian, *V. H.* II, 31: Sextus Empiricus, *adv. Math.* IX, 55 ff.; Clemens Alex., *Protrepticus* I, 18, 7) cites among others, Anaxagoras, Protagoras, Aristotle, and Theophrastus as philosophers who drew down upon themselves the charge of *asebeia*.

20. Cf. H. Lietzmann, *The Beginnings of the Early Church*, London, 1935, I, ch. 9; P. Wendland, *Die Hellenistisch-Römische Kultur*, 2nd ed., Tübingen, 1912.

21. The Christian apologists continually feel the need of defending Christians against the charge of atheism: Athenagoras, *Supplicatio pro Christianis*, ch. 4 ff., Justinus, *Apology*, I, 46, p. 83; II, 13, p. 81, 6; Minucius Felix, *Octavius*, ch. 8. Cf. A. von Harnack, *The Mission and Expansion of Christianity*, Eng. transl. London, 1909, vol. I, p. 169; John Juster, *Les Juifs dans l'Empire Romain*, Paris, 1914, vol. I, p. 256 ff.; cf. also Edward Gibbon, *The Decline and Fall of the Roman Empire*, ch. 16 (vol. II, Oxford, 1827, p. 150).

22. *De Natura Deorum* is the title of Cicero's work on this subject. The words with which Socrates defends himself in Plato's *Apology* against the charge of atheism, brought against him by Meletus, show clearly how little the Greek philosopher thought he was denying the divinity of cosmic bodies like the sun and the moon, when he declared them merely to be of stone and earth: 'You say that I do not myself believe in god at all? . . . You amaze me, Meletus! Do I not even believe that the sun or yet the moon are gods *as the rest of mankind do?*' 'No, by Zeus, since you say: "the sun is a stone and the moon earth"' . . . 'But for Heaven's sake, do you think this of me that I do not believe there is any god? This man appears to me very violent for he seems as it were by composing a puzzle to be making a test: "Will Socrates, the wise man, recognize that I am joking and contradicting myself?" For he appears to me to contradict himself in his speech as if he were to say: "Socrates is a wrongdoer because *he does not believe in gods but does believe in god."*' The contradiction pointed out by Socrates is significant. However the philosopher conceives the nature of the gods, their existence remains unquestioned. Concerning Protagoras' famous work *On the Gods*, cf. T. Gomperz, *Greek Thinkers*, vol. I, ch. VI, 4, and W. Jaeger, *Humanism and Theology*, 1943, p. 38: 'Protagoras does not deny their [the Gods] existence,' ibid., p. 46, 82: 'It is the task of philosophical theology to determine the *nature* of God.' Concerning Aristotle, see below, note 28.

23. For this the medieval philosophers are accustomed to call upon the authority of Paul (Romans I. 19). 'That which may be known of God is manifest in them [namely in the heathen]; for God had shewed it unto them. For the invisible things of Him from the creation of the world are clearly seen, being understood by the things that are made.' Cf. St. Thomas, *Summa Contra Gentiles* I, 12 (Engl. transl. 1924, p. 22); *Summa Theol.* I, qu. I, 6; XII, 12, C; CXI, 1 ad. 2.

24. Thomas Aquinas, basing his argument on St. Paul (Romans I. 19), Boethius, and Augustine, emphasizes that human reason can only prove that God is, but not what He is, His Existence, but not His Essence. (*Summa Theol.* I, 12, 12 contra, and *In Boethii de Trinitate* I. 2.) But even that does not suffice to uphold the validity of the Greek proofs, for although one admits that the cosmological argument actually proves the existence of an unmoved mover, this still does not really say, as Duns Scotus (*Opus Oxonium: In Primum Librum Sententiarum,* distinctio 8, questio 5) correctly saw, that the unmoved mover must be the personal God of Christianity, who is distinct from the world. The 'wicked genius' of Descartes and the Dionysus of Nietzsche indeed are likewise unmoved movers. Similarly the objection can be made to the teleological argument, that though it may well prove the existence of a formative power in nature or even of a demiurge, an architect of the world, the demiurge himself can also be a wicked genius, and indeed the Gnostics did consider the demiurge of this world to be just such an evil demon. Therefore Kant is right in saying that the cosmological and the teleological arguments alone cannot prove a true and creative God who is not of this world, but need to be rounded off by an additional argument, which the ontological proof precisely is in a position to offer. (*Critique of Pure Reason,* 2nd ed., p. 658; cf. *Critique of Judgment* § 86; *Fortschritte der Metaphysik,* ed. K. Vorländer, Leipzig, 1905, p. 134).

25. No less authority on medieval and ancient philosophy than C. Baeumker (Witelo, pp. 290 ff.) says that Anselm of Canterbury was the first philosopher who planned to give a rigorously formulated proof of the existence of God.

26. To be sure, the basic thought of Anselmian argument can be found already clearly expressed in a passage of Augustine's *Confessions* (VII, 4, 6), as J. Gibb and W. Montgomery in their edition (London, 1927, p. 171) note. Since Anselm himself says (in the preface to his *Monologium,* Migne, Patrologia, CLVIII, 143) that in his works there is nothing which is not most inwardly related to the writings of Augustine, he may well have had this passage of the *Confessions* in mind. The departure which his formulation takes from Augustine, then, is all the more significant: whereas Augustine, following Plato and the Platonists, defines God as the Summum

and Optimum Bonum, Anselm tries to express the idea of God in purely ontological terms of existence. With this, however, he arrives at an entirely new philosophical concept of existence and thus the Anselmian argument signifies the beginning of a new epoch of philosophical thought. In him for the first time, human thought becomes conscious of the problem to which the name 'ontological' was later given. Greek philosophers like Plato, Aristotle, and Plotinus still believed that they could directly grasp being through *nous*. A Christian philosopher like Anselm knows that it is no longer possible through thought alone to conceive of God.

27. Anselm, *Proslogium,* ch. 1. Cf. the edition of F. S. Schmitt, Secconii, 1938, p. 106): God is 'aliquid quo majus nihil cogitari potest.'

28. Cf. Aristotle, *Physics,* II, 1, 193a3: 'Any attempt to prove that nature exists would be childish.' Cf. note 10 to ch. VI.

29. Even though faith based on divine revelation is for Anselm the indispensable hypothesis preceding every attempt to explain divine things, he is nevertheless far from being a mere fideist. He desires a rational inquiry into the content of faith, corresponding to Augustine's 'credo ut intelligam,' or as he himself expresses it: 'I do not seek to understand that I may believe, but I believe in order to understand.' On the other hand, he is anything but the representative of an exaggerated rationalism, in which guise he is often pictured. The first title of his treatise was *Fides quaerens intellectum* (Faith in search of understanding) and its form is that of a prayer: it is a *Proslogium.* (Cf. *Deus Homo,* I, 2; *De Fide Trinitatis,* 2, and M. Grabmann, *Scholastische Methode,* 1909, vol. I, 258 ff.)

30. It is the principle of all criticism of religion to take our conception of God as a mere product of our human nature. And it is this principle against which the Anselmian argument is directed. Anselm seeks to make clear to the atheist that in the moment in which he looks upon his idea of God as an idea produced by himself, he no longer is thinking of God, but of something quite different, namely, of his abstract conception of God. (Cf. the interesting interpretation of Karl Barth, *Fides Quaerens Intellectum, Anselm's Beweis der Existenz Gottes,* Munich, 1931.

31. This contemporary is the monk Gaunilo of the Convent of Marmoutier, who in his *Liber pro Insipiente Adversus Anselmum* contested that the argument was convincing for an atheist.

32. Kant is familiar only with the imperfect form in which the Anselmian argument appears in the works of Descartes, Leibniz, or in those of his own contemporaries, like Mendelssohn. Most later philosophers in turn have become acquainted with it from Kant. Moreover, it was not until Kant's time that the designation of this argument as ontological became customary. Even the word 'ontology'

does not appear before the seventeenth century and is supposed to serve the purpose of designating the problem of Being (in contrast to consciousness) in terms of Cartesian philosophy. (Cf. E. Frank, *Kants Prinzip der Dialektischen Synthesis*, Berlin, 1911, pp. 16 ff.)

33. Hegel correctly emphasized this in his criticism of the Kantian criticism of the ontological argument. (Cf. *Science of Logic*, vol. I, pp. 98 ff.; *History of Philosophy*, Engl. transl. vol. III, p. 71 etc.)

34. For this reason also Thomas Aquinas' criticism does not invalidate Anselm's argument (*Summa Contra Gentiles*, I, 10 ff., *Summa Theol.* I, qu. II, art. 1. *In Sententiarum Librum* I, distinctio III, qu. I, art. 2.): Anselm does not maintain that the essence of God is adequately known to our intellect, and has no intention at all of wresting from the essence of God proofs of His existence.

35. See Kierkegaard's penetrating interpretation in *Philosophical Fragments* (p. 33): 'And how does God's existence emerge from the proof? Does it follow straightway without any breach of continuity? Or have we not here an anology to the behaviour of these toys, the little Cartesian dolls [in Danish: 'dukker,' which literally means divers]. As soon as I let go of the doll it stands on its head. As soon as I let it go—I must therefore let it go. So also with the proof for God's existence, as long as I keep my hold on the proof, i.e. continue to demonstrate, the existence does not come out, if for no other reason than that I am engaged in proving it; but when I let the proof go [i.e. in the act of faith] the existence is there.'

36. Cf. A. E. Taylor, in Hastings' *Encyclopedia of Religion and Ethics*, XII, 280: 'It is probably true to say that it is primarily due to Kant's influence that in our time it is mainly upon the moral argument that popular theistic philosophy continues to base itself.'

37. I follow Dostoevski in the formulation of the nihilistic point of view.

38. Plato already notes in his analysis of philosophical dialectic (*Seventh Epistle*, p. 343D) that every philosophical thesis can easily be disproved by its opposite and that in such discussions, due to the weakness of the arguments, it is usually the opponent who holds the upper hand. (Cf. *American Journal of Philology*, 1940, p. 40.) In very much the same words Kant gives expression to this idea in the *Critique of Pure Reason*. (Cf. the chapter, The Interest of Reason in these Conflicts, 2nd ed., pp. 494 ff.)

39. Cf. Pascal, *Pensées*, nr. 277 (ed. by L. Brunschvicg).

40. Cf. William James, *The Will to Believe*.

41. This is the foundation of what is called Pascal's wager, by which he tried to vindicate the belief in the existence of God against the modern Sceptics. (Pascal, op. cit. nr. 233. Cf. the interpretation of his argument by Sully Prudhomme, *La Vraie Religion selon Pascal*, 1905, 264 ff.) Kant (*Critique of Pure Reason*, 2nd ed.

p. 852) defines 'pragmatic belief' as 'such contingent belief which yet forms the ground for the accurate employment of means to certain actions.' It is such a faith which the doctor, for example, has, who must do something for the patient in danger. And then Kant continues: 'The usual test for continuing the firmness of someone's belief is whether he ventures to make a wager on it or not.' The similarity between Kant's idea and that of Pascal is striking.

42. Cf. Kierkegaard, *Philosophical Fragments*, pp. 29-36.

43. William James, *Pragmatism*, 1910, p. 201. 'True Ideas are those that we can assimilate, validate and verify. False ideas are those we cannot.' Cf. *A Pluralistic Universe* (1909), p. 325: 'The type of union . . . is what I call the strung-along type, the type of continuity, contiguity or concatenation.' *Talks to Teachers on Psychology* (1899), p. v: 'The truth is too great for any one actual mind, even though that mind be dubbed the "absolute," to know the whole of it. The facts and worths of life need many cognizers to take them in.' Cf. R. B. Perry, *In the Spirit of William James*, New Haven, 1938, pp. 137 ff.

44. Cf. Thomas Aquinas, *Summa Theologica*, II, 2, qu. 1, 4, c: 'The apostle says, Hebrew XI, 1, that "faith is the evidence of things that appear not." Faith implies assent of the intellect to that which is believed . . . Now the intellect assents . . . through an act of choice, whereby it turns voluntarily to one side rather than to the other: and if this be accompanied by doubt and fear of the opposite side, there will be opinion, while, if there be certainty and no fear of the other side, there will be faith.' Cf. H. A. Wolfson's analysis of the concept of faith in Aristotle and the medieval philosophers. (*Jewish Quarterly Review*, 1942, pp. 257 ff.): 'The new element that Saint Thomas' interpretation introduces into the definition of faith is the view that the knowledge of which faith is the judgment of truth . . . must not be absolutely certain on purely intellectual grounds. Intellectually there must be some element of uncertainty and doubt about it. Only by an act of the will does it become certain knowledge.' (Cf. *Summa Theologica*, II, 2, qu. 2, 1, c.)

45. John Scotus Erigina (*De Divisione Naturae*, I, 1: Migne, *Patrologia*, CXXII, Paris, 1853, p. 443) says, for example: 'Whatever evades not merely the senses but also understanding and reason, as God does, because of the excellency of His nature, seems indeed not to be . . . and yet God is after all the One, who alone is true, the Being of everything, or as Dionysius Areopagite says: "everything has being, but only Godhood has super-existence."' This thought goes back to Plato, who, in the famous passage of the *Republic* (VI, p. 509B) defined the Idea of Good, the absolute principle, as beyond being and thought. (Cf. Plotinus, *Enneads*, III, 8, 9; V, 2, 1; V, 3, 13; V, 4, 1, etc.) It is this idea on which Plato's whole

dialectic is based. Plato's thought was transmitted to medieval philosophers mainly through Dionysius and Augustine. Thomas emphasized again and again, with reference to the authority of Dionysius, that God for us remains in truth an Unknown and that the attempt to grasp God's essence in a positive way must yield to a negative procedure: 'The divine essence by its immensity surpasses every form to which our intellect reaches. But we have some knowledge thereof by knowing what it is not . . . The more completely we see how a thing differs from others, the more perfectly we know it.' (*Summa Contra Gentiles,* I, 14, Cf. I, 13; *Summa Theologica,* I, qu. 4.; *In Boethii De Trinitate,* I, 2, ad. 1; VI, 3.) Cf. n. 44 to ch. IV.

This is the method of negative theology, as first developed by Plato in his *Parmenides.* 'No statement about God,' says Thomas, 'can tell us what God really is. In order to perceive God in all His truth, we must reject everything about Him which we think we know: The assertion that "God is," denotes not *what* God is, but only an endless and unlimited ocean of substance. If we therefore advance towards God on the path of cancellation, we deny firstly anything corporeal about Him, and secondly anything intellectual or mental, at least in the respects in which this element is found in living creatures, as, for instance, kindness, wisdom, etc.—and then there remains in our intellect only the idea *that* God *is* and nothing further. Finally we remove even this idea of "being" itself, in so far as this idea of "being" is present in living creatures, and then God remains in a dark night of ignorance, and it is this ignorance in which we come closest to God in this life, as Dionysius (*De Divinis Nominibus,* ch. VII) says. For in such mists, they say, does God dwell.' (*In Librum I Sententiarum,* distinctio VIII, qu. 1, art. 1, ad. IV; cf. *De potentia,* VII, 5.) The traits of negative theology to be found in Thomas are strongly emphasized by A. G. Sertillanges, *St. Thomas,* Paris, 1910, and *Les Grandes Thèses de la Philosophie Thomiste,* Paris, 1928, p. 67 ff.

46. Concerning the principle of analogy, see pp. 161 ff.

# The Copy Shoppe

2507B Hearst Ave., Berkeley, Calif.

845-5330

DEC 1971

| Pick Up | Order No. |
|---|---|
| Am Pm | 33402 |

| Total Paid | |
|---|---|
| $ | |

PRESENT THIS RECEIPT WHEN PICKING
UP YOUR ORDER.

*Thank You*

# III. Creation and Time

NATURE, according to the traditional religious belief,
has been created by God, who holds the universe together, using it merely as a means for his ultimate ends.
This conception implies that the earth is the pivot of the
universe, which not only actually but also in a spiritual
sense revolves around man. Modern science has put an
end to such a naïve notion of the world. Since the discoveries of Copernicus we no longer believe that the earth is
the centre of the world; the firmament no longer signifies
the boundary line of the universe. Our present-day concept of nature seems to be diametrically opposed to the
idea of creation. Nature, to modern man, is the sum-total
of blind forces which, regardless of man and his aspirations, relentlessly follow their own laws; and it is precisely
this absolute indifference that is characteristic of nature.

Nature, then, is a complex system of relations, a chain
of causes and effects which seem to have no beginning or
end in time or space. With such a concept of nature, does
it still make sense to speak of the creation of the world
and of man? Is it not actually the rejection of the anthropomorphic way of thinking, the postulate that all mani-
festations of nature and of human life should be explained
through merely natural causes, that has brought about the
stupendous discoveries of modern science and the progress
of modern civilization? To the human intellect, spontaneous generation is inconceivable, for all understanding is
based on the assumption that *nihil ex nihilo fit*—nothing
comes of nothing, every phenomenon has its natural cause

in some other phenomenon through which it can be explained and understood.

It was the Greeks who, in following this rational principle, discovered that concept of 'nature' according to which every phenomenon had its clearly comprehensible cause.[1] Thus the world was freed of all foggy superstition, of all vague spirits.[2] For the first time nature appeared to man in all its beauty, harmony, and rational order, as a cosmos, i.e. as something which in spite of certain persistent enigmas still gave evidence of a character both kindred and discernible to the highest faculty of the human spirit: Reason. To this day all science and philosophy are based on this concept of nature, which no sensible person is likely to abandon again. For a truly scientific understanding of the world, no principle except that of reason, no method other than an empirical one, will suffice. To reintroduce into science the concept of creation, with its implication of supernatural intervention, would verge on absurdity.

But this is not the question. The idea of creation does not infringe upon the precincts of natural science. It is a religious idea, and its realm is so far remote from that of science that a confusion of the two spheres would endanger not only scientific understanding but religious truth as well. The notion of God as the creator of heaven and earth, which was to remain the fundamental presupposition of Christianity, was first formulated in the initial sentence of Genesis. Who would seek scientific information today in such a document of the far distant past when there was not yet science in the modern sense of the word? Scripture was concerned with religion, not with science; it was meant to reveal religious truth, rather than to transmit exact knowledge. Still we must ask: has the idea of creation lost all its religious or philosophical significance? Is it mere folly to take it seriously? Or is it not true, on the contrary, that the real meaning of this concept can become clear only if it is cleansed of all the accidental cosmological connotations which seem to challenge a purely scientific explanation of the world?

Let us consider the signification of the word 'creation.' What does it mean, to create? [3] We speak of the creative forces of nature, but in fact we should speak rather of its productive forces. Actually we mean only that spontaneous faculty of nature for developing continually from its seeds and for reproducing that which they potentially contain. Creation in the true sense of the word is utterly impossible in nature: an ultimate origination, an absolute coming into existence which is not dependent upon any cause of a similar order of being is unthinkable. This is precisely what makes the universe a stable order that can be comprehended by man's reason. Everything that comes into being must be understood as an effect of certain causes, or as an unfolding of certain potencies which previously existed.[4] Strictly speaking then, nothing new ever does happen in nature. Yet this does not imply that in a relative sense nothing novel can come into existence.[5]

With regard to man, we speak of creation in a different sense when we refer to his creative achievements in science, art, philosophy, industry, and so forth.[6] But even the finest accomplishment of the human spirit is not real creation, for all human creation presupposes as its matter the world which man has not created himself. All he can do is to give this material a new shape, the form of his own mind or imagination. More important: man has not created himself, nor his spiritual powers which follow their own natural laws; all his creative work is merely an unfolding of his natural, given faculties. It is precisely this fact which reveals the limitation and finiteness of human existence.

Creation in the traditional religious sense, on the other

hand, means something quite different. It means the bringing forth of something out of nothing, absolute origination—a thing which man can neither experience nor understand.[7] This religious idea, though it cannot be defined
in its positive content, is all the more important as a negative concept, as a philosophical warning that nothing in
the world should be considered absolute. For if we assume
that the world and man have been created by God, neither
the world nor man can be independent in their existence
but must be relative, contingent, accidental; in other
words, they cannot have their origin and meaning in themselves. The relation between the world and a God who is
not of it but different from it is conceivable only as the
relation between creature and the creator. That is why
in the history of religion the idea of real creation first
appears when God, instead of being considered a merely
natural force, becomes a transcendent Being. We do not
know this God through experience or reason but through
faith, and we know of the mystery of creation by the same
means.

Such a concept of creation was utterly foreign to Greek
philosophy. For the Greeks, the world was god; nature
itself was of divine character. The world had its beginning
in itself. It had sprung from an original state, chaos or
matter, which in a somewhat changed form, as its true
'nature,' remained inherent in it.[8] To be sure, Plato in his
transcendent Idea of Good visualized an absolute 'Principle' beyond this world. He even believed that this world
had been created by a divine Being—anticipating in some
measure the Jewish-Christian concept of creation. But the
Platonic god did not really create the world out of nothing; he only transformed the chaos into a cosmos.[9] God
was not a true creator, he was merely an artificer, an architect who had shaped the world out of the everlasting
matter which was there, and which he had not created.

This universe he built in conformity with the Idea—which again was an everlasting pattern independent of the artificer. The notion of true creation is only to be found in the Jewish-Christian religion.[10] The Christian philosophers were fully aware of the fact that their idea of creation, just as their idea of God, was based on their religious faith, on revelation, not on intellectual reasoning. No matter how earnestly they tried to find a philosophical justification for their religious creed, the creation of the world remained a mystery beyond human understanding, the miracle of all miracles.[11]

According to this idea of creation the unalterable order of nature is itself created. This is a thought which need not imply a depreciation of the rational order of the universe. It only means that this world is not everything, but has its limits in a superior Power by which it has been posited; it has the origin of its existence not in itself but in something beyond itself. The idea of creation, then, limits the realm of nature and at the same time the extent of our scientific understanding.

To confuse the idea of creation with the metaphysical assumption that the world had a beginning in time means a complete misunderstanding of the significance of creation.[12] Such procedure is characteristic of those modern philosophers who, in accordance with the exact methods of science, want to understand, to prove or disprove, ideas which to the medieval philosophers had been the inexplicable mysteries of faith.[13] Since it is precisely the temporal character of the world that is indicative of its essence, a beginning of the world in time would imply that the world had a beginning within itself. But the fact that the world was created does not mean that it has a limit in time, it rather indicates that the world itself and consequently also time border on something which is beyond time and therefore eternal.

Eternity is an idea of which we can have no notion or experience. Yet, in our thinking we always have recourse to a truth that seems independent of time.[14] The Christian term 'eternity' should be distinguished from the Greek term *aeon* which means 'everness.' For the Greek philosopher, *aeonion* is that which is *always (aei)*, unending, and conveys the idea of infinite duration.[15] Everness means an everlasting now, a perpetual present.[16] It is in this sense, that to the Greek philosopher, the world was everlasting, immortal, was divine. The Christian concept of eternity, on the contrary, means absolute timelessness, something beyond time and incommensurable with it.[17] The transcendent creator who is beyond this world must also be beyond time.

To the ancient mind, the Jewish-Christian thesis that the world had been created seemed utterly paradoxical and absurd. Both pagan and early Christian thinkers alike felt the threat to the traditional picture of the world in the new idea of creation. Thus a man like Galen, the great physician of the second century A.D., says: 'Moses' opinion greatly differs from our own and from that of Plato and of all the others who among the Greeks have rightly handled the investigation into nature. To Moses, it seems enough that God willed to create a cosmos, and presently it was created; for he believes that for God everything is possible, even if out of ashes He wanted to make a horse or an ox. We, however, do not hold such an opinion; for we maintain, on the contrary, that certain things are impossible by nature, and these God would not even attempt to do; rather would His reason choose the best among those things for which it is possible to come into being.' [18] It was on account of similar arguments that even among early Christian thinkers the concept of creation was absorbed only gradually and not without reluctance.[19]

Augustine is the first to have understood the idea of

creation in all its implications. But even his discussion of
the problem reflects the spiritual struggle that had preceded. He starts his contemplations by saying: 'If asked
why man was not created during these countless and infinite ages of the past, why he came into being so late that,
according to Scripture, less than 6000 years have elapsed
since he was created, I would reply, just as I replied regarding the origin of the world: if it offends you that the
time since the creation of man is so short, take this into
consideration, that nothing that has a limit is long, and
that all the ages of time being finite, are very little, or
indeed nothing at all, compared to the interminable eternity. Consequently, if there had elapsed since the creation
of man, I do not say five or six, but even sixty or six hundred thousand years, or millions or trillions of years, or
this sum multiplied until it could no longer be expressed
in terms of numbers, the same question could still be put:
Why was he not made before?' [20] Augustine's own words
make it sufficiently clear that in my interpretation of the
concept of creation I am by no means applying modern
philosophical terms to a traditional religious idea. The
very foundation of Augustine's understanding of the problem is, that creation is a miracle the idea of which human
reason alone cannot grasp. The conception that the world
was created is an integral part of the Christian Revelation.[21] That does not mean that the belief in the truth of
creation is based merely on the outward authority of the
Bible, on the letter. On the contrary, this conviction rests
on its own inner evidence, which makes it immediately
acceptable to the human intellect: 'We look upon the
heavens and the earth, and they cry aloud that they were
made. For they change and vary . . . They cry aloud that
they did not make themselves: "We did not exist before
we existed in order that we might give ourselves exist-

ence!" And their evident appearance is itself the voice with which they speak.' [22]

These words of Augustine can be taken in a way which has significance for us even today. The free individuality and spontaneity of all things in the world, and particularly of man, constitute the peculiar character of reality. Yet, reason alone which explains everything merely through universal causes is unable to account for this character of reality. The concept of creation, on the other hand, acknowledges both the rational and the irrational elements in the world. For creation means that free and individual beings are brought forth, or, from the point of view of the creator, it signifies that he has infused his own being into another thing which thereby has taken on an independent existence of its own and may later on itself become productive.[23] Thus the idea of creation, although transcending human experience, serves to explain the world as it really is in its twofold character of individual autonomy and universal dependence.[24]

Augustine, however, did not conceal the fact that the idea of creation nevertheless presents a serious difficulty to the human intellect—the relation between creation and time. We are indeed likely to ask: at what moment was the world created, how many years or centuries ago? If in our mind we move backwards into the past, there is no reason for us to stop at any one point. For how could we imagine a temporal limit to the world, we who ourselves are in it and surrounded by it and who in measuring time express only our own relation to this world? In any measurement of time two relative factors are always presupposed: the existence of the world on the one hand, and of man who contemplates it on the other. Yet, if the world and man are created, time must have been created together with the world; and in this case, it was not the world that had a beginning in time, but rather time itself that had a beginning and is therefore limited.

The problem of creation, thus, is most closely connected with that of time. But what is the peculiar character of time? The greatest philosophers have tried to solve this question, but they have all confessed to the same experience that every one of us has had: as long as nobody asks us, we seem to know what time is, but as soon as we are forced to give an account of it, we are unable to define it without getting into serious difficulties.[25] It is for this reason that the present-day positivists flatly refuse to answer the question regarding the true nature of time. They restrict themselves to pointing out that, according to mathematico-physical laws, time is an independent variable, and that beyond this fact the word time has no meaning.[26]

But even if it were true that we should never be able to find out anything definite about the real nature of time, in some fashion we do know this thing that we call time. We take it into account every moment; we consider it the most certain factor in our life.[27] Why is it, then, that we cannot understand this seemingly most familiar phenomenon? Why does it appear to be so contradictory? Is time not a matter of experience? Will anybody deny its objective existence? It is this selfsame question from which the whole difficulty arises. For we call only that which we can perceive as actually or potentially present an objective fact; yet time as a whole is not present. The nature of time consists in that it passes, that, as soon as it turns from future into present, it has passed again and has become past. Shall we say, then, just as the Greek philosophers maintained, that the true nature of time can be comprehended only in the present moment, in the now? Yet, is it possible at all to grasp this present moment? [28] We call present sometimes this century, sometimes this year, or again this month, this day, this hour, this second. But not even the smallest time unit is ever present, for it is time only in so far as it passes. The 'now' is only an indivisible instant, separating the future from the past, without any perceptible existence of its own, something like the mathematical point in the continuum of space. Such a point of time, however, without any extension is not time, it is merely a time limit. The present time, then, cannot be grasped at all, since it exists only in passing, i.e. in becoming past. If this were not so, the present would not be time at all, but eternity. For it is in this way that our mind is wont to imagine eternity, as an eternal now, as a *nunc stans*, as perpetual present.

But where is the future that is not yet and the past that is no more if even the present time cannot be grasped? Time always contains an element of non-existence, and yet it exists. It is the all-inclusive principle; everything else in its dynamic process of becoming and perishing is determined by this contradictory character of time. Nothing in this world lasts forever. In fact, it is a strange irony that the higher and more valuable an existence, the more perishable it seems to be. The dead mineral may last a long time, the loveliest blossom lives but a short while, and the highest exaltations and visions of the human soul flash up only for a moment in order to disappear again in the darkness.

Yet, in spite of all this, we measure time in a way similar to that in which we measure space, which we apprehend as being simultaneously present. According to the revolution of sun, moon, and stars, we measure time in years, days, and hours. That is, we measure the past and the future, though actually these are non-existent for us. Where is the abyss of non-existence out of which emerges the present, and into which it sinks back again? What is time really?

Since the days of Plato and Aristotle philosophers have

never ceased to raise this question, and in present-day thought, with Bergson, Alexander, and Whitehead, the problem of time has once more become the center of philosophical interest.[29] Aristotle in his profound analysis of time says that the dynamic process of change and movement is the essential phenomenon on which time is based, while our actual notion of time is merely an abstraction. In correcting this formulation he then states that time is the measure of change and movement in relation to the before and the after.[30] This definition, however, as he himself adds with amazement, would seem to presuppose a soul which contemplates, counts, and measures the movement of time.[31]

Could it be true that there is no time unless there is a soul to apprehend it? Aristotle restricts himself to raising this question without giving a definite answer to it. It remained for Augustine to understand this problem in all its philosophical consequences. He says that even if time were nothing but the measure of actual movement in the world, still the problem would remain, how we can measure something that is no more, or is not yet.[32] For how can we measure time and call it long or short, if it exists only in passing, if the present has no dimension but is merely a point? And still, this is precisely what we are doing; we perceive intervals of time, we compare them one with another, we measure them one by the other, although they are time units which are passing, which change from non-being into being, and from being again into non-being.[33]

Where then is time, that non-existent thing which we measure and compare in this way? There is only one acceptable answer, that given by Augustine and repeated by Kant: it is in our soul, in the faculty of our imagination to perceive something even though it is not present.[34] The past is nowhere except in our memory, that is, in our imaginative faculty to recall that which once was present to our senses. It is here alone, in our imagination, or whatever term we may use, that the past can possibly be present, just as on the other hand it is in our expectation, in our intention, in our planning and designing, that the future has a similar presence. From the depths of our memory we can draw forth the images of things past whenever we think of them or want to speak of them. The act of sense-perception lasts only a short instant, but the objects by passing through our senses leave their imprint, as it were, thus forming the ideas which we have of them in our soul, and which we can easily reproduce in our imagination. My childhood is not real at this moment, yet I can remember it and visualize it as though it were present. In a similar way, the future is in my soul, as for instance when I think of that which I intend to do or to say the next minute, and still, what I intend is not yet real. Our subjective existence is essentially that process through which the memory of the past and the anticipation of the future are fused into the sense of the present.

This psychological analysis of time has one indisputable result: time essentially is a non-existence which exists, and this mysterious being has its place in our own soul. Still, time is not merely subjective, it is not simply a figment in our soul outside of which it has no meaning whatever. Who can doubt that the order of succession in time is a phenomenon which is objectively founded in nature and its processes—that in measuring time we understand something real as regards the objects of this world? [35] Yet this implies rather than excludes the fact that the phenomenon we call time is realized in its entirety only in the human soul, in our act of measuring it. This is so because only through this operation does it acquire its entelechy, that complex meaning which the word time holds for us. Certainly no one will doubt that the sun and the planets,

even without our measuring their movements, will follow
their course in the firmament just the same. But the universe, though it exists objectively in time, cannot measure
its own time. The universe does not think—man does.

To the Greek philosophers, to Plato, Aristotle, and
Plotinus, the problem of time was of a somewhat different
character.[36] For them, the world was animate, it was divine. Therefore, they did not have difficulty in ascribing
soul or reason or thought to it, or in speaking of a world-
soul, a world-*Nous,* which could measure time.[37]

For modern man, such a way of thinking is no longer
acceptable.[38] Through the Christian idea of creation, the
world once and for all has ceased to be divine or animate; [39]
it has become an entirely prosaic nexus which can be understood simply as a chain of causes and effects. But the
idea of creation also brought about a new interpretation
of the phenomenon of time which is completely different
from that of the Greek philosophers: the subjective time
of the soul is distinguished from the objective time of
nature.[40]

The Greeks thought that time was the time of this
world since it was objectively determined by the revolution of the firmament. Time itself, in their opinion, was
a circle—a periodical recurring of the same, a cycle in
which even the life of the human soul was involved.[41] Just
as every year the succession of the seasons is the same, so
in every human life youth is followed by manhood, manhood by old age. It was thought that the whole process of
nature repeats itself in ever-recurring world periods, during which the souls are reborn in ever new bodies. Thus,
according to most Greek philosophers, the human soul—
even though in this life it may have reached its goal—was
drawn back again into the life-cycle, into a new body
where it had again to live through all the misery of this

world. Man, accordingly, had no definite aim, no real future. Time, to him, was essentially past.

With Christianity, however, man acquired a new understanding of time. Here he sees himself as a unique, un-
repeatable individuality, created by God; thus, the soul
has no past, it has a future. And that absolute future is
God, eternal blessedness, a future which transcends time
and becomes the eschatological aim of all human desire.
With this idea the magic cycle of time has been broken;
it is transformed into a straight line which leads into the
future towards a definite goal.[42] This is our modern concept of time.

It took the passion of a new faith to shatter the idea of
a cyclic time and to enable man to experience time as
something upon which he is not only objectively dependent, but which he himself may subjectively determine
through his own freely willed actions. The human soul,
in its longing for a God beyond this world, reached out
beyond its own limits and beyond time. Believing that the
world had been created, man found within himself, in his
own soul, in his volition and his thinking, a power which
was stronger than all the forces in this world. It was only
logical that Nietzsche, the fanatical opponent of Christianity and its view of creation, tried to revive the ancient
concept of the circular movement of time and of the eternal recurrence of the same events.[43] But modern man cannot return into the narrowness of this ancient concept of
time. No matter how far he may have fallen away from
the traditional dogmas of religion, time, to him, can never
again mean the revolving time of nature. Time now is
directed towards a future which he has set before himself.

Time has thus acquired a new meaning. It is not merely
a cyclical process of nature which unfolds what potentially
had existed before, but it points to the future, to something new. Life, therefore, means struggling for a future.

for progress compared with which all that is present and all that has passed fades into a mere shadow and loses its importance.[44] With the coming of Christianity the human soul became conscious of itself, of its own peculiar power, 'forgetting those things which are behind and reaching forth unto those things which are before.' [45] The soul freed itself from the past, from the world over which it was then trying to rule as its own realm. Nothing which is of this world can satisfy the human spirit; it is the future in which man believes. Even the most irreligious person clings to that concept of time which was inaugurated by Christianity as to the most self-evident presupposition of his existence.

This new Christian view of time naturally resulted in a new concept of history.[46] For if the world has been created, it must have had a beginning and consequently a history. Creation is, as it were, that moment in which eternity touched upon time. In a similar way Christ's advent in the world means that eternity again invaded time and thus a 'new creation' came about.[47] Both Creation and Redemption are absolutely unprecedented; they are unique events which are fixed in time. 'Christ died and rose from the dead only once; he will not die again.' [48] His death was an event which will never recur. It belonged to a definite moment in time which, through its lasting importance, gave the merely natural course of time a new content, a meaning. Thus it became history; that is time, filled with meaning. According to the Christian idea of history, something new happens in time, something that did not exist before and that turns everything which preceded it into the past—into something that will never recur. History, thus understood, is not an eternal repetition of the same events, as it had been for Plato and Aristotle.[49] History, on the contrary, is a sequence of creative moments in which something new enters the world and deter-

mines the future. For the Christian philosopher, Creation
and Redemption signify fixed points in the history of the
world. This idea marks a new historical interpretation of
the world and of the events which happen in time. Our
modern concept of history, no matter how rationalized and
secularized it may be, still rests on that concept of historical time which was inaugurated by Christianity. Here history is understood as the progress of time, as a sequence
of moments in which something new happens and thus
gives meaning to the merely natural course of time.

Whatever we may think of the purely objective time
of nature, that consciousness through which alone time
acquires complete and true meaning for us has its seat in
the human soul, in the ability of the imagination to envisage future goals. The ultimate principle of time must
be sought, therefore, in our own soul, in that imaginative
power which enables us to transcend merely objective
reality. That is why it seems to us that time would go on
even if in the universe all time were to come to a stand-
still, even if the sun and the moon were to stop following
their courses, even if the universe ceased to exist. Still, the
human soul would perceive time. For the life of the soul,
as far as it can be grasped at all, is inseparably connected
with that process in which the two opposite faculties, that
of remembering the past and that of anticipating the future, are fused into the awareness of the present. It is for
this reason that our consciousness knows itself as a transi-
tory process in time and can never for a second cling to
the present.

The only present which we can conceive as really present is the presence of God. It is in the act of faith alone
that the soul realizes true presence, in so far as it is itself
present to God. 'It is here alone that the restless soul may
find a resting point.' [50] The imperfection and finiteness of
man thus manifests itself in his temporal limitation. His

apprehension of the present is merely the consciousness of an absence of the present, of transitoriness. From this feeling springs the desire for the unattainable, for true presence, true existence. Whether we speak of this urge as the Eros of Plato or the Love of the New Testament— under any name it is simply the desire that true being, which is a thing of the future, should become a thing of the present. In this life, however, man cannot attain true existence, this absolute present which lies in a future beyond time, for he remains time-bound and restricted by the limits of time.

Time is the outgrowth of our imagination; [51] therefore the soul is essentially connected with time. No matter how passionate its love, how ardent its religious desire—in this life the soul can never grasp the Beyond as something present in the same way as it experiences the objects of this world. It can only hope for this Beyond as for its own future; in other words, it can only believe in it. That is the philosophical meaning of the Biblical saying, 'we walk by faith, not by sight.' [52]

In his relation to a transcendent God, man cannot immediately perceive Him, as the Greek philosopher perceived his god. Since he can only believe in Him, hope for Him, his relation to God remains dependent upon time. Even if man thinks that in his own soul he has felt the immediate presence and proximity of God, even if in mystical ecstasy he believes he has seen God directly, such an experience lasts only a short moment and cannot be retained.[53] It remains open to subsequent doubt; we can never be sure that we did not fall prey to our excited senses or to our fantasy. Be the remembrance of such an experience ever so deeply engraved upon our memory— we can do little more than believe that it was truly an experience of reality. This belief consists in our hope for a goal beyond time, when this future shall become the true present. This is the only possible relation that man in his temporal limitation can have to the eternal. The act of belief, however, like the act of love which is fundamentally identical with it, always implies mutual confidence. Belief means that I trust in another being's belief in myself, that I comprehend that by which I am likewise comprehended.

As we have seen, the far-reaching implication of the concept of true creation is this: through it alone can man understand the significance of his own temporality. It is clear now that all metaphysical speculation regarding the moment in which the world or the individual soul may have been created is senseless. For the notion that the world and the soul have been created means just this, that they were not created within the limits of time, but that time was created along with them. It is for this reason that the life of the soul in this world is inseparably connected with time.

There is a profound meaning in the traditional dogma, according to which man was created in the image of God and his soul is the *imago Dei*. We may interpret this metaphor to mean that all creative power of the human soul is a mere shadow of true creation. Human creation is in fact merely the work of man's imagination, but imagination seems to be the expression of man's real essence. We may admit that the human concept of creation itself is an idea of religious imagination for which there is no adequate example, either in the universe, or in man himself. With this concept our imagination, by trying to grasp a truth beyond the limited possibilities of sense-perception, transcends its own boundaries. But even if creation can be pictured only by our imagination, this fact need not impair the objective meaning or the truth of this idea.

The seemingly superstitious notion of creation, if freed from all the unessential cosmological connotations with which tradition has imbued it, sits in judgment, as it were, upon all our apparent truths and our imaginary aspirations. In this negative sense, the idea of creation is acceptable even to philosophical reason. That does not mean that through the concept of creation any natural or human phenomenon could be explained in a scientific way. It only serves to indicate the limits of reason and of human existence. The individual wakes up to the fact that he has been thrown into this alien world as an utterly dependent being. He does not know whence he came or where he is going. Our origin and our destiny remain inscrutable to reason. That is the fundamental fact from which all philosophy has to start. If in spite of this, man wants to believe that his own existence, his volition, his thought have a meaning and a truth, he can do so only by relating himself to an absolute truth through which his existence and his thought are determined. It is this absolute dependence which is meant by the idea of creation. This concept, although it cannot rationally explain the riddle of human existence, serves to point to it and to make man aware of it. The greatness of the religious idea of creation consists in this: that amidst this finite and dependent world it keeps alive in man a sense of his own mysterious place within that creation.

## NOTES

1. Aristotle calls the dogma that 'nothing comes into being out of what is non-existent' a doctrine common to all physicists (*Physics*, I, 4, 187a27; cf. *Metaphysics*, III, 4, 999b6; VII, 7, 1032a13; b31). This principle, attributed by Aristotle (*Physics*, III, 4, 203b6 ff.) already to Anaximander was expressly formulated by Parmenides (*Fr.* 8, 9, Diels) and by his pupil Melissus (*Fr.* 1, Diels). Cf. also Epicurus (Diogenes Laërtius, x, 38) and the even more pointed statement of Lucretius, *De Rerum Natura*, I, 150: 'Nothing is ever produced by divine power out of nothing.' Cf. ibid. 159; cf. also C. Giussani in

his edition of Lucretius, Torino, 1923, *ad loc.*, p. 30. How strongly the Greek concept of nature in general is determined by the idea that 'everything has its natural cause, and nothing occurs without a natural cause' becomes evident from the Hippocratic writings (e.g. Hippocrates, *On Air, Water, and Situation*, ch. 64K. Cf. W. A. Heidel, *Proceedings of the American Academy of Arts and Sciences*, XLV, 1910, pp. 79 ff.; H. Burnet, *Early Greek Philosophy*, 1908, p. 12; F. J. E. Woodbridge, *Philosophical Review*, 1901, pp. 359-74; A. O. Lovejoy, *Philosophical Review*, 1909, pp. 369 ff.).

2. Cf. Epicurus in Diogenes Laërtius, x, 87: 'For in the study of nature we must not conform to empty assumptions and arbitrary laws, but follow the promptings of the facts.'

3. Concerning the problem of Creation in general, cf. A. N. Whitehead, *Process and Reality*, New York, 1929, p. 528; J. Ward, *The Realm of Ends*, 1920, pp. 225 ff.; E. S. Brightman, *Personality and Religion*, 1935, p. 55 f.

4. Aristotle elaborated on the concept of potentiality as differentiated from that of actuality precisely in order to maintain the principle of the 'nihil ex nihilo fit,' cf. *Metaphysics*, IV, 5, 1009a31.

5. Cf. A. N. Whitehead, *Religion in the Making*, 1926, p. 90: 'The creativity whereby the actual world has its character of temporal passage to novelty' constitutes 'the formative character of the actual temporal world'; cf. the same, *Process and Reality*, p. 31: 'Creativity is the principle of novelty' (ibid. p. 248; p. 324), and J. Ward, op. cit. p. 245 (below, n. 23). S. Alexander, *Space, Time and Deity*, London, 1927, Vol. II, 14: 'Mind is an "emergent" from life, and life an emergent from a lower physico-chemical level of existence.' C. Lloyd Morgan, *Emergent Evolution*, London, 1927, pp. 9 ff.; H. Bergson, *Creative Evolution*, New York, 1923, pp. 128 f., 163 f., 339 f.

6. Cf. Whitehead, *Process and Reality*, p. 474; cf. also J. Ward, op. cit. p. 239, who fittingly compares Aristotle, *Nic. Eth.*, IX, 7, 4, p. 1168a7: 'He that has created a given work loves his work . . . for the work produced displays in actuality what existed before potentially.' (Transl. by D. P. Chase, London, 1925, p. 222.)

7. The term 'creatio ex nihilo' is a rational expression evidently coined as a counterpart of the philosophical formula 'nihil ex nihilo fit.' It is foreign to Scripture, where the idea of creation did not yet constitute a philosophical problem. It first occurs in the second century B.C., in the Greek version of the second Book of the Maccabeans (7. 28), a passage the Vulgate renders as follows: 'ex nihilo fecit illa Deus.' Of later writings cf. *Apoc. Baruch Syr.*, 48, 8; Philo, *De Spec. Leg.*, IV, 187, p. 367; *Corp. Herm.*, I, 48, p. 334 Reitz. Subsequently the formula is used by Christian thinkers whenever

they wish to express their idea of creation in terms of Greek philosophy, cf. Romans 4. 17; Hermas, *Visio*, I, 1, 6.

8. The term 'nature' was used by the early Greek philosophers originally in the sense of 'material cause' or 'elemental constituent.' They understood the genesis of the world as a process similar to the growth of an animal from its seed. (Cf. Heidel, op. cit. p. 101 and p. 86, n. 32: 'The philosophers were in effect giving the genealogy of the world.') According to them, things did not originate through creation but rather through generation from a primary substance. Whatever was brought forth in this way is that which actually exists, while that from which it emanated recedes and turns into past. The guiding principle of Greek thinking is the Nous, the intellection of that which exists. That which the Nous perceives as being present actually exists and at the same time must needs be as it is; it is an *eidos*, an 'idea,' something that can be seen (cf. A. E. Taylor, *Varia Socratica*, Oxford, 1911, p. 178 f.; cf. also below, n. 16 and note 37 to ch. VI.)

9. Plato, *Timaeus*, 30A: 'The god took over all that is visible—not at rest, but in discordant and unordered motion—and brought it from disorder into order' (transl. by F. M. Cornford, *Plato's Cosmology*, 1937, p. 22); cf. *Laws*, x, 897A ff.; Plutarch, *De Animae Procreatione*, 1014a ff., seems to give the most adequate interpretation of this Platonic concept of creation. (Cf. Kant, *Critique of Pure Reason*, 2d ed., p. 655.)

10. The difference between the concept of creation of the Old Testament and that of Plato is most adequately formulated by Philo, *De Somniis* I, 13, 76: 'God, when He gave birth to all things, not only brought them into sight but also made things which before were not, not just handling material as a *demiurge*, an *artificer*, but being Himself its *creator*' (cf. *De Vita Mosis* II, 48). It is for this reason that the translators of the Septuagint in rendering the corresponding Hebrew word did not choose the Platonic word *demiurge*, which signifies the craftsman who shapes material with his hands, but rather the word *ktistes*, a word which in classical Greek means 'the founder,' especially the founder of a city. The creation of the world is a spiritual process which may actually be compared with that of a ruler who through his will alone founds a city out of nothing; cf. *Theologisches Woerterbuch des Neuen Testaments*, ed. Kittel, *s.v. ktistes*; G. F. Moore, *Judaism*, 1927, I, p. 380; R. Smend, *Alttestamentliche Religionsgeschichte*, 1893, p. 40. I wish to point out that the passage cited from *De Somniis* is the only one in which Philo shows a clear understanding of the difference between the Jewish and the Platonic conception of creation. Everywhere else he appears completely dominated by the Platonic idea of God as the artificer, the demiurge, which presupposes the eternal

existence of matter. Cf. E. Brehier, *Philon d'Alexandrie*, 1908, pp. 79 ff.; C. Siegfried, *Philo*, 1875, pp. 230 ff.; J. Drummond, *Philo Judaeus*, vol. I, London, 1888, pp. 267 ff.; 292 ff., 300 ff. Cf. H. A. Wolfson, *Philo*, 1947, I, 301.

11. Cf. Augustine, *Confessions*, XI, 3, 5; ibid. 5, 7, 9, 11. Cf. n. 13.

12. The same misunderstanding of the meaning of the idea of creation is in Kant's *Critique of Pure Reason*, 2nd ed., p. 454. (First Antinomy: 'The world has a beginning in time.' But cf. p. 478.) Cf. J. Ward, op. cit. p. 231; A. N. Whitehead, *Process and Reality*, 1929, pp. 528 ff. But even those recent philosophers who are trying to deduce from the latest observations and discoveries of astronomy an argument for the truth of the thesis that the world was created are guilty of the selfsame mistake. Even if it were possible to demonstrate that our world is but a finite number of years old, this would still be no proof for the assumption that this world must have been created out of nothing. It would still be possible to assume the existence of some kind of primordial matter prior to the beginning of the world. Plato showed in the *Sophistes* that we can understand only relative non-existence whereas absolute nothingness cannot be grasped by our thinking. Cf. M. B. Foster, 'The Christian Doctrine of Creation and the Rise of Modern Science,' *Mind*, 1934, p. 446.

13. Thomas Aquinas formulated this medieval opinion in the *Summa Theologica*, I, qu. 46, art. 2 contra: 'The article of faith cannot be proved demonstratively, because faith is of things not seen (Hebr. XI) . . . Therefore the newness of the world is known only by revelation . . . Hence that the world began to exist is an object of faith, but not of demonstration or science.' (Vol. II, pp. 247 ff. Cf. *Summa Contra Gentiles*, II, 38.)

14. The word 'Eternity' is used in at least three different senses: (1) To denote *unending time*. This is the general Greek usage of the word as we can find it, e.g. in Aristotle, who says: 'The world as a whole was not generated and cannot be destroyed, as some [for instance Plato] allege, but is unique and eternal, containing infinite time and embracing it in itself' (*On the Heavens* II, 1, 283b26, cf. *Physics* IV, 12, 221b3). This is a kind of eternity that even modern philosophers are ready to recognize. As an example I mention J. Royce, who claims that 'the temporal world must needs be when viewed in its wholeness an eternal world' (*The World and the Individual*, New York, 1901, Lect. III esp. p. 133). Cf. W. James, *A Pluralistic Universe*, 1928, p. 43, 232 f.; A. O. Lovejoy, 'The Obsolescence of the Eternal,' *Philos. Review*, 1909, p. 479; J. Ward, *The Realm of Ends*, p. 468 ff.; D. Balsillie, *Mind*, 1911, p. 357. (2) To denote *the timelessness of truth*. This is evidently Plato's conception of eternity as it is ascribed to his Idea in contraposition to the ever-changing world in time. But since Plato considers time as

'the moving likeness of eternity' (cf. F. M. Cornford, *Plato's Cosmology*, pp. 98, 102), he does not understand eternity as something incommensurable with time. In this second sense also modern idealists use the word in speaking of eternal values, ideals, or truths. (3) To denote *the timelessness of existence*. This is the meaning of eternity that in Scripture is an attribute of the God who is above World and Time. The Hebrew words *nezach, olam* and the like, which since the Septuagint we are used to render with 'aeon' or 'eternity,' originally do not imply any relation to time but are the equivalent of 'hard, powerful, life, triumph,' words that signify God's superior force. This true Eternity therefore 'belongs to God alone and is God's substance itself' (Augustine, *De Natura Boni contra Manicheos*, 39; *Enarratio in Psalmum* 101, 10; *Sermones* 117, 10). 'God is outside the order of time' (Aquinas, *Summa Theologica*, Part I, q. 10 ff., p. 96 ff.). This is the kind of Eternity that modern philosophers are inclined to deny. About the modern discussion of the problem of Time and Eternity, cf. J. E. McTaggart, *Mind*, 1909, p. 343; MacKenzie, 'Eternity,' *Encyclopaedia of Religion and Ethics;* Pringle-Pattison, *The Idea of God*, Lect. XVIII; F. von Hügel, *Philosophy of Religion*, London, 1926, p. 78; and in general T. A. Gunn, *The Problem of Time*, London, 1929.

15. Cf. Aristotle, *On the Heavens*, I, 9, 279a22. 'Indeed, our forefathers were inspired when they made this word "*aeon.*" The total time which circumscribes the length of life of every creature, and which cannot in nature be exceeded, they named the *aeon* of each. By the same analogy also the sum of existence of the whole world, the sum which includes all time even to infinity, is *aeon*, taking the name from "ever" (*aei*) being.' (Cf. C. Lackeit, *Aion*, 1916; Kittel, *Theolog. Woerterbuch*, 1933, s. v. *Aion*, p. 197.) Cf. W. Gouge, *A Commentary on the Epistle to the Hebrews*, I, 8 (1655): 'The Greek word here translated ever, *aeon*, according to the notation signifies *everbeing*' (quoted in *English Dictionary on Historical Principles*, ed. J. A. H. Murray, Oxford, 1888 ff., vol. E, p. 341).

16. The idea that absolute being means an ever-lasting 'now' is first to be found with Parmenides, *Fr.* 8, Diels: 'The one Being never was nor ever will be since it is *now* all at once' (cf. F. M. Cornford, *Plato's Cosmology*, p. 102). It remains the characteristic expression of the Greek concept of being. Later on, the phrase *tota simul* is much used by Christian thinkers, for instance, by Aquinas to describe Eternity, and Aquinas was influenced by Boethius, whom in his own discussion he quotes often (e.g. *Summa Theologica*, I, 1, q, 10, 1 ff.).

17. Cf. E. Rohde, *Psyche*, Engl. transl., 1925, p. 253: 'When a Greek says "immortal," he says God; they are interchangeable ideas.' Concerning the difference of this concept of immortality from that

of true eternity, cf. Augustine, *De Natura Boni contra Manichaeos,*
Ch. 39; *De Trinitate,* xv, 5, 7 f.; *Sermones,* 65, 3, 4; and Boethius,
*The Trinity,* iv, 65: 'The expression "God is ever" denotes a single
Present . . . *Philosophers* say that "ever" may be applied to the
life of the heavens and other immortal bodies . . . But as applied
to God it has a different meaning . . . Our present connotes changing time and sempiternity; God's present, unmoved, connotes eternity.' Thomas Aquinas, *Summa Theologica,* i, 1, qu. 10, art. 4, shows
that 'Time and Eternity' do not have 'the same kind of measure
(mensurae unius generis),' Engl. transl., p. 103.

18. Galen, *De Usu Partium Corporis Humani,* xii, 14 (iii, p. 905,
Kuehn). I am indebted to my friend L: Edelstein for drawing my
attention to this important passage.

19. Like Philo, many of the early Church Fathers (cf. above, note
10) fail to make clear the principal difference between the Platonic and the Biblical concepts of creation; they simply interpreted
the creation of Genesis in terms of Greek philosophy. Cf., e.g. Justin
Martyr, *Apologia,* i, 59 f.; Clement of Alexandria, *Stromateis,* v, 14,
92, 12, 78; *Protrepticus,* 5, 3 ff.; *Comm. in Joh.,* i, 19, 114; cf. E. de
Faye, *Origène,* Paris, 1928, iii, p. 66. Augustine expressly attacks
such Platonizing interpretations wherever he tries to elucidate the
true meaning of the idea of creation in all its philosophical consequences (cf. esp. *Confessions,* xi, 4; *De Civitate Dei,* xi, 23; xii, 14).
The Greek philosophers after Plato frequently discussed the problems of cosmology and anthropology in the form of commentaries
on the *Timaeus.* In an analogous way, Philo and the Church Fathers,
in treating the same subject, used *Genesis* i, 1-3 as their text (cf.
A. Harnack, *History of Dogma,* London, 1897, iii, p. 247). Augustine,
*Confessions,* xi, 2, begins his discussion of these problems by con-
trasting the fables of the Greek philosophers with the initial words
of Genesis, and then expounds his own ideas in the course of an
interpretation of this account.

20. This is an abridged translation of Augustine, *De Civitate Dei,*
xii, 13. The final sentence reads as follows: 'For the past and infinite
eternity during which God abstained from creating man is so great
that, compare it with what vast and untold number of ages you
please, so long as there is a definite conclusion of this term of time,
it is not even as if you compared the minutest drop of water with
the ocean . . . That space of time which starts from some beginning
I know not whether to say we should count it the very minutest
thing or *nothing at all*' (transl. by M. Dods, p. 233).

21. *Confessions,* xi, 2, 4, end; cf. ibid. 3, 5; *Civitas Dei,* xii, 26;
cf. also *De Genesi ad Litteram Imperf. Liber,* i, 1.

22. *Confessions,* xi, 4, 6 (cf. transl. by F. J. Sheed, New York,
1943).

23. Cf. A. N. Whitehead, *Process and Reality*, 1929, p. 31: 'Creativity is the principle of novelty'; cf. ibid. p. 324: 'An entity is at least a particular form capable of infusing its own particularity into creativity.' Cf. E. S. Brightman, *The Problem of God*, p. 153; *Philosophy of Religion*, 1940, pp. 149 ff.; cf. below, n. 41.

24. Cf. J. Ward, *The Realm of Ends*, p. 245: 'The idea of creation like the idea we admit is altogether transcendent . . . But if the idea of creation will carry us further and if nothing else will, then that idea, it is maintained, is rationally justified though it be not empirically verified.'

25. Cf. Plato, *Parmenides*, 156D; *Timaeus*, 37D; *Symposion*, 206D; Aristotle, *Physics*, IV, 10 f.; Plotinus, *Enn.*, III, 7. Augustine, *Confessions*, XI, 14, 17.

26. R. von Mises, *Kleines Lehrbuch des Positivismus*, 1939, p. 168 f.; P. Frank, *Kausalgesetz*, Vienna, 1932, pp. 142-6; 285; the same, *Between Physics and Philosophy*, Cambridge, Mass., 1941, p. 92. Cf. note 36. Cf. Russell, *Analysis of Matter*, 1927, p. 131: 'Time seems equally obvious . . . From this happy familiarity with the everyday world physics has been gradually driven by its own triumphs. The space-time of relativity is very far removed from the space and time of our unscientific experience.'

27. For the following compare Plato, *Parmenides*, 156D ff.; Aristotle, *Physics*, IV, 10-14, and VIII, 1 f.; *On the Heavens*, I, 9; Plotinus, *Enn.*, III, 7; esp. Augustine, *Confessions*, XI, 13-31.

28. Cf. Aristotle, *Physics*, IV, 13, 222a10 ff.; cf. also Plato's pupil Xenocrates, *Fr.* 9, in Porphyry, *In Harm. Ptolemaei*, p. 30 (ed. Döring).

29. Cf. W. R. Inge, *Philosophy of Plotinus*, London, vol. I, 1923, p. 169-91: 'The problem of Time is one of the hardest in metaphysics . . . From the first dawn of speculation till now, from the time of Parmenides and Zeno to that of Mr. Bradley and M. Bergson, there has been no other problem that has seemed so baffling as that of Time.' S. Alexander: 'To realize the importance of Time is the gate of wisdom' (*Space, Time and Deity*, Vol. I, London, 1927, p. 36); Russell: 'To realize the unimportance of time is the gate of wisdom' (*Mysticism and Logic*, London, 1919, p. 22). It is generally agreed that in our day Bergson was the first philosopher to give serious consideration to the problem of time (cf. Alexander, op. cit. p. 44). But it was J. M. Guyau, in his work *La Genèse de l'Idée de Temps*, who, in the eighties of the last century, first attacked the problem and stimulated Bergson to produce his own work. In the same decade, stirred by the experiment of Michelson, the physicists became interested in the problem of time in relation to the measurement of objective time. M. Palágyi's *New Theory of Space and Time* (1901) furnished the basis for Minkowski's con-

ception and 'without Minkowski's idea the general theory of relativity would perhaps have got no further than its long clothes' (Einstein, *Theory of Relativity*, Engl. transl., p. 57). About the historical development of the problem of Time and the vast literature concerning this subject see the interesting book of J. A. Gunn, *The Problem of Time, An Historical and Critical Study*, London, 1929.

30. *Physics*, IV, 11, 219a8: 'Time must either itself be movement, or if not, must pertain to movement and change . . . Movement, then, is the objective seat of before- and afterness.' Cf. *De Gener. et Corr.*, II, 10, 337b23; *Met.* XII, 6, 1071b9, etc. *Physics*, IV, 11, 219b1: 'This is just what time is, the calculable measure or dimension with respect to before- and afterness.' Cf. 220b8; VIII, 1, 257b28.

31. *Physics*, IV, 14, 223a21. 'The question remains, then, whether or not time would exist if there were no soul and consciousness; for if there cannot be someone to count there cannot be anything that can be counted, so that evidently there cannot be number and measure.' Cf. Simplicius, *In Categorias*, p. 350. Cf. Thomas Aquinas, *Commentary on Aristotle's Physics*, IV, Lect. 23, ed. Leonina. tom. II, Romae, 1884, p. 223.

32. Cf. *Confessions*, XI, 16, 21 ff.

33. Cf. *Confessions*, XI, 18, 23-21, 29.

34. Kant had as little intention as Augustine of explaining time as a purely subjective phenomenon which had no basis in objective nature. His discussion in #62 of his *Critique of Judgment* (cf. *Critique of Pure Reason*, 2nd ed., esp. pp. 71 ff.) proves this. When Kant denies the form of time to the 'Thing in itself,' he is doing nothing but what the Christian metaphysicians have always done. For towards the end of the *Critique of Pure Reason* it becomes clear to everyone that in the last analysis Kant, by the 'Thing in itself' really understands God. The interpretation of Kant as a subjective idealist and an antimetaphysical epistemologist seems to be ineradicable in spite of all Kant's assurance that his intention was to refute this very idealism (*Crit. of Pure Reason*, 2nd ed., pp. 274 ff., 406 ff., etc.) and to give a 'metaphysics of metaphysics' (letter to M. Herz after 11 May 1781). In reality Kant's basic metaphysics is not at all so different from Aristotle's as the interpreters of Kant make it appear. Form and matter are also his fundamental principles. Aristotle says that 'Reason, the mind, is the form of forms and sense the form of sensible things' (*On the Soul*, III, 8, 432a2). Kant tries to analyse this 'form' of Reason, though in the subjective terms of modern philosophy. But even Aristotle apparently knew that the phenomenon of time reaches its actual form, its 'entelechy' in the soul which counts it (cf. n. 31). Augustine on the other hand sought the origin of time in a

very much deeper stratum of man than did Kant, who in this respect does not get beyond Aristotle's concept of time as the time of nature. Russell's criticism of Kant's argument (*Problems of Philosophy*, London, 1915, p. 155; *Our Knowledge of the External World*, London, 1915, pp. 155 ff.) does not invalidate Augustine's conception of historical time.

35. For the opinion of modern physicists regarding this problem, cf. J. A. Gunn, *The Problem of Time*, ch. v, pp. 173 ff.; A. S. Eddington, *The Mathematical Theory of Relativity*, 1923, p. 225; and F. A. Lindemann, *The Quantum Theory*, Oxford, 1932, p. 144.

36. According to Plato, *Timaeus*, 37E ff., and Plotinus, *Enn.*, III, 7, 11-12, the true origin and nature of time are to be found in the life of the world soul. For the Christian, however, there can be nothing between God and our mind (*inter mentem nostram et veritatem nulla interposita creatura est*: Augustine, *De Vera Religione*, 55, 113). Therefore Augustine could find the origin of time only in the life of the individual soul, for God, to him, is beyond time. In this sense he enlarged upon the Platonic-Plotinian concept of time.

37. Cf. Plato, *Phaedrus*, 245C; *Laws*, x, 892 ff., and Aristotle, *De Anima*, II, 1, 412a19; cf. also R. D. Hicks, *Aristotle De Anima*, Cambridge, 1907, p. 311 ad loc.

38. And yet contemporary metaphysicians who deal with the problem of time have fallen back into this Greek mode of Panpsychism, despite the fact that they are deeply affected by the findings of recent science. Bergson makes *durée* or real time the dynamic of the evolutionary process of Nature, thus reviving Plotinus' conception of Time in the subjective terms of our modern language. S. Alexander regards time as the *élan vital* of the universe. It is not easy to characterize briefly Whitehead's profound theory of time, but the panpsychistic or vitalistic tendency of his whole metaphysics can hardly be denied. These ideas of old have not lost their charm for us and strangely satisfy our speculative imagination. But while the Greeks found absolute truth in such metaphysics, modern man sees in it a free play of abstract thought. Today no one of us would in sober earnest regard the Universe as a kind of living and conscious being, that is as God. Augustine was the first to free himself from these fantastic ideas. In his analysis of time he drew the consequences resulting from his fundamental change of view and sought the source of our time-consciousness in a stratum of man's existence which is different from the world. In this Augustine's concept of time is superior to that even of contemporary metaphysicians and this is the reason why I have followed not their interpretation but the lucid analysis of Augustine.

M. Heidegger's interpretation of time (*Sein und Zeit,* Halle, 1927, p. 231 ff.) is not fundamentally at variance with that of Augustine, since Heidegger too tries to grasp the root of the time phenomenon in man's existence so far as that is different from the objective existence of the world. But to him human existence becomes merely subjective and in the last analysis his concept of time reminds one more of Bergson than of Augustine (cf. J. A. Gunn, op. cit., esp. p. 257). S. Alexander, on the other hand, says that 'the world and everything in it is historical because the world is a world of events.' (*Philosophy and History: Essays presented to E. Cassirer.* Oxford, 1936, p. 11 ff.) But by the word historical we certainly mean more than this, and Augustine is concerned with the analysis of genuinely historical time. (Cf. Collingwood's statement quoted in note 1 f. to ch. v.)

39. It is characteristic that Kepler argued against the Aristotelian as well as the Ptolemaic theory, on the ground that they implied that the 'planets know mathematics.' Cf. note 2 to ch. 1. For the discussion among the Church Fathers concerning the problem whether the stars are conscious see Migne, *Patrologia Graeca,* XVII (Origenes, 7), pp. 973 ff.; St. Thomas, *Summa Theologica,* I, i, qu. 70 ff.; and C. C. J. Webb, *Studies in the History of Natural Theology,* Oxford, 1915, p. 273 f. Cf. also Hegel, *Philosophy of Religion,* II, p. 184.

40. This new interpretation of time is the important achievement of Augustine. He no longer believes that 'the motions of the sun, moon and of the stars were the very true times,' as the Greek philosophers did (*Confessions,* XI, 23, 29. Cf. Diels, *Doxographi,* 1879, p. 318.)

41. Aristotle, *Physics,* IV, 14, 223b21, says: '. . . and so time is regarded as the rotation of the sphere [cf. ibid. IV, 10, 218 b1: 'the revolution of the all-embracing heaven'] . . . And this is the reason of our habitual way of speaking; for we say that human affairs and those of all other things . . . seem to be in a way circular, because all these things come to pass in time and have their beginning and end as it were "periodically." ' The best-known examples of this circular concept of time are the Stoic doctrine of the world periods and the Pythagorean-Platonic notion of the migration of souls according to which the individual soul is re-incarnated in every world period. Yet, in a broader sense this periodical concept of time occurs with most Greek philosophers, with Heraclitus and Empedocles no less than with Parmenides and even with Aristotle, as is evident from the above quoted passage. (Cf. W. Jaeger, *Aristotle,* Oxford, 1934, p. 133 f.; A. O. Lovejoy and G. Boas, *History of Primitivism,* Baltimore, 1935 passim.) This idea is closely connected with the scientific doctrine of the world year

or the world cycles. Basing their assumptions on the age-old astronomical observations of the Egyptians and Babylonians the Greek astronomers thought that just as the sun, the moon, and the planets at the end of certain regular periods returned to the same positions which they held at the beginning; so was this also true of the other heavenly bodies. Even the changes in the movement of the world were believed to take place according to a periodic law. Eudemus, a pupil of Aristotle, in a lecture on the concept of time and of temporal identity, used the following words: 'But if one may believe the Pythagoreans . . . then some day I myself, with this staff in my hand, shall talk to you who will sit in front of me, just as you are sitting now, and the same will be true of everything else.' (Eudemus, *Fr.* 51, ed. Spengel; cf. T. Gomperz, *Greek Thinkers*, Engl. transl., vol. I, ch. 5, Sect. 4). It is the same concept of time which Augustine finds current even among philosophers of his own time and which he characterizes in the following words (*De Civitate Dei*, XII, 14): 'Some philosophers have introduced cycles of time in which there should be a constant renewal and repetition of the order of nature . . . For men were before us and are with us and shall be after us; and so all living things and plants . . . According to these philosophers, the same periods and events of time are repeated: as if for instance the philosopher Plato having taught in the school of Athens which is called the Academy, so, numberless ages before, at long but certain intervals, this same Plato and the same school and the same disciples existed and so also are to be repeated during the countless cycles that are yet to be.' Ibid. XI, 23: 'They say that souls in proportion to their various sins merited divers bodies as prisonhouses; . . . *Origen* is justly blamed for holding this opinion.'

42. Augustine, *De Civitate Dei*, X, 30; XI, 4; XII, 14 ff.; XII, 21. Cf. P. Brunner, *Zeitschrift f. Theologie u. Kirche*, 1933, pp. 1 ff.

43. G. A. Morgan, *What Nietzsche Means*, 1941, pp. 287 ff.; K. Löwith, *Nietzsche*, 1935, pp. 101 ff.

44. It is this character which distinguishes our concept of time from that held by all other civilizations. We become conscious of it only by being confronted with a different time experience, for example, that of the Chinese as it is graphically described by an American: 'Time in China has no immediacy as in America. Here I find the swift passage of our few earthly years accepted as naturally as the fall of flower and leaf. This philosophical acceptance of the individual life as just a part of the life of the race, which goes on as the life of the tree goes on, makes time limitless. A century past or a century in the future is not considered far off. I hear and speak a language in which grammar has no tense. Both scholars and illiterates, in ordinary speech, tell an event of centuries ago as

casually as an incident of the hour. Only as my knowledge has accumulated have I been able to know whether something related happened just then or in some past dynasty. Even now, after twelve years, I often do not know.' (Nora Waln, *The House of Exile,* New York, 1943, p. 45.) The time consciousness of the Greeks as it is expressed, e.g. by Homer (in *Iliad,* VI, 145 ff., etc.) is half-way between our experience and that of the Orientals.

45. In *Confessions,* XI, 29, 39 (cf. also 23, 30, and 28, 30) Augustine by interpreting this passage of St. Paul's Epistle to the Philippians III. 12-14, expounds his new concept of time. St. Paul says: 'Not as though I had already attained or were already perfect: but I follow after, if that I may apprehend by any means that for which also I am apprehended of Christ Jesus . . . this one thing *I do,* forgetting those things which are behind, and reaching forth unto those things which are before, I press towards the mark to the prize of the supernal vocation of God in Christ Jesus. Let us therefore, as many as be perfect, be thus minded and . . .' In the act of reaching forth, in the soul's distorting itself beyond the limits of time instead of merely extending itself, Augustine sees the true nature of the soul and of its concept of time. This conviction makes him feel free of servitude to time which for Plotinus is still the inescapable destiny of the soul: 'The soul renders itself temporal . . . and causes that which is generated to be *a slave to* time, making the whole of it to be in time' (*Enneads,* III, 7, 11, transl. by T. Taylor, London, 1817, p. 208).

46. Cf. Augustine, *De Civitate Dei,* XII, 10-28.

47. For the Christian as 'a new creature,' cf. St. Paul, Galatians 6. 15; II Corinthians 5. 17; Romans 8. 10. The change of the psychic man (the first Adam) into the spiritual man (the second Adam) takes place in an indivisible particle of time (*in atomo*), cf. Augustine Sermo 362, 17, 20; 277, 11, 11. In such a moment time touches upon eternity. Cf. Kierkegaard, *The Concept of Dread,* ch. 3 and note 29 to ch. VI.

48. Augustine, *De Civitate Dei,* XII, 14 (edit. by E. Hoffmann, Vienna, 1899, p. 589).

49. E.g. Plato, *Timaeus,* 22A ff.; *Critias,* 109D; *Laws,* 677 ff.; *Politicus,* 269-74; Aristotle, *On the Heavens,* I, 3, 270b16; *Meteorology,* I, 3, 339b19; *Metaphysics,* XII, 8, 1074a38; *De Animae Motu,* 3, 699a27; *Polit.,* VIII, 10, 1329b35, *Frs.* 13 and 53 R.; Theophrastus in Philo, *De Aeternitate Mundi,* 130; cf. Lucretius, *De Rerum Natura,* V, 328 ff. Cf. W. W. Jaeger, *Aristotle,* Engl. transl., 1936, p. 138, J. Bernays, *Theophrastos,* 1866, p. 46 ff.

50. Cf. Augustine, *Confessions,* XI, 11, 13.

51. For Augustine's interesting theory of imagination see *De*

*Genesi ad Litteram,* XII, esp. 30, 58. Cf. C. Butler, *Western Mysticism,* 1927, pp. 49 ff. and notes 26, 32 to ch. IV.

52. II Corinthians 5. 7; cf. Romans 8. 24: 'But hope that is seen is not hope; for what a man seeth, why doth he yet hope for?' Cf. Hebrews 11.1: 'Now faith is the assurance of things hoped for, the evidence of things not seen.' Cf. I Peter 1. 8: 'Whom having not seen, ye love; in whom, though now ye see him not, yet believing, ye rejoice with joy unspeakable . . .'; cf. I John 4. 20.

53. St. Paul in II Corinthians 12. 2 ff.: 'I know a man in Christ above fourteen years ago . . . caught up to the third heaven . . . yet of myself I will not glory, but in mine infirmities.' Concerning St. Augustine see C. Butler (op. cit. pp. 78 ff.) who quotes *De Genesi ad Litteram,* XII, 28, 56: St. Paul also 'was rapt into this transcendent vision, wherein we may *believe* that God vouchsafed to show him that life wherein, *after this life,* we are to live forever.'

# IV.  Truth and Imagination


THE concept of creation, in spite of its religious and philosophical importance, proves to be an idea of imagination. The same may be said of other religious ideas which serve to reveal the nature of God and our relation to Him. They are not verifiable by anything that we know in the world. Are not the Positivists right, then, in maintaining that our religious concepts are empty words, products of poetical fantasy without any serious claim to truth? [1] Such a criticism of religion should be examined with more concern than is usually shown by the opponents of Positivism. For it cannot be denied that religions have always been revealed in terms of human imagination— terms which obviously do not have the same truth as mathematical or scientific statements. [2]

But what is truth? According to Aristotle: 'To say that what is is, and what is not is not, is true'; and it is indeed correspondence to reality which constitutes the truth of our thought. [3] Still, the same philosopher recognized the fact that 'the soul never thinks without a phantasmal picture.' [4] If this is true, are we to conclude that the external world itself, with which our knowledge is supposed to coincide, is essentially a figment of imagination? Obviously not, for the object of our understanding is independent reality, the very criterion by which so many of our conceptions are proved to be mere fantasies. 'Nature,' in the usage of modern philosophers, is a name for all that actually is, or at least for all that is outside the mind and yet legitimately knowable. Where is there room, then, for anything supernatural? More crucially, is not the mere idea of supernatural being a contradiction in terms? [5]

Let us consider more exactly what 'Nature' is. What is this concept of an objective reality compared with which everything else appears to be merely a projection of imagination or a vague feeling? [6] Nature obviously is the totality of all that is present or may become present to our senses. Perception is then the final test by which our reason distinguishes being from mere semblance; on the other hand, imagination, under the influence of our emotions and practical interests, makes reality appear in a fashion not in keeping with sober experience. Thus, in science we rigidly and methodically exclude all the effects of subjective feelings and of fantasy—even all those vague notions which are suggested by human language. [7] Man has learned to discriminate in this way between the essence of things, their real 'nature,' and their sensory appearance.

But what does essence mean? Is not 'essence' that which has passed, the past which is ever present? Aristotle himself defined it as 'what it *was* for it to be.' [8] This we cannot grasp except through our memory, that is by means of our imaginative power. This, too, was observed by Aristotle, who says: 'It is from memory that man acquires experience'; [9] what we call experience is precisely that which enables us to apprehend as recurring in the present object something that actually has passed. The significance of this fact becomes clear in the light of our analysis of time, which proves that we can comprehend and measure a time that has passed only by means of our imagination.

Moreover, do not all categories by which we think of nature, or of anything real at all, express some relation of time? Is substance anything other than that which persists throughout its changing modifications? And is not cause that which is still present in its effect? [10] To be sure, modern physicists are doubtful regarding the traditional concepts of substance and even of causality. They have restricted themselves to describing observable events of nature in terms of mathematics; [11] and the Positivists of today pretend to see even in the law of causality only a conventional expression of those differential equations in which time is an independent variable.[12] Thus, in modern physics time has become a dimension of timeless space, and is devoid of its essential temporal character.[13] But even in this denaturalized form, time, and consequently imagination, remains an ineradicable constituent of our concept of nature.

Our scientific understanding of nature is impossible, therefore, without imagination, which alone enables us to conceive objects in their absence.[14] Those philosophers who wish to deduce all our concepts from sense perception, and who consider all other knowledge as potential in it, seem to forget that sense perception itself is by no means the simple phenomenon it appears to be in their theories. True, all general concepts and natural laws originally were abstracted from our sensory experience. But what is sense perception itself? The physical act of sensation may be the *conditio sine qua non* of our conception of the world, yet it does not suffice to explain it. Our senses open for us a window through which we get a limited glimpse of reality as it appears spread out before our eyes in all its manifold colours.

Yet, how are we to understand the fact that this reality exists simultaneously within ourselves and without? 'The stone does not exist in the soul, but only the form of the stone.' Thus Aristotle tried to express the problem in the categories of his philosophy.[15] Still, even if we accept this definition, what is this form within ourselves? Is it not actually a product of our imagination rather than of our sensation? Is it not our imagination which integrates the particular and successive impressions of a given object into a unified picture of it? What we actually apprehend through our senses can be no more than a casual impression, a superficial aspect of the object. An all-round representation is gained only when we join these partial experiences together into a unity; what we may actually have perceived at different moments of the past is simultaneously present before our inner eye. And, furthermore; whatever we grasp in this way, we understand merely as an accidental and external quality of the real object, or as its impress upon our senses; [16] chronologically the thing itself must have preceded its effects. Some of the celestial bodies may have vanished even while we are looking at them. Thus our sense perceptions are always related to the past, and nature itself, being the sum-total of that which is perceptible, is as it were the past from which all the present stems: the past which appears to us as present only through our imagination.

Habit has been called second nature. But one might just as well reverse this metaphor and with a certain amount of justification say that nature itself may be a first habit.[17] Ever since the planets first happened to revolve around the sun, they have kept on repeating the same course, following the same mathematical laws. It is characteristic of nature that what happened in it once and came into existence tends to persist in it. This tendency to persist has been expressed in the law of inertia and in the principle of the conservation of energy. But in physical laws nothing is said about location in time: the chronological changes of a given quantity are represented here as definite functions of the momentary value of that quantity. The ultimate presupposition of the scientist is the conviction that the natural laws which he discovers at a certain moment have determined and shall continue to determine the course of nature at all times.[18]

This certainly does not mean that in nature nothing

new can ever happen. A certain creativity, a creative or
emergent evolution, is an indisputable characteristic of the
process of nature, a fact which modern philosophers have
emphasized. But even this factor of novelty and creative
power in nature can be understood only as the actualization of certain potentialities which were inherent in it
from the beginning. Even in its creativity—nay, here especially—does nature remain a manifestation of forces which
have always been immanent in it. Nature is the world's
memory, the preservation of all past existences.

Our conception of nature, then, is not merely an impression of the senses, but is also a projection of our imagination, which in its struggle for a uniform picture of
reality is guided by certain logical ideas and mathematical
principles that it supposes to be true. It is for this reason that man's sensory picture of the world is so flexible
and varies according to the intellectual presuppositions
by which it is determined at various periods of history
and in various schools of thought. The most recent psychological research has demonstrated sufficiently the adap-
table character of sense perception and its dependence
upon imagination.[19] We know that the Greek philosophers
saw the world with eyes different from ours, and the conception of nature following from the latest scientific findings differs considerably from that of even a few decades
ago.[20]

To be sure, the Pragmatists will rightly object that our
picture of reality is not the result of our theoretical knowledge, but rather that of our practical understanding. In
our theoretical attitude we are passive and thus our object
seems inaccessible to us. But is not action also a way of
knowing? In acting we approach the object itself, and in
its reaction to our interference it seems to reveal to us its
true nature.[21] The successes of the experimental method
have shown how by this means we may actually lift the

veil of nature. But can we dispense with the power of imagination even in the process of acquiring practical knowledge through trial and error? Are not all our practical actions determined by a definite end that lies in the future and does not yet exist, by a vision that will come true only in so far as we are able to actualize it? How can we consider, however, something that lies in the future, except through our imagination—which alone permits us to identify that which we anticipated in our fantasy with that which we subsequently perceive?

No sensible person will ascribe to nature real intention.[22] Nature, we are convinced, acts blindly, in conformity with its own laws. Of real design and teleology in a literal sense we can speak with reference to man alone; and even there it may be only man's interpretation of his own doings and his attempt to justify what he would have done in any case. But the mere fact that he is able to act upon certain intentions and to gain his ends proves the analogous character of nature, which makes such subjective aims and their achievement possible. Even where nature is opposed to our aims, and here especially, our incongruous actions reveal its specific structure to which we must try to adapt ourselves.[23] No matter how carefully we bar from our scientific understanding of nature all teleological concepts, some direction towards the future remains a peculiar character of its living process, a relation of time which we can detect only through our imaginative power.

As all theoretical understanding is related to the past, so all practical knowledge is related to the future. But in the final analysis the pragmatic interpretation of understanding is just as one-sided as is the opposite theory, namely, that all our practical action is only an application of theoretical knowledge.[24] The process of experience consists in the combination of theoretical and practical functions which mutually condition and correct each other, and form a unity difficult to analyse. Neither of these can claim absolute primacy. From their reciprocal actions results the truth in which we are wont to believe as revealing objective reality. But in whatever way we approach reality we cannot avoid using imagination.

Important as the power of imagination may be, however, in both our theoretical and practical understanding it remains merely reproductive. It has a subservient function and its conceptions are rectified according to an objective criterion of reason. In art and poetry, on the other hand, fantasy frees itself from the narrow bounds of reason and seems to be truly creative. In the works of artistic imagination man believes that he finds a peculiar truth, one which he has felt in the unconscious depths of his soul without being able to give it an adequate expression in his daily life. Beyond the hazy horizon of objective reality, as he understands it both in theory and practice, man in his own hidden impulses divines still other forces to which he responds in bold images of fantasy.

But what kind of truth do such creations of imagination have for us? Their elements evidently are taken from our sense-perception, but under the influence of some vague impulsion they are put together in such a way that the final picture is never an exact copy of reality.[25] Is this fantasy, then, not merely a kind of exalted memory? Perhaps so, but even ordinary memory is not merely reproductive, or only a source of delusion. By remembering an absent object we lift it out of all the relations in which it was actually embedded; memory thus is at the same time oblivion. It idealizes that which is absent—far-away lands and times, the dead, other things unknown and distant— thus enduing them with a peculiar charm. Reality, in losing the cumbersome weight with which it oppressed us while it was present, gains in our minds a new significance and a beauty ordinarily hidden by the toil of the day. In dreams of youth, of hope, of love and happiness, man lives in the expectation of a future which may never be realized. Yet, in such visions he becomes aware of certain aspects of life which otherwise would remain unknown to him for ever. In the state of inebriation, in exuberant feasting, in every exhilarated condition of mind, an excited fancy is capable of lifting us out of the immediate present.[26] Freeing us from the subjective fetter and burden of the moment, it elevates us above our captivity to the senses or to the petty interests of the day, and opens a vista into a new dimension of reality—its truth, its beauty, and its freedom.

In ordinary life, to be sure, all visions of beauty are bound to be shattered on the hard rock of reality. In the works of art and poetry, however, human imagination creates a reality of its own which maintains its place and rank in the world. Its figures represent a truth and wisdom deeper than that expressed by abstract science or philosophy. A work of art often may reflect the truth just in those features in which it differs from reality. Even when the realistic artist of our time tries to depict nothing but objective reality, his picture is no less imaginary than that of the idealist of earlier times.[27] The only difference consists in that the one, following the *sursum corda* of his feelings, tries to grasp the beauty of marvellous things, whereas the other, determined to remain within the limits of this world, seeks beauty in everyday life—even in ugliness. Still, this does not mean that his work is merely a copy. Every true piece of art, no matter how insignificant or particular a phenomenon its object, through its form conveys an image of the whole world. Even if its individual features in no way coincide with reality, in their harmony they impart to us an impression of natural truth.

The imagination of the genius is like a magic wand

through which the colours of the world regain their original freshness.[28] In the eyes of the artist the most ordinary reality becomes interesting and full of wonders. The world of our everyday experience is dull and benumbed; its diverse features have no inner connection one with another; they are not merged into the unity of a whole. In the creations of art, however, reality acquires an eye with which it looks at us, a voice that speaks to us and sings in our own language.[29] The genius does not arrange the elements of reality in the logical order habitual to our prosaic minds. And therefore he can communicate an idea of nature that is as infinite as nature itself. Thus, in the creations of the genius, a human faculty becomes apparent which remains an unfathomable mystery to our reason.

In the fine arts the artist reveals the visions of his fantasy through objects of the senses whereas the medium of poetry is human language, which is itself an immediate expression of human imagination. Language in its essence is metaphor and simile, although in ordinary life this original character of language has gradually become obscured; words are commonly used as signs for certain definite concepts and objects.[30] In the mouth of the poet, however, language has kept its original power of expressing the inner feelings and visions of man. Poetry therefore gains in significance to the extent that man himself and his spiritual life become its central problems; its true greatness it reaches in drama and tragedy, where man is represented in his inner conflicts and in his struggle with fate. The poet seems to understand everything—heaven and earth, man and all his feelings. In the world of the poet even the stones seem to speak. Not that he has real knowledge of all this; he does not need experience, for he creates the whole world anew, as if he were familiar from birth with its inmost laws and all the hidden secrets of the human heart.

Thus the world of art constitutes another creation. Still, this creation is but a shadow of true creation. Wherever we wish to understand reality in an objective way and wherever we wish to master life effectively, the artistic genius cannot teach us anything. He is well aware of his shortcomings as far as mundane affairs are concerned. He is like one who walks in his sleep. In his dream he can do more than anybody who is wide awake; no heights or depths seem inaccessible to him; but when he awakes from his dream and is faced with everyday reality, he is bound to stumble. Yet one may justly say of him: 'If others while waking dream and are tortured with monstrous delusion from their every sense, he lives through the dream of life like one awake, and thus he is at once a teacher, a prophet and the friend of gods and men.' [31]

These words express in poetical language what many people feel today. Art and poetry, to modern man, seem the revelation of a superior truth; the genius now enjoys a position not unlike that of the prophet or saint of earlier generations. But how can his merely imaginary figures have such truth? Obviously they can be true only in so far as they are an adequate expression of the human soul in its relation to the world. Through our senses we perceive physical objects. Imagination, on the other hand, being able to picture things that may not exist, is a source of delusion. But, in this faculty of deluding itself, the soul becomes aware of its own peculiar subjective character, which distinguishes it from its objects. *Si fallor sum,* if I am deluded, I am. Granted that imagination is a cause of our errors, its visions and dreams are uniquely ours and in this its truth consists.[32]

Thus understood, figments of imagination may have truth, although—or rather just because—they do not pretend to coincide literally with their factual counterpart. The greatest poets and artists have never tired of present-

ing, in the colours of their fantasy, the Invisible, Heaven
and Hell, Creation, and the Last Judgment. With all such
ideas of supernatural existence, our power of imagination
runs counter to its own sensory limitations; while using
pictures taken from the visible world, it reaches toward
things beyond the boundaries of sense perception; and it
is this inner tension of the imagination which allows us
to have a certain grasp of something that is beyond us.
Michelangelo's Creation of the World in the frescos of the
Sistine Chapel is one of the most magnificent paintings of
all times. Every line, every configuration of this work,
seems surcharged with a meaning which strains at the
capacity of the medium. Such works of art transcend their
own content. We feel that they represent their objects just
because they are inadequate to them.[33]

Even though modern man pretends that in the products
of the artistic genius he can find a truth more profound
than any which science or practical experience or even
ethics may convey to him—in the final analysis he does
not really believe in this truth. His relation to art is merely
aesthetic; for him its creations remain nothing but figments of imagination. The beauty of appearance alone in
his eyes constitutes the worth of art. The modern artist
therefore is strangely divided in his attitude. He is unable
to overcome the conflict between objective reality and the
ethical concepts which he recognizes as the ultimate cri-
teria of truth on the one hand, and the merely aesthetic
value of his art on the other.[34] A merely aesthetic conception of the world, quite evidently, does not satisfy the
principal need of our soul.

In the religious consciousness the conflict between aesthetic and real existence is resolved. Here the beauty of
the world has gained full significance and does not clash
with our ethical or theoretical demands.[35] Artistic imagination therefore showed its greatest power in the early

stages of civilization when religion still held its sway over
the whole soul and existence of man, when all reality
appeared to him in the light of mythical fantasy, when
the world had not yet become prosaic. But in the measure
to which the various interests of life—politics, ethics, science, philosophy—have gained through seeking independent truths different from that of religion and even contrary to it, the arts have lost their original force. Men are
really creative in their imaginative power only as long as
their art, poetry, and music are the expressions of religious
belief and do not serve exclusively to glorify life or to
provide aesthetic enjoyment.[36] Dante believed in the truth
of those ideas to which his fantasy gave visible form. The
modern artist, however, no longer seriously believes in the
truth of his art although it itself is to him the ultimate
revelation. Goethe in his *Faust*—the tragedy of modern
man and his this-worldly character—tried in vain to cope
with the greatest examples of classical poetry; his imagination lacked the creative power to find an expression
comparable to the forms of the *Divine Comedy* or the
Greek tragedy.[37]

But even the religious poet is merely playing with figments of his creative imagination. Nay, religion itself cannot do entirely without fantasy. Is it not revealed in terms
of human language and thus in forms of human imagination? [38] Man in his discourse with God can use only his
own words. If he speaks of God as Our Lord and Father,
of His will, His providence, all such concepts are taken
from human life; they are not to be understood literally
but rather as metaphors.[39] These ideas, however, just because they are entirely human, are the perfect expression
of the relation which man has to his God. All rationalistic
censure of religion may be reduced to that argument
which its oldest critic has so poignantly formulated: 'If
oxen and lions had hands, and could paint with their

hands, and fashion images, as men do, they would make the pictures and images of their gods in their own likeness; horses would make them like horses, oxen like oxen.' [40] This observation certainly is correct. But it is not an argument against the truth of religion, but rather for it. The oxen and lions would be quite right indeed; in their religion they would not be sincere were they to believe in human gods.

The Greeks imagined their divinities no longer in the shape of animals, as primitive people do, but of human beings. Their gods were untrue, not, as their philosophers wanted them to believe, because they were too human, but rather because they were not human enough.[41] It is in Christianity that man in his own heart, in his soul, discovers the true nature of God. In the sphere of religion, the most human, the most deeply felt expression is the most truthful.

As man himself, as his conscience is, so is his God. But this does not mean that man venerates as his God nothing but his own ideal projected into the Absolute.[42] For the religious person the true idea of himself is not that one which he holds, but that one which God has of him. In his religious consciousness man feels himself totally determined by the presence of God: In faith 'I follow after Him if in any way I may comprehend wherein I am also comprehended'; [43] I believe in God's belief in myself and find the truth of my existence in that idea which God has of me. Therefore, I must express my relation to Him in terms of my whole existence and that is in terms of imagination.

Reason, on the other hand, striving for an objective truth, understands all our knowledge as a relation to an object which itself differs from our apprehension of it. The philosopher, for the content of his thought, draws upon sense perception, science, practical experience, ethics, art or religion. Yet, considering this content under the aspect of eternity, he distinguishes the object from his idea of it. Therefore the truth of all philosophical concepts must be abstract and negative. For in these concepts we try to envisage the Absolute by cancelling our subjective idea of it.[44] Wherever man, not content with religion and its figurative truth, tries by philosophical reasoning to find a more adequate conception of God, he achieves not a broader or higher understanding of Him but finds only abstract ideas which cannot satisfy religious needs.[45] The philosopher should have learned from Plato that he can approach God, or the Absolute, through reason only in a negative sense, by distinguishing his object from his own idea of it.[46] In religious experience man knows himself present to God in his total existence, not only in one particular part of his being, such as his reason. Even the most rational idea of God retains a finite element which makes it inadequate. A positive theology, a concrete knowledge of God in the whole manifoldness of His being, can be gained through faith alone.

But can our knowledge have any truth if, as a human concept, it never really coincides with its object? There is truth and falsity not only in thought but also in being, as Aristotle remarked. A being is true in so far as in its existence it adequately expresses what it is. Whatever exists, however, exists not only in itself but also in relation to other things. Thus it also may be said that a being is true so far as, in its relations to others and to itself, it exhibits its real nature. With regard to thought itself, modern thinkers including sceptics are inclined to recognize only cognitive truth—as if our knowledge had no existence of its own.[47] Granted by reasoning we understand our knowledge as different from its object and thus as relative and subjective, the relation of knowledge and object cannot be relative also. Thus as a kind of being, as a mode of human existence, our knowledge is true to the extent in which it adequately expresses its essential relation to its objects—a relation by which knowledge itself is determined.

This conclusion holds for the knowledge of the world, of oneself, and of God. It is in imagination that man's relation to himself finds its expression. Thus there can be no knowledge which does not contain an element of imagination. In science and practical life we rectify our subjective ideas by reason, i.e. by our essential relation to other things. Religious faith expresses our essential relation to God, the Presence by whom our entire existence is determined. But in each of these types of knowledge—in imagination, sense perception, and faith—truth can consist only in the fact that these modes of our existence adequately express the relation to an object, a relation in which knowledge has its true essence.

Mathematics has cognitive truth in the highest sense. Here our thoughts literally correspond to their objects, since we produce them by thinking them.[48] But mathematics has no existential truth because its objects do not refer to anything beyond themselves. On the other hand, ideas of religious imagination do not claim to be literally adequate to their object. But they have certainly existential truth because they express uniquely man's total determination by a Being beyond himself.

Thus, in the concept of essential truth or ontological truth, to use the traditional term, we see the solution of our problem of truth and imagination. For in an existential or essential sense a religious idea may well be true even though, or because, it does not entirely coincide with its object, provided that the total existence of man in his relation to his object is adequately expressed in it. All our knowledge, even the most elevated, always remains a form of human existence, which as such differs essentially from its object. We cannot speak of the logical truth of a sense perception because logical truth belongs only to a proposition.[49] And yet we rely on our senses, since they express our relation to our object. For the actuality of the sensible object and that of the percipient sense are one and the same actuality. In an analogous way the ideas of religious imagination are the adequate expression of man in his relation to God, the expression of that faith in which he is present to Him. They have truth only so far as our human existence in its totality and its inwardness is determined by a real relation to Him. And is not all man's struggling concerned with this one aim: to attain real existence; or, in terms of religion, to become immortal and to find salvation?

## NOTES

1. Cf. B. Russell, *Religion and Science*, New York, 1935, esp. pp. 178 ff.; *The Problems of Philosophy*, New York, 1915, p. 201: 'A belief is *true* when it *corresponds* to a certain associated complex, and *false* when it does not.' R. Carnap, *Introduction to Semantics*, Cambridge, Mass., 1942, pp. 24 ff. W. O. Quine, *Mathematical Logic*, New York, 1940, pp. 1 f., 27 ff. P. Frank, 'Logical Empiricism and the Philosophy of the Soviet Union,' in *Between Physics and Philosophy*, Cambridge, Mass., 1941, p. 147: 'According to this doctrine [of 'concrete truth'] the truth of a proposition can be judged . . . only by examining the practical conclusions that can be drawn from it . . . By religion should be understood a concrete organization which seeks to propagate the belief in a supranatural being among men and in this way deter them from the struggle against their oppressors.'

2. This is not denied by St. Thomas either. Cf. *Summa Theologica*, Part I, q. 1, 9: 'Whether Holy Scripture should use metaphors?' '*Objection*: It seems that Holy Scripture should not use metaphors. That which is proper to the lowest science [viz. poetry] seems not to befit this science which holds the highest place of all . . . Therefore to put forward Divine Truths by likening them to corporeal things does not befit this science . . . *I answer that* . . . it is natural to man to attain to intellectual truths through sensible objects, because all our knowledge originates from sense. Hence in Holy Writ spiritual truths are fittingly taught under the likeness of material things. This is what Dionysius says: *We cannot*

*be enlightened by the Divine rays except they be hidden within the covering of many sacred veils* . . . Then it is clear that these things *are not literal descriptions* of Divine Truths . . . because this is more befitting the knowledge of God that we have in this life. For what He is not is clearer to us than what He is.' (Engl. trans., p. 14. Cf. *Summa Contra Gentiles* I, 30, ibid. p. 74.) Cf. also E. Gilson, *The Philosophy of St. Thomas Aquinas*, St. Louis, 1939, pp. 187 and 201 note, and A. G. Sertillanges, *La Philosophie Thomiste*, 1928, pp. 73 ff.

3. Aristotle, *Metaphysics*, IV, 7, p. 1011b27. The other passages concerning Aristotle's concept of truth are collected and discussed by H. A. Wolfson in his paper 'The Double Faith Theory,' *Jew. Quart. Rev.*, 1942, p. 215 f. Cf. Kant, *Critique of Pure Reason*, 2nd ed. p. 82: 'The nominal definition of truth, that it is the agreement of the cognition with its object, is granted.' (Transl. by F. M. Mueller, 1881, p. 48.) Russell, *The Problems of Philosophy*, 1915 (cf. note 1); *Philosophy*, New York, 1927, p. 254 f.

4. Aristotle, *On the Soul*, III, 7, p. 431a16. Cf. R. D. Hicks, *Aristotle De Anima*, Cambridge, 1907, p. 141: 'This is why the soul never thinks without an image [phantasm].' Ibid. p. 530: 'That the image or pictorial presentation is indispensable to thought is often affirmed [by Aristotle],' e.g. 432a8, 13 sq., 403a8, *De Mem.* 1, 449b31) cf. St. Thomas, *Summa Theologica*, I, qu. 11, art. 12 (Engl. transl., p. 143): 'Objection 2: "The soul understands nothing by natural reason without the use of imagination." But we cannot have an imagination of God, Who is incorporeal: therefore we cannot know God by natural knowledge.'

5. Concerning this problem see the discussion of E. S. Brightman, *Philosophy of Religion*, New York, 1940, pp. 209 ff.

6. Cf. Russell's illuminating discussion of the problem in *The Problems of Philosophy*, London, 1915, p. 224 ff.

7. Concerning the problem of Language, see Russell, *Philosophy*, New York, 1927, p. 256 ff.; *An Inquiry into Meaning and Truth*, New York, 1940, *passim;* and R. Carnap's analysis of language in his *Foundations of Logic and Mathematics*, Chicago, 1939, pp. 3 ff.: 'The elements of the language are signs, e.g. sounds or written marks, produced by members of the group in order to be perceived by other members and to influence their behavior. Since our final interest . . . concerns the language of science we shall restrict ourselves to the theoretical side of language.' A. Korzybski (*Science and Sanity*, An Introduction to Non-Aristotelian Systems and General Semantics, Lancaster, Pa., 1941) and Stuart Chase (*Tyranny of Words*, New York, 1938) try to show 'the dangers concealed in an uncritical acceptance of traditional language.' In opposition to this campaign against 'verbalization' P. W. Bridgman (*The Nature of Thermodynamics*, Cambridge, Mass., 1941 p.x.) emphasizes that our

'traditional verbal habits may have the highest guiding and constructive value.' Concerning the general problem of language cf. G. A. de Laguna, *Speech*, New Haven, 1927; W. M. Urban, *Language and Reality*, London, 1939, *passim*; R. Hönigswald, *Philosophie und Sprache*, Bâle, 1937; E. Cassirer, *Symbolische Formen*, vols. I and III, Berlin, 1929.

8. Aristotle often calls a thing's 'formal cause' its 'essence,' the τὸ τί ἦν εἶναι of it, a formula which can be rendered by 'what it *was* for it to be.' Cf. G. R. G. Mure, *Aristotle*, London, 1932, p. 13, and H. Bonitz, *Index Aristotelicus*, Berolini, 1870, pp. 763b50 ff. The grammarians are wont to call the Greek imperfect tense, which expresses timeless being, 'philosophic.' Cf. W. W. Goodwin, *The Moods and Tenses of the Greek Verb*, London, 1897, p. 13: 'The philosophic imperfect may express something which is the result of a previous discussion with reference to which the past form is used.' One may indeed say that this mode of expression is characteristic of the thought of Greek philosophy. In a similar manner, Hegel, playing on the etymology of the German words, defines essence (*Wesen*) as 'that which has been' (*das gewesene*): 'Language has in the verb *Sein* [to be] preserved *Wesen* [Essence] in the past participle *gewesen* [been]; for Essence is Being, which has passed away, but passed away non-temporally.' (*Science of Logic*, vol. II, 1929, p. 15.)

9. *Metaphysics* I, 1, p. 980b29. In his treatise *On Memory*, p. 451a14, Aristotle emphasizes the fact that in memory imagination is implied. Cf. *On the Soul*, III, 3, 428a6: 'Sensation is either potential or actual . . . but imagination occurs when neither of these is present, as when objects are seen in dreams. Secondly, sensation is always present but imagination [*phantasia*] is not.' From Aristotle comes the traditional definition of imagination as 'the faculty of representing an object even without its presence in intuitive perception' (cf. Kant, *Critique of Pure Reason*, 2nd ed., § 24, p. 151, and Berkeley, *De Motu*, § 53).

10. Concerning the relation between the ontological categories and time, cf. Kant's analysis in the *Critique of Pure Reason*, 2nd ed., pp. 176-265, esp. p. 263: 'Our "analogies" [viz. the principles of Substance, Causality, and Coexistence] therefore really portray the unity of nature in the connection of all appearances under certain exponents which express nothing save the relation of time . . . according to rules.'

11. The truly positivistic scientist does not interpret the concepts by means of which he understands nature, in the same way that the philosopher does. Newton used the concept of attraction only as an auxiliary term: 'I use the words attraction, impulse or propensity of any sort towards a centre, promiscuously and indifferently one for another, considering those forces not physically

but mathematically: wherefore the reader is not to imagine that by those words I anywhere take upon me to define the kind or the manner of any action, the causes or the physical reason thereof or that I attribute forces in a true and physical sense to certain centers, which are only mathematical points.' (Sir Isaac Newton's *Mathematical Principles,* transl. by A. Motte, ed. by F. Cajor, Berkeley, 1934, p. 14.) Cf. W. Dilthey, *Works,* vol. I, Leipzig, p. 365, and E. Zimmer, *The Revolution in Physics,* London, 1936, pp. 213 ff.; 225 ff.

12. P. Frank, *Between Physics and Philosophy,* Cambridge, Mass., 1941, pp. 18 ff.; 24: 'The law of causality and with it all of theoretical science have as their object not empirical nature but the fictitious nature of which we spoke above.' Cf. P. W. Bridgman, *The Logic of Modern Physics,* New York, 1927, p. 88: 'The conviction . . . that the future is determined by the present and correspondingly the present by the past, is often phrased differently by saying that the present causally determines the future. This is in a certain sense a generalization of the causality process. It is one of the principal jobs of physics to analyse this complex causal connection into components, representing as far as possible the future state of the system as the sum of independent trains of events started by each individual event of the present.' Cf. note 11 to ch. II and P. W. Bridgman's recent formulation of his operational theory (in *The Nature of Thermodynamics,* Cambridge, Mass., 1941, p. 61): 'It seems to me that we are satisfied that our characterization of a body is complete if, whenever in the future the body again is characterized in the same way, every feature of its behavior again is the same . . . This criterion patently assumes that we are dealing with "causal" systems. That is, systems in which the future behavior is connected by regularities which can be formulated with present condition and past behavior.'

13. Bergson emphasized the fact that 'the representation of time as spatial [by the scientists] deprives time of its real character.' Cf. Bergson, *Les Données immédiates de la Conscience,* Engl. transl., p. 98: Such time is 'nothing but the ghost of space.' The contemplation of time from the point of view of space is a feature characteristic of most of the thinkers of the seventeenth and eighteenth centuries, of Hume as well as of Kant. Concerning 'the spatializing of Time,' cf. S. Alexander, *Space, Time and Deity,* vol. I, p. 148, and the historical study of J. A. Gunn, *Time,* London, 1927, esp. pp. 246 ff.

14. Cf. notes 4 and 9.

15. Aristotle, *On the Soul,* III, 8, p. 431b28: 'Sensation is a form which employs the forms of sensible objects.' Therefore *'the soul is the place of forms';* cf. 429a28 and 431b20: 'Now summing up

what we have said about the soul, let us assert once more that in a sense *the soul is all the existing* universe.' According to Aristotle, sensation is not merely a passive process, not merely a simple change of state but the realization of potentiality: '[knowledge is] the growth into its real self, that is to actuality.' (Ibid. 417b6, cf. W. D. Ross, *Aristotle*, New York, 1927, p. 136.)

16. This traditional Aristotelian formulation appears correct even to us, although, with Plato and the modern scientists, we do not assume static substances to be the sub-stratum of the perceptible universe but rather dynamic processes, relations governed by mathematical laws. Aristotle, to be sure, regards as axiomatic that 'which is per se, i.e. *substance*, is prior in nature to the *relative*—for the latter is likewise an offshoot and accident of being' (*Nicomachean Ethics*, 1, 6, p. 1096a21, transl. by W. D. Ross, Oxford, 1925. Cf. *Metaphysics*, xiv, 1, p. 1088a23 ff.). This is one of Aristotle's main arguments in his criticism of Plato (cf. W. D. Ross, *Aristotle*, p. 165 f.), and rightly so from his point of view, since for him the world is eternal and therefore absolute substance. If, however, the world is taken as created, as it is by Plato and in Christianity, then neither the world itself nor anything in it can truly be substance, rather does the ultimate essence of all these things lie in their dependency, that is, in their being relative. (For 'every relation signifies dependency': St. Thomas, *De Veritate*, qu. 21, 1, etc.) Inspired by the revolutionary thought of Plato, Galileo and Kepler created modern natural science, which disclosed to us the true nature of the world. (Concerning Galileo's Platonism cf. A. Koyré, *Études Galiléennes*, 3 vols., Paris, 1939, esp. 1, 7 ff.; III, 267 ff.; L. Olschki, *Galilei*, Halle, 1927, pp. 164 ff., and *Philosophical Review*, 1943, p. 355. In regard to Kepler, see D. Mahnke, *Unendliche Sphaere*, Halle, 1936, pp. 138 ff.; and my book on *Plato and the Pythagoreans*, Halle, 1923, pp. 31 ff.) Among contemporary philosophers Whitehead has best understood the basic idea of that philosophy of mathematics which Plato presented in his course of lectures 'On the Idea of Good' and which we unfortunately only know from Aristotle's biased criticism. On the subject of this lecture course Aristotle wrote a special critical study, ['Plato's] Idea of Good,' of which only a few fragments are preserved. (Cf. *Aristotelis Fragmenta*, ed. V. Rose, 2nd ed., Berolini, 1885, fr. 27-31; L. Robin, *La Theorie Platonicienne des Idées et des Nombres*, Paris, 1908; W. Jaeger, *Aristotle*, 1936, p. 174.)

17. Cf. Pascal, *Pensées*, ed. L. Brunschvicg, n. 93, and L. Brunschvicg's note ad loc. (Cf. also Leibniz, *Discourse on Metaphysics*, ch. 7, and Pierce, *Coll. Papers*, v, 25.) Pascal's characterization of the concept of nature reminds one of Kant's definition of nature as 'synthetic unity of the manifold unity according to rules.' (*Critique of Pure Reason*, 1st ed., pp. 126 f.) Aristotle calls habit a second nature: 'Habit

is a thing not unlike nature: what happens *often* is akin to what happens *always*, natural events happening always, habitual events often.' (*Rhetoric*, 1, 11, p. 1370a7.) For Aristotle, however, this conception of habit has also ethical significance. For according to him 'moral virtue comes about as a result of habit whence also its name [*Ethics*] is one that is formed by a slight variation from the word *ethos* ["habit"].' (*Nicom. Eth.*, 11, 1, p. 1103a17. Cf. *Eudem. Ethics*, 11, 2, 1220a39, and *Magna Moralia*, 1, 6, 1185b38.) Thomas à Kempis (*De Imitatione Christi*, 1, 21, 2) on the other hand, says: 'Strive manfully; habit is overcome by habit.' (Cf. J. C. Murray, *Christian Ethics*, Edinburgh, 1908, p. 33: 'As the supreme principle of Christian morality, love . . . must be habitual.') Also in other points, Thomas à Kempis attempts to rectify Aristotle on the basis of Christian faith (cf. W. Jaeger, *Humanism and Theology*, Milwaukee, 1943, p. 14). The contrast between our present-day conception of morality and that of Aristotle finds its most striking expression in Miguel De Unamuno's statement: 'To fall into a habit is to begin to cease to be moral' (*Tragic Sense of Life*, tr. by J. E. Crawford Flitch, London, 1931, p. 206).

18. The possibility of applying differential equations to physical problems rests on the assumption that if at a given moment one cuts a cross-section through nature, then the values and laws observed in this cross-section are valid at any time. Laplace imagined a Spirit who at a given moment knew all the forces existing in nature, and the relative position of all existing things or elements composing it. If this omniscient Demon were able to submit all these data to mathematical analysis he would be able to comprehend in a single formula the motion of the greatest heavenly body and of the lightest atom. Nothing would be hidden to him; future as well as past would lie open before his eyes. The present-day physicist, however, does not accept this deterministic view of nature. Schrödinger, for example, says: 'If we state the laws of causality in the form: "If we know the present, we can calculate the future" it is not the conclusion but the premise which is false; for we can never know the present completely in full detail.' (E. Schrödinger, *Science and the Human Temperament*, New York, 1935, pp. 60 ff.; see also W. Heisenberg, *The Physical Principles of the Quantum Theory*, Chicago, 1930, pp. 58 ff.; P. Frank, *Between Physics and Philosophy*, 1941, pp. 107 ff.; cf. the popular survey in E. Zimmer, *The Revolution in Physics*, 1936, pp. 5, 213, 225 ff.; P. W. Bridgman in note 12 and M. Planck in note 11 to ch. 11.)

19. Concerning this problem, cf. Charles Spearman, *The Abilities of Man*, New York, 1927; *Creative Mind*, New York, 1931; G. Révész, *Tastsinn*, Haag, 1938, vol. 1, 189 f., vol. 11, 120 f., and espe-

cially the work of the so-called Marburg School on 'eidetic imagery.' (See E. Boring, *History of Experimental Psychology*, New York, 1929, p. 590; G. Murphy, *Modern Psychology*, New York, 1929, pp. 259 f.; 437 ff.; H. Klüver, *Psychological Bulletin*, 1928, pp. 69 ff.) Kant seems to have been the first to emphasize the important rôle which our imagination plays in sense perception: 'Psychologists have hitherto failed to realize that imagination is a necessary ingredient of perception itself.' (*Critique of Pure Reason*, 1st ed., p. 120.) On the other hand, see Aristotle, *On the Soul*, p. 417b6 quoted above, note 15 (in general cf. F. C. S. Schiller, *Formal Logic*, London, 1912; T. Ribot, *Creative Imagination*, Chicago, 1906).

20. Cf. A. O. Lovejoy, *The Great Chain of Being*, Cambridge, Mass., 1936; A. O. Lovejoy and G. Boas, *Primitivism and Related Ideas in Antiquity*, Baltimore, vol. I, 1935. And above all, W. Dilthey's important contributions collected in the edition of his *Works*, esp. vol. II, 1923.

21. W. James, *Pragmatism*, New York, 1907; cf. R. B. Perry, *The Thought and Character of W. James*, Boston, 1935; J. Dewey, *Logic*, New York, 1938; W. P. Montague, *The Ways of Knowing*, New York, 1925. Concerning W. P. Bridgman's 'operationalism,' see note 12.

22. Even Aristotle does not attribute purpose in a literal sense to nature. In a literal sense he speaks of purpose only with regard to an artefact which differs from a product of nature by the very fact that it has its cause and end not within itself but in some external agent (Cf. *Physics*, II, 1, 192b8, 193a35).

This is the reason why an artefact has no true existence, no real 'form,' as Plato had already emphasized (*Metaphysics*, I, 9, p. 991b7, 1070a18; Alexander, *In Metaph*. p. 549 etc.). On the other hand, the fact that man acts according to purpose is an expression of his imperfection, of a lack on his part. He needs art in order to exist, and in this he differs from the animal. (Cf. Plato, *Protagoras*, pp. 321A ff., etc.) His 'Techne' fills, as it were, the gaps that nature has left. To take the example of medicine, nature itself heals most of the damage done to our body. But if nature fails, medical art must come to our aid and perfect the healing process. Aristotle stresses the point that we must therefore understand man's Techne after the pattern of nature and not nature after the pattern of art: 'For art imitates nature but it is not true the other way round that nature imitates art.' (*Physics*, II, 2, 194a21; II, 8, 199a15, and Aristotle's own interpretation of this basic idea in fr. 11 of his dialogue *Protrepticus*. Cf. R. Walzer, *Aristotelis Dialogorum Fragmenta*, Firenze, 1935, p. 47; W. Jaeger, *Aristotle*, Oxford, 1934, pp. 74 ff.) Thus the products of human Techne have a kind of existence inferior to those of Nature. But man's purposive activity itself is a phenomenon of nature: 'Just as in man we find Techne and Wisdom, so in certain animals there exist some other natural potentialities akin to these.' (*Hist. Animal*, VIII, 1, 588a29.) The subject of Aristotle's analysis is not the product but the activity of man's Techne. That is why Aristotle's favorite example for the formal cause is not any product of Techne but Techne itself: 'for the Techne (the art of building) is the form of the house' (*Metaph.*, VII, 9, p. 1034a24) and 'the medical art is the formal cause of health' (ibid. XII, 4, p. 1070a30. Cf. 1070b33; 1032a32).

Techne, this pragmatic activity of man, discloses to him the inner logical structure of nature although discursive thought divides into successive steps what in nature might be present all at once: 'In any operation of human art, where there is an end to be achieved, the earlier and successive stages of the operation are performed for the purpose of realizing that end. Now when a thing is produced by Nature, the earlier stages in every case lead up to the formal development in the same way as in the operation of art and *vice versa* . . . Thus if a house were a natural product, the process would pass through the same stages that it in fact passes through when it is produced by art [There would also be a foundation and a roof resting on the walls, etc.] . . . We may therefore say that the earlier stages are for the sake of the later [although they may be present all at once] and generally speaking art partly completes Nature, partly it imitates Nature' (*Physics*, II, 8, 199a8; cf. above p. 107). True, in speaking of teleology in Nature, Aristotle employs anthropomorphic terminology which may easily be misunderstood. But when he says: 'Nature *like* a good housewife economizes and throws away nothing' (*Gener. Animal.*, 744b16) or 'It is *as if* Nature has foreseen the Future' (*On the Heaven*, II, 9, 291a4), it is manifest that he is entirely aware of the analogical character of his words. In the last analysis he does not maintain anything other than what even the most recent physicists concede when they speak of the principle of 'least action' or of 'economy' (E. Mach, *The Science of Mechanics*, Chicago, 1919, Introduction, #6), or when they consider physical events determined by the future (see note 18 and note 10 to ch. II).

Aristotle's final concept of nature is that of 'entelechy' (or 'energeia'), a concept which defines nature as a process which has its goal and product in itself. With regard to this idea one speaks of 'immanent teleology' (W. D. Ross) or of 'natural purpose' (Kant). The distinctive character of human purposiveness lies in the fact that it places the object of purpose beyond oneself. But this very character is cancelled in Aristotle's conception of 'entelechy.' Kant is justified in calling such a 'natural purpose,' which is not really a purpose, a contradiction in terms (*Critique of Judgment*, #64), but the very contradictoriness constitutes the philosophical profundity of this concept.

23. This process of adaptation is reciprocal: on the one hand, we try to adapt nature to our aims and to force our will on it; on the other hand, we adapt our activity to nature by abstracting our aims from nature, within and without ourselves, and by then adjusting these aims to the natural course of experience.

24. The concept of *theoria,* the philosophical ideal of pure contemplation, was first formulated by Aristotle (Cf. *Nicomachean Ethics,* Books VI and XI). In opposition to this view, Aristotle's pupils, Aristoxenus and Dicaearchus, found the real source of philosophical thought in practical knowledge, above all in political activity. They can therefore be considered the first pragmatists. Cf. my discussion in *American Journal of Philology,* 1943, p. 223.

25. This traditional theory of imagination is best formulated by Hobbes: 'Imagination is nothing but decaying sense . . . Imagination is only of those things which have been formerly perceived by sense, either all at once, or by parts at several times; the former is simple imagination when one imagineth a man, or horse . . . The other is compounded; as when from the sight of a man at one time, and of a horse at another, we conceive in our mind a centaur.' (*Leviathan,* I, ch. 2.)

26. Through such experiences it becomes manifest that imagination does not consist merely in reproduction of sense-impressions (Cf. W. Wundt, *Outlines of Psychology,* Engl. transl., London, 1907, pp. 298 ff.; *Grundzuege der Physiol. Psychologie,* Leipzig, 1911, 6th ed., vol. III, pp. 603 ff.). What we call soul, the proper existence of man, seems to find its most adequate expression in the very power of imagination and imagination seems to be the real medium of our life. This does not mean that our soul is but a projection of imagination; rather it means that our soul can grasp its own presence only in imaginary pictures. It is Augustine who emphasized again and again that we must see the proper cognitive faculty of our soul in its power of imagination (Cf. esp. *De Genesi ad litteram,* XII, 30, 58 and note 51 to ch. III). Our soul becomes aware of its distinctive character in the very process of deluding itself: *Si fallor sum* (cf. below note 32). Being dependent upon its imaginative power the soul can imagine its own presence in temporal forms alone. In memory the soul imagines its present as past, casting an enchanting glamour over the distant. In dreams of hope and love the soul imagines its present as future, in states of exaltation and inebriation as present. Though this may all be mere self-deception, we certainly feel that in these moments the very core of our existence reacts upon the world and thus reveals the soul's true nature. It was Plato who first realized that the problem put

before the philosopher is to understand the existence of deception and error. (Cf. *Sophistes,* p. 236-68, and Aristotle, *Metaphysics,* IV, 2, p. 1004b17, etc.)

27. In conscious opposition to Dante's *Divina Comedia,* Balzac wrote his *Comédie Humaine.* He characterized his realism in the following way: 'I take man as he is created by nature. I dare to picture even his repugnant features. I love exceptional creatures; I am one myself . . . But I am more interested in vulgar creatures. I *magnify,* I *idealize* them in their stupidity and ugliness. I give to their deformities frightening and grotesque proportions.' (My italics.) Cf. E. P. Dargan, *Studies in Balzac's Realism,* I: *Balzac's General Method,* Chicago, 1934, pp. 29 ff.

28. 'The genius differs from any other man by beginning as primitively as Adam.' (S. Kierkegaard, *Concept of Dread,* ch. III, Sect. 3.) Shaftesbury (*Characteristics,* I, 136), on the other hand, says: 'Such a poet is indeed a second maker: a just Prometheus under Jove.' The effect this idea of genius had on Continental romanticism, on Carlyle and Emerson, is well known. But the symbol of Prometheus as well as that of Adam had its origin in the Middle Ages: Giotto was compared by his contemporaries with Prometheus and after Dante (*Conviv.,* IV, 12) the return to the pristine natural state of Adam became the ideal of the poets and painters (Cf. K. Burdach, *Reformation, Renaissance, Humanismus,* Leipzig, 1926, pp. 159-69).

29. This is a characteristically modern feeling. Cf. H. Miller, *The Wisdom of the Heart,* Norfolk, Conn., 1941, p. 64: 'I want that the pictures should look back at me; if I look at them and they don't look at me too then they are no good. In all his pictures there was an eye, the *cosmological eye.*' The same idea has already been expressed by Hegel in similar words: 'Art gives to her forms the dilation of a thousand-eyed Argus through which the inward life of Spirit at every point breaks into view.' (*Philosophy of Fine Art,* vol. I, 210; cf. vol. II, 282 ff.)

30. 'Language is a perpetual mythology,' says G. Santayana (*Reason in Art,* New York, 1928, pp. 83 f.). Kant regards language as a kind of art—the primary art of expression after which all other arts are modelled (*Critique of Judgment,* § 51). A penetrating analysis of the historical process through which the originally metaphorical nature of language gradually became rationalized is to be found in the recently published lectures of the historian J. D. Droysen (*Historik,* Berlin, 1937, § 63, pp. 221 ff. Cf. the short '*Outline of the Principles of History,*' of the same author, transl. by E. B. Andrews, Boston, 1893, pp. 39 ff.). The way in which the ancient critics understood this process of rationalization is interesting: 'Critias [the great sophist, Plato's uncle] . . . did not have recourse

to words borrowed from poetry; his was the kind of elevated language that is composed of the most ordinary and appropriate names of things and is quite natural.' (Philostratus, *The Lives of the Sophists*, ch. I, 16.)

31. Goethe, *Wilhelm Meister's Apprenticeship*, II, ch. 2, transl. by Thomas Carlyle, London, 1888, Vol. I, p. 68. In this passage Goethe evidently tries to revive the Greek ideal of the poet, as expressed, for example, in the famous line of Aristophanes: 'We the poets are teachers of men' (*Frogs*, 1055). Homer, 'the great teacher of all that goodly band of tragic poets,' was regarded even by Plato as the founder of the Greek way of life, and as 'the leader of all education.' (Cf. J. Adam, *The Republic of Plato*, Cambridge, 1929, vol. II, pp. 399, 385 ff.)

32. St. Augustine, *City of God*, XI, 26: 'I am not at all afraid of the arguments of the Academicians [i.e. of the Sceptics] who say: What if you are deceived? For if I am deceived I am.' Cf. *De Trinitate*, X, 10, 14; *De Vera Religione*, 39, 72; *Contra Academicos*, III, c. 11; *Soliloqu.* II, 1, 1; cf. also E. Gilson, *St. Augustine*, Paris, 1929, pp. 46-52. Augustine's important theory of imagination has not yet found a congenial interpreter. Cf. above note 51 to ch. III and note 26 to this chapter; concerning Descartes' relation to Augustine see E. Gilson's *Commentary of the 'Discours de la Méthode,'* Paris, 1925, pp. 295-8.

33. Cf. Kant's interesting definition of an 'aesthetical Idea' (*Critique of Judgment* § 49) 'An *aesthetical Idea* cannot become a cognition, because it is an intuition [of the imagination] for which an adequate concept can never be found. A *rational Idea* can never become a cognition, because it involves a concept (of the supersensible), corresponding to which an intuition can never be given.' In regard to the general problem of Form in Art see, M. C. Nahm, *Form in Art: A Bryn Mawr Symposium*, 1940, pp. 275 ff.

34. The ambivalent attitude of modern man towards art and aesthetic beauty finds characteristic expression in Santayana's *The Sense of Beauty*, New York, 1896, pp. 9 ff., and p. 190: 'If we are distrustful in general of our prophetic gifts, why should we cling only to the most mean and formless of our illusions?' *Reason in Art*, 1905, p. 172: 'Beauty gives men the best hint of ultimate good . . . The ideal dignity of art is [however] merely symbolic and vicarious,' cf. p. 218, and R. B. Perry, *W. James*, 1935, vol. II, p. 403. E. Hemingway, *The Green Hills of Africa*, 1935, pp. 26-7: 'Do you think your writing is worth doing . . . as an end in itself?' 'Oh, yes.' Thomas Mann gives the following analysis of Goethe's attitude: 'In what did Goethe really believe? Did he believe even in Art? Was Art holy to him as good people say? There are certain remarks of his which give evidence against such an assumption.

One day he made the paradoxical statement to a perplexed inter-
viewer: "A poem? A poem is really nothing. What is my poem of
the Fisher and the Nix? It is nothing . . . Every poem is like a
kiss one gives to the world—but out of mere kisses do not come
children." ' ('Goethe as Representative of the Bourgeois Age,' in
Thomas Mann, *Werke*, Berlin, 1935, p. 33. Cf. similar statements in
R. Wagner's *Letters*, transl. by J. S. Shedlock, London, 1890, p. 172;
and those of other modern artists.

At the end of his life, Goethe summarized his experience in the
following words: 'I am old enough to want peace. I have, however,
no faith in the world and have learned to despair.' (Cf. F. von
Biedermann, *Goethes Gespraeche*, 1910, IV, p. 282.) Dante, on the
other hand, was inspired by his faith in his mission. Like Joachim
of Floris, St. Francis, and the 'Spirituals' of his time, he sincerely
believed in the regeneration of the human soul and of the whole
world through the Spirit, and his poem is intended to give expression to this faith and help to realize it. (Cf. note 27 and note 19
to ch. VI.)

35. 'Equilibrium between the aesthetical and the ethical in the
composition of Personality' is the problem of Kierkegaard's 'Either-
Or' (*Collected Works*, Copenhagen, 1901, vol. II, pp. 141 ff., Engl.
transl., p. 131). It is the leading idea of Kierkegaard's interpretation that religion 'is a sphere unto itself where the aesthetic relation appears again though paradoxically as higher than the ethical;
normally it is the other way about.' (Cf. the *Journals*, transl. by
A. Dru, no. 887.)

36. Gian Battista Vico may have been the first to formulate this
idea clearly. (Cf. his *Principi di una scienza nuova d'intorno alla
commune natura delle nazioni*, 1744, esp. Part II, first chapter;
H. P. Adams, *Giambattista Vico*, London, 1935, p. 122; T. G.
Robertson, *Genesis of Romantic Theory in the Eighteenth Century*, Cambridge, 1923, p. 179.)

37. Concerning the second part of *Faust* (Helena), cf. Goethe's
own words: 'If only the crowd of spectators take pleasure in what
is obvious, the initiated will detect the higher meaning. Such has
been the case with the *Magic Flute*.' And as Eckermann adds, 'There
is no precedent, indeed, in the records of the stage, for beginning
a piece as a *tragedy* and ending it as an *opera*.' (F. P. Eckermann,
*Conversations with Goethe*, 29 January 1827, transl. by S. M.
Fuller, Boston, 1852, p. 198 f.)

38. See Thomas Aquinas quoted in note 2. Cf. also R. Kroner,
*The Religious Function of Imagination*, New Haven, 1941.

39. Only primitive peoples think of their gods as the fathers of
men in a literal sense. True, even Homer presents his heroes as

genuine sons of Gods. But Homer was a poet. Cf. note 31 and note 1 to ch. I.

40. Xenophanes, Fr. 15 [Diels], transl. by Charles M. Bakewell, *Source Book in Ancient Philosophy*, 1907.

41. Cf. Hegel, *Philosophy of History* (*passim.*, esp. p. 325), and his *History of Philosophy* (vol. III: *Introduction to Mediaeval Philosophy*).

42. L. Feuerbach, *The Essence of Christianity*, transl. by M. Evans, London, 1881, p. 29: 'Man—this is the mystery of religion —projects his being into objectivity and then again makes himself an object to this projected image of himself thus converted into a subject, into a person.' Feuerbach's criticism of religion prepared the ground for Marx. Cf. F. Engels, *L. Feuerbach*, Engl. transl., New York, 1935, p. 28: 'Then came Feuerbach's *Essence of Christianity*. With one blow . . . it placed materialism on the throne again . . . Nothing exists outside nature and man, and the higher beings our religious fantasies have created are only the fantastic reflection of our own essence. The spell was broken. The "system" [of Hegel] was exploded and cast aside . . . One must have experienced the liberating effect of this book to get an idea of it. Enthusiasm was general; we all became at once Feuerbachians. How enthusiastically *Marx* greeted the new conception and how much—in spite of all critical reservations—he was influenced by it one may read in *The Holy Family*.' Cf. notes 17 ff. to ch. VI.

43. Cf. St. Paul's Epistle to the Philippians 3. 12 (quoted above in note 45 to ch. III). This passage expresses the essence of faith in the most perfect way so that Augustine used it as starting point for his analysis of the new Christian consciousness of time. Modern philosophers, on the other hand, seem to have a quite different understanding of faith. Kierkegaard characterizes this modern concept of belief as follows: 'What Schleiermacher calls "Religion" and the Hegelians "Faith" is at the bottom nothing but the first immediate condition for everything—the vital fluidum—the spiritual atmosphere we breath in—and which cannot therefore with justice be designated by those words.' (*The Journals*, transl. by A. Dru, no. 78.)

44. Upon this principle rests Plato's dialectic as evolved in his *Parmenides*. In this dialogue Plato inquires into the concepts of 'Being' and of 'Unity,' which even according to Aristotle 'might best be supposed to embrace all existing things and to be most of the nature of first principles since everything *exists* and is *one*' (*Metaph.* X, 1, 11, p. 1059b30). And yet in Plato's dialogue even 'Unity' (the *'One'*) proves to be 'being' as well as 'not being,' and thus contradictory in itself. In trying to grasp any existent object, thought must cancel itself and thus reveals itself as contradictory

in itself. Even by thinking 'Existence' or 'Reality' we think this object as something different from our thought and independent of it; thus we think it as something which we do not really think. All philosophical thought consists in such polar tension of antagonistic tendencies (cf. above, note 45 to ch. ii).

45. Cf. A. N. Whitehead, *Religion in the Making*, New York, 1926, p. 20 (A Metaphysical Description): 'We know nothing beyond this temporal world and the formative elements which jointly constitute its character . . . These formative elements are: 1. The creativity whereby the actual world has its character of temporal passage to novelty. 2. The realm of ideal entities, or forms . . . 3. The actual but non-temporal entity whereby the indetermination of mere creativity is transmuted into a determinate freedom. *This non-temporal actual entity is what men call God*—the supreme God of rationalized religion.' (My italics.)

46. It is in Plato's dialogue *Parmenides* that the idea of 'Negative Theology' has its origin. (Cf. note 43.) To medieval philosophers this idea was transmitted, above all through Dionysius Areopagite, who applied Plato's dialectical method to the problems of Christian faith. (Cf. above note 2 and note 45 to ch. ii.)

47. Modern philosophers recognize only cognitive (or subjective) truth. In so doing they can hardly claim for themselves the authority of Aristotle. He clearly distinguishes cognitive and existential truth and restricts logical truth to the sphere of the *logos,* i.e. to 'sentences affirming or denying one thing from another' (*De Interpretatione* 4, p. 17a2 etc.). Since affirmation or negation is part of a contradiction, the principle of contradiction evidently is the ultimate axiom of this kind of truth (*Anal. Post.,* I, 2, p. 72a11; *Priora,* I, 1, p. 24a16; *Metaph.,* iv, 3, p. 1027b20, etc.). So far 'falsity and truth are not in things but only in thought' (*Metaph.* 1025a5; 1027b25; 1028a2; 1065a25 etc.). According to Aristotle, however, there is falsity and truth also 'in things outside of thought' (ibid. 1024b17, 1028a2, 1051b21, 1065a25, etc. Cf. Alexander ad Ar., p. 666,20 Hayd. and H. Maier, *Syllogistik d. Arist.,* vol. I, 1896, p. 7 ff.). And it is this kind of truth which I call *existential.* Aristotle declared: 'To *say* that what is is, is true.' Analogously one can define existential truth: 'To *be* that which one is, is true.' No being exists only in itself but it exists also in relation to others, making its appearance in this interrelationship with others. A being is true in so far as it adequately expresses its being in its appearance. The same definition applies to man's existence. Man, however, does not only exist but knows that he is; he is an existence which is to itself. Thus in man's knowledge not only the object but also his own existence makes its appearance as a being which is reciprocally related to its objects. The awareness of this relationship we call rea-

son; in this sense Aristotle may be justified in saying that 'Nous is always true' (430b27). For by reasoning we understand our knowledge as different from its object and therefore as subjective and relative; and this difference cannot itself be relative. Knowledge can be true only so far as it adequately expresses its relation to its object. Thus our sense-perception expresses the relation of our senses to their object adequately; this is why Aristotle can say that 'the perception of a specific sensible quality is always true, whereas most imaginations are false' (*On the Soul*, III, 6, p. 427b12; 428a4; b18-25). And yet even imagination can be true. In our vain efforts to imagine what is unimaginable, in the inner tension of this struggle, we may adequately express our true relation to this object. Analogously the philosopher tries to grasp reality by cancelling his subjective idea of it. (Cf. above, note 44.) In spite of their general sceptical tendency, modern philosophers often consider human knowledge as something completely different from its object, from existence, as something that has, so to speak, no existence of its own. Thus, however, they make knowledge (consciousness) absolute. But knowledge is itself existent just as, on the other hand, its object is knowable. Hence the opposition between Knowledge and Being is not absolute but dialectical. (Cf. the penetrating analysis of G. A. de Laguna, 'Being and Knowing: A Dialectical Study,' in *The Philosophical Review*, 1936, pp. 435 ff.) Neither of them can be regarded as an ultimate principle. On the contrary, as the ultimate presupposition we must assume a third principle which makes Being knowable and Knowledge able to know. This has been the epoch-making insight of Plato (*Republic*, VI, p. 509 f.; note 59 to ch. VI).

48. Since mathematics is a science of abstract relationships, the mathematician is not concerned with any existence which may be expressed in those relationships. Cf. note 47. This is the reason mathematics can be applied to any object.

49. This is the traditional interpretation of Aristotle as it is to be found, e.g. in Kant: 'The senses do not err—not because they always judge rightly but because they do not judge at all.' (*Critique of Pure Reason*, 2nd ed., p. 350.) Nevertheless, Aristotle does speak of the truth of sense-perceptions, and according to him truth and falsity do not belong only to propositions. Cf. note 47.

# V. History and Destiny

MAN'S whole life is a struggle to gain true existence, an effort to achieve substantiality so that he may not have lived in vain and vanish like a shadow. Whether he is a believer or a sceptic, whether he is a Metaphysician or a Positivist—this idea of existential truth is the driving force of all his thought and action. Everything else in the world simply exists; man, however, knows that he is, and he wants to be what he has recognized as his truth, as his true existence. What he seeks is not only satisfaction of his material or spiritual needs, for at the bottom of all contentment lingers the fear that it may be merely an illusion. What man really wants is existential truth, the actualization of his true destiny.

Yet, in his endeavor to fulfil his destiny man does not stand alone; he is inextricably entangled in the lives of others. He is determined by the social, economic and intellectual conditions of the community into which he is born; in short, he is moulded by history. No one can make an absolute beginning, nor can he wholly consummate himself in time. The situation in which the individual finds himself is the result of that which he himself and others before him have been and done and thought, of historical decisions that cannot be revoked. It is only by taking account of this past that man can think and act and be. In this the historicity of his existence consists.[1]

History is a sequence of critical actions which bring a new present into existence, making that which was present irretrievably past. It is in history, not in nature, that

man recognizes himself. The object of historical understanding is not a thing in itself, independent of the mind
which contemplates it.[2] The past is present to us only in
so far as we deal with it, accept or deny it, or simply try
to comprehend it. The aims of men, seen from an absolute point of view, may be subjective, or they may be the
contingent results of the process of nature. Still, we are
able to understand the ideas of diverse peoples and of
distant times—be they ever so much opposed to our own
ideals—precisely because they are subjective and thoroughly human. The history of mankind reveals to man
potentialities that he has realized in the past and that
may be beyond the narrow horizon of the immediate present and its interests. Thus from the study of history even
the philosopher may profit, in so far as it enlarges his
knowledge of human nature and makes him see his own
struggle for true existence in the context of the whole of
which he is but a part.

But what is the true destiny of man? Can history give
us an answer to this question? Throughout the ages we
see men fighting bitterly about the truth of their different
conceptions of destiny; there are as many conflicting views
on this issue as there are periods, nations, civilizations.
Does man's true destiny lie beyond this world and beyond
time, in his relation to God, as religion teaches? Or is it
to be found in this world, in man himself, in the development of all his natural and rational faculties—in short, in
the perfection of civilization, as modern man believes? [3]
Since the Renaissance the peoples of the Occident have
taken an increasingly hostile stand against the religious
interpretation of history, according to which mankind
is guided by divine Providence.[4] Modern man sees his
destiny in this world; he has decided to take his fate into
his own hands. Even the religious person will hardly deny
that this is the real task that God has set for man in this

life: to make use of all his faculties and so to become a real man; to build a world of truthfulness, of justice and morality in which the diverse nations may co-operate with all their strength towards the realization of their common ideals, so as to make the earth a more perfect dwelling place for humanity.

Filled with enthusiasm for this noble task of mankind, the philosophers of the eighteenth century, starting with Voltaire and Hume, built the foundation of that modern concept of history which, freed from all religious premises, has finally become openly opposed to religion. The history of mankind no longer appears as a religious drama, but rather as a natural genetic process which has gradually led from primitive beginnings to ever-higher stages of civilization. For us every historical occurrence finds sufficient explanation in some other phenomenon of history.[5]

The historian of today, in trying to grasp the essential forces by which certain events have come about and to bring order into the seeming chaos of historical data, has recourse to human and natural factors alone. In his struggle for objectivity he has learned to abandon as merely legendary an increasing number of traditional features. Our picture of the past thereby has lost a great deal of the poetical charm and the heroic grandeur it had for former generations. But the same enthusiasm for empirical reality which fills us in regard to the present makes itself felt in our understanding of the past and enlivens the letter of documentary tradition.

Even religion itself and its concepts of man and his destiny thus have come to be regarded as merely historical phenomena. These concepts are now understood as historically conditioned expressions of certain primitive forms of human thought which gradually had to yield to the more enlightened insight of later generations. In-

deed, how could modern man find a God or even a trace
of divine Providence in history which, he is convinced,
he has made himself, according to his own will? If the
world is out of joint, it is his responsibility to set it right
again; the destiny of the human race is to be determined
by man himself.[6]

For us history has thus become a history of civilization,
a 'struggle for individual and social perfection, a battle
against ignorance, disease, and the harshness of physical
nature.'[7] The deeds of great individuals and the contest
for power among nations may still have their place in
history, yet it is the progress of humanity as a whole with
which the historian is really concerned and which gives
history its unity and significance. War, like an incomprehensible natural catastrophe, may again and again inter-
rupt this steady advance. The outbreak of religious passion and the aggressive and expansive lust of certain individuals or nations may disturb the serene dominance
of reason. Still, this cannot shake modern man in his basic
conception of history; such calamities, on the contrary,
confront him with the task of inquiring into their causes
so as to avoid similar disaster in the future.

Philosophers of history from the time of Turgot and
Condorcet have made every effort to convince modern
man that history itself is proof of the fact that man's true
destiny lies in his unlimited perfectibility. Exact science,
to which man owes his mastery over nature, indeed has
given modern civilization a new and secure foundation.
The feeling that now he stands on firm ground, that he
sees before him a clear goal and a practical way by which
to reach it, distinguishes modern man from all previous
generations. And the rise of this feeling is itself perhaps
one of the most decisive events of history.[8]

Still, can this scientifically founded belief in progress
sustain the test of an unbiased investigation? There is a

strange contradiction in such a concept of progress. For
modern science owes its certainty precisely to the per-
sistence with which it has excluded from its understanding of reality all teleological concepts on account of their
merely subjective character, whereas the belief in progress
expressly introduces such a teleological principle into the
explanation of history. But do we know the real end of
history, so that we can judge if, a certain development
really means progress or regress? [9] True, the history of
human reason, of science and technology, gives proof of
a certain advancement. How could it be otherwise, since
the results of mathematical investigation are the logical
presuppositions of physics, which in turn form the theoretical foundation of chemistry and all the other branches
of science; and these again shape the economic, social, and
political structure of our time? Thus, certain stages of
theoretical knowledge and practical skill must have been
reached before the next higher step could be taken.[10]
Yet, is this fact sufficient for the conclusion that the history of the human race must follow the same law of
progress? If this were true, the meaning of history would
be seen exclusively in the perfection of science and technology, that is, in the external organization of society.
Man, however, is primarily interested in himself, in the
advancement of his moral faculties, his freedom, his happiness. Are we justified, then, in speaking of real progress
in this respect also? [11]

Condorcet in expounding his idea of progress in history was seriously convinced that all man had to do was
to overcome his religious prejudices and use his reason
—and war, tyranny, persecution, and all the other evils
from which his time was suffering would become a legend
of the past; man would approach the millennium.[12] During the eighteenth and nineteenth centuries the actual
decrease in the number and violence of wars may have re-

assured man in this expectation. But today, in view of
our recent experiences, it seems hardly possible to maintain such a belief. It is the strange irony of our time that
all progress in science and civilization, nay, in moral and
social consciousness, is turned eventually into a means for
war and destruction. Even those peoples who do their
utmost to prevent such a tragic reversal are forced to submit to the necessity of history. To the extent to which
man, through his reason, has learned to control nature,
he has fallen victim to the catastrophes of history.[13] Thus
his dream that he may be entirely free to shape his future
according to the ideals of his own reason is frustrated by
history. Man is thwarted by man himself, by his own
nature.

Out of the dissolution of the humanitarian idea arose
a new concept of history. Man began to recognize that
the course of history is marked by the divergence between aim and accomplishment. Man's goal may be set
by his own will, yet the results following from his actions
do not conform to his intentions.[14] But do we not call
the indeliberate result of a purposeful action chance? [15]
Whether we interpret the power which counteracts our
own will as chance or as historical necessity—it is in this
power that modern man, compelled by the experiences of
his time, sees the primary force of history.

History thus has become for him a continuous process
which seems to move with a necessity similar to that of
nature and which has a decisive influence upon man's
entire existence—upon his thought, his volition, his religious and moral convictions. Modern realism is based
on the belief that it is not his thought which determines
man in his being, but on the contrary, it is his being
which determines his ideas. But if all his activities appear
as secondary results of a process which is beyond human
control, man's theoretical concepts and moral values be-

come entirely conditioned and relative, mere reflections of the objective forces of nature and of history. The only freedom left to man, then, consists in his recognizing these powers within and without himself, in admitting the fact that they are not subject to his will, and in yielding to them voluntarily instead of being ruled by them against his will. In this way, he may hope within certain limits to gain control over them and to direct their course, thereby taking again an active part in the process of history.[16] But even so, his freedom is not truly creative; man has no existential truth in history, no destiny of his own which he must fulfil.

For such a point of view, even the idea of humanity appears only as one 'ideology' among many, as the expression of a definite historical and social situation.[17] But if our noblest ideas are merely relative and subjective, then it remains for success and force to decide which one of these ideals shall determine the future of mankind. Modern reason having turned against itself and against its most sublime idea, that of humanity, in this way has led to historical scepticism and relativism and thus to inhumanity. Man has returned to the ancient Greek idea, according to which history was merely a natural process, an idea from which Christianity had tried to free him through the creative liberty of the spirit.

Through this dissolution of humanitarian ideals, however, the philosopher has regained the liberty to admit the power of religion in history; he has become free again to recognize religion as the source from which the whole process of rationalization and secularization draws its vitality, even where it has turned against its own origin.[18] Ideas, such as those of truthfulness, freedom, justice, and morality, of the unity and progress of mankind, were inspired by Christianity; and yet, the same ideas have constituted the main incentives of the fiercest opposition against religion.[19] The whole scope of that process which we call history becomes evident only in the polar tension of religion and reason. The true essence of history finds its symbolic expression in the contemporaneousness and opposition of Caesar and Christ.

Caesar is the most conspicuous example of what human reason may accomplish in this world.[20] He is the great political genius who through the superiority of his intellect always recognized the right means for his ends. His aim was one of the most ambitious that man can set for himself: the political and moral rebirth of his declining people. This goal he reached, as far as that is humanly possible. If the ultimate freedom that man can attain is his power over reality, this Caesar had. At the end of his life he had subjugated the whole world; there was no one who really could oppose his will. That is more than anybody has been able to claim for himself either before or since. Caesar conquered the world in the full sense of the word. For this ancient world he determined forms of civilization which outlasted it and have even left their imprint upon modern life.

The historical development of the ancient Orient had reached its climax in the Persian empire of Darius, which integrated the currents of Eastern civilization. When Alexander conquered the East, he opened that region to the influence of Greek culture, which up to his time had had a relatively indigenous development. Thus Hellenism rose to the rank of a world-civilization which later was bequeathed to Rome. But it remained for Caesar to complete this universal historical process. By conquering all Western Europe he made that territory accessible to Graeco-Roman civilization, thereby setting a new stage for future history. The ends of his empire—which excluded India and the Far East—to this day mark the boundaries of two worlds and represent the limits of

Western civilization. Not until the discovery of the Americas were these limits widened. If we measure the greatness of an individual by the durability and consequence of his accomplishment, Caesar undoubtedly is the greatest character in history. With unfailing certainty he recognized behind the political phrases by which others were deceived the real forces of his time; with superior wisdom he knew how to direct them according to his own aims. This deep insight into the dynamics of human life and of history, this spontaneous understanding of the particular historical situation, enabled him to make quick and firm decisions which secured him success. He put an end to the freedom of the Republic because he saw that the religious, moral, and political principles upon which it was based had disintegrated and that the civil strife by which the nation was torn could be settled no longer by political means, but by military force alone.[21]

Yet, no matter how intelligently and carefully he planned everything, he always remained aware of the fact that in all human affairs it is fortune, chance, which tips the scale and which defies human foresight.[22] Just because he considered himself merely the tool of destiny did he contemplate himself so objectively, so indifferently, repeatedly gambling with his life in the mystical belief that by staking everything he might force destiny to his will.[23] 'Better to die once for all than to be always expecting death,' was his maxim,[24] and through this inner superiority and freedom in the face of destiny Caesar surpasses all similar figures in history.

True, all such men feel themselves somehow in secret agreement with Fate, and this conviction gives them the strength for their superhuman deeds. Still, in their inmost hearts they never cease watching with anxiety the signs of destiny which are written in the stars; they remain for ever fearful lest Fate may turn against them and crush them relentlessly. Caesar alone felt himself in complete harmony with the destiny of history, so much so that his personal fate was of no consequence to him. Brutus could destroy the man Caesar, but not his work, which continued to live.

What is so disturbing about Caesar or Napoleon or similar figures is the fact that the noblest moral forces of their times, which try to oppose them in order to defend freedom and morality, seem to be doomed to failure from the outset. Nothing seems capable of resisting these individuals in whom the passions and desires of the masses seem to be concentrated. All moral forces combined seem powerless against them.[25] Such men break forth upon mankind with the blind violence of natural catastrophes. This tragic pattern is clearly visible in the hopeless fight of Brutus against Caesar: wherever the realization of his ultimate aims was concerned, Caesar had no moral scruples. He liked to quote the lines from Euripides:

'If wrong must be, when empire is the prize
    The noble cause gives glory to the wrong.' [26]

Brutus, on the other hand, the philosopher and Platonist, was convinced that in resisting Caesar he was fighting at the same time for the highest ideal of philosophical morality. When he was finally beaten and saw that his cause was lost, he is said to have committed suicide with the words of the Greek tragedian on his lips:

'O wretched virtue, thou wert but a name,
    And yet, I worshipped Thee as real indeed.
    But now, it seems Thou wert but Fortune's slave.' [27]

Yet, is this really the final word that the philosopher has to say in view of the relentless course of history? Was Caesar right in his sceptical contempt of all human ideals? Is morality really the slave of historical Fate? Caesar's vic-

tory over the Roman Republic meant the end not only
of that social order, but of its religion, morality, philosophy as well, which now fell an easy prey to dogmatic petri-
fication or sceptical dissolution. True, after a century of
anarchy and senseless bloodshed Caesar had restored peace,
law and order; his contemporaries hailed him as a 'God
on earth,' the 'Saviour of mankind,' or the bringer of a
new 'Gospel.' [28] Still, the edifice erected by him and his
successors furnished merely a temporary shelter in which
the old world and its ideals seemingly lived on; they kept
their appearance, while their inner vitality had for ever
vanished. Even the supreme political wisdom of a Caesar
failed to produce something new.[29] To the world which
was craving for freedom and peace, he could give nothing
but the despotism of an empire which was a mockery of
true freedom and offered only the peace of the graveyard.[30]

If a new and truly productive life was to rise from the
ruins of the old world, a new faith was needed, a belief in
real peace, in higher justice, in a truer freedom than had
been envisioned by the ancient world. It was through
Christ that this truth was revealed to mankind. In Christ,
not in Caesar, did the truly creative power in the history
of that age manifest itself. While contemporary historians
took great pains in recounting the noisy deeds of the
Caesars, they failed to notice that in a far corner of the
world, among people who hardly seemed worth the attention of the educated, certain things were taking place that
were of an entirely different nature and of far greater importance for the history of the world than anything they
had written in their books. The modern historian who, following these ancient authors, understands the history of
that age merely as the reign of the Caesars and the decline
of ancient civilization, similarly fails to understand the
significance of those events that were to shake the world
to its foundations.[31]

Indeed, these happenings cannot be grasped in the same categories of rational historical interpretation as the deeds of the emperors. That is why all attempts to give a historical picture of the life of Christ are so unsatisfactory. The historian may try to depict the historical background and the spiritual world from which Jesus came, he may describe his parents, his education, his words, deeds, and miracles, he may praise his talents, his character, his moral teachings; he may compare him with Socrates and rank him even above the Greek sage. He may find him faultless, as did Pilate; he may be impressed by the fact that with Christ, everything seemed natural, as though it could not be otherwise, coming forth clearly and unhampered as the spring flows from the depths of the earth.[32] But the more enthusiastic the historian is about his subject, the more he tries to do it justice, the less convincing or adequate does his account appear, the more disproportionate do the external historical data seem to the significance he gives them. This is not solely due to the fact that apart from the Gospels we have no historical reports written by eye-witnesses. Were we in possession of the most accurate contemporaneous sources that might give account of every moment of Christ's life, we should still not have gained anything; [33] we should still be aware of the inadequacy of all such narrations compared to the greatness of their subject. As long as we see Christ only as a historical figure of the past, like Socrates or Caesar, we do not have the right approach. Even to the Apostles, Christ while he was alive was not the same as he appeared to be afterwards, the one who endowed them with the Spirit that dwelt within them, the Comforter who guided them 'into all truth.' [34]

This experience is beyond the reach of historical method. It is an experience of the soul, of the spirit, accessible only to him who holds the belief that in all those events which seemed of little importance a new truth had come into the world, a truth through which he who has faith in it may become a new man. It is the nature of religion that through it, man experiences the presence of God, who, being the absolute truth, determines his whole existence. To consider this experience as a merely human and subjective phenomenon and seek to explain it historically or psychologically means to deny its truth. But the belief in that truth which was revealed through Christ— whether man is passionately opposed to it, or whether he makes every effort to realize it as his own destiny—has been *the* driving force of history ever since.

For those who had this faith, the ancient world and its ideals vanished before the vision of a new kingdom, which was to be based on the infinite value and the freedom of the individual soul. In striving towards this 'community in heaven' the whole human race was to find its unity, its true historical destiny. To be sure, the earliest Christians misunderstood this idea of a kingdom that was to come, and yet is ever present; they expected the world literally to come to an end. The external world did not perish, rather did the Christians in struggling for their kingdom enliven the rational and political forms of the old civilization with a new spirit.[35] With their ideal of the unity and destiny of mankind, history finally became truly universal. This does not mean that the world has actually become a place of justice, peace, and brotherly love, or even that it has made a definite advance towards that end. The Christian kingdom is not of this world, it belongs to the realm of the spirit. In this world, it is always Caesar who is bound to be victorious, while Christ will for ever be crucified. Whoever will follow Him and work towards the fulfilment of His kingdom must take up his cross.[36] The position of the human soul in this world, despite the external progress of civilization, has at all times been the same. If there were any progress in this respect, the Chris-

tians of today would be more perfect than were the
Apostles.

Yet, though the kingdom of the soul is not of this world,
it is from the realm of the spirit that this world draws its
true vitality. Manly virtue was the cause of the grandeur
of Rome and the supposition of its Republican freedom.
When that source ran dry, nothing but the external might
of Caesar could hold the world together.[37] But even Caesar
was able to win his battles only as long as the Roman
soldier felt morally bound to his oath, to the 'sacrament,'[38] and was willing to die for it at his post. Wherever
spiritual strength gives out, the development of political
freedom inevitably follows the cycle from patriarchal mòn-
archy through aristocracy and democracy to the tyranny
of a Caesar.[39] In experiencing the dire necessity of history,
however, man becomes aware of his true destiny as being
the very thing which he has lost and which he can regain
in the realm of the spirit alone.

To recognize this ethico-religious consciousness as one
of the principal forces of history does not imply, however,
that one has to reintroduce into history God or Providence as the primary cause of external historical phenomena. How could modern man discover divine guidance
in this domain of his own from which he purposely has
excluded God? In such a world he can feel only complete
desertion and utter remoteness from God. The forces that
are active here are entirely independent of religion—
they are openly opposed to God. To see with modern
philosophers an immediate manifestation of divine Providence in the political and social history of mankind means
to reduce God to a political ruler, to turn society and its
order into 'visible Gods.'[40] Providence is a religious idea;
it does not signify God's interest in political parties or
social agents, but rather His concern about the ethico-
religious individual and the secret of his soul. Only in the

spiritual sphere is it appropriate to speak of Providence.
The history of religion and its moral ideals may be understood as progress towards an ever more profound understanding of the true nature of God and of His relation to
man and to the world. In this sense, Augustine was justified in interpreting the chronological sequence of paganism, Judaism, and Christianity as a meaningful and logical
development, as a manifestation of Providence; [41] and
from this presupposition it may be permissible to see even
in the external historical evolution some reflection of divine Providence.

But when man has consciously detached himself from
religion, as he has done in our time, the only true relation
to God discernible in history is the uprising against Him
and against all religion. In fact, a steady growth of such
revolutionary tendencies can hardly be denied today.
Wherever modern man speaks of progress in history, he
actually means this advance towards enlightenment and
rationalization which has finally led to a determined revolt
against God. This development has come about through
an inner necessity which the individual seems unable to
evade. If in any historical fact, it is here that we cannot
help recognizing a manifestation of divine Providence.

Apparently, then, there is a profound truth in the old
saying: 'No one contends with God except God Himself.'
For if there is a God, those Promethean powers which
antagonize Him must in some manner be ordained by
Him; they must be understood as His most imposing and
awe-inspiring manifestation. And is it not precisely the
same fundamental principles of ethics and religion, the
ideals of truth, freedom, and brotherly love, by which even
this insurrection against religion is inspired in the soul of
modern man?

The enigma of reality with which all religion and philosophy is confronted is the fact of evil in the world, that

compelling force which is opposed to man's moral freedom and which never ceases to frustrate him in his highest aspirations.[42] Even where human reason believes it has attained its ultimate freedom, its greatest power, as it did with Caesar, it knows that at the same time it is merely the tool of an all-pervading necessity. Fate is the opposite of Providence, but the religious consciousness discovers in the necessity of Fate a shadow of Providence.[43] It feels that the human aspect of necessity and of evil is not the final truth; it recognizes that in some way unfathomable to reason, the blind necessity of Fate, even evil itself, may serve as a means towards the realization of good, that is, of freedom.[44]

For the philosopher, then, the problem of history and destiny is identical with that of freedom and necessity. True freedom is not gained where man, liberated from reality and necessity, finds himself in a vacuum. Truly free is only he who in his subjective freedom can find a true, that is, an essential, content. However philosophical reason may define the concept of freedom, it always returns to the conclusion that freedom, in so far as it is truly creative and effective, must consist solely in the recognition of a superior necessity and in obedience to its law. The only question is in regard to the character of this necessity. The Positivist and the Materialist, for whom nature is the absolute principle, see it as the necessity of natural laws or of the similar laws of the social and economic development. The leap into freedom, from this supposition, is the recognition of these laws.[45] For the psychoanalyst, it is the understanding of the psychological mechanism which sets man free.[46] For a figure like Caesar, it is the necessity of Fate which he must voluntarily follow in order to gain his inner freedom. A rationalistic philosopher like Kant finds the ultimate necessity in the general moral law of reason; his will delivers itself by obeying this law of its own.[47] Yet, in none of these cases does man find that truly creative freedom which would liberate him even to the depths of his existence. In all these instances it is only a part of his being, his material, psychological, social, political, rational, or ethical nature, not his existence in its entirety, that finds its freedom.

Man truly liberates himself only when his freedom becomes the source of a new life, delivering the real essence of his existence. Nothing in the world can be considered truly good except creative freedom, which makes man aware of the fact that whatever he may do of his own free will is at the same time an ultimate necessity. The only evil consists in the loss or the betrayal of this freedom for the sake of some seeming, external necessity. Yet, man cannot escape the power of necessity and of evil merely by insisting stubbornly and with vain defiance upon his formal freedom and upon the preservation of his subjective existence. In this way, he gets only more deeply entangled in the net of psychological automatism, while his soul becomes empty.

True freedom is conceivable only on the basis of the idea of creation. For this concept implies that the absolute cause, God, has posited *vis-à-vis* of Himself free beings who, in their very freedom, realize their true and necessary existence, their destiny in this world. Only if man believes in the possibility of such inner freedom which is stronger than all worldly necessity, can he be certain that whenever he obeys with utter sincerity the voice of his conscience, he will follow out the intention of creation. On this condition alone can there be freedom and truth for man, can he believe that even if he is frustrated by the necessity of history he may still fulfil his true destiny. This idea of creative freedom is of course a religious concept. Its truth can never be proved through the principles of philosophical reason; yet, reason must recognize the fact that it can maintain its own truth and its own freedom only if it accepts this religious presupposition. The problem of history and destiny finds its solution in the belief in the creative freedom of the human spirit.

## NOTES

1. The concept of 'historicity' was used by S. Alexander to signify 'the timefulness of things.' In his essay on 'The Historicity of Things' (in the volume on *Philosophy and History: Essays presented to E. Cassirer,* Oxford, 1936, p. 11 f.) he expresses the view that 'a world laid out in space and moving forwards in time' is 'a world of events'; that 'novelty is of the essence of history and so it is of the world of things,' for 'there is an "emergence" of novel characters in things.' In a similar way Whitehead says that 'cosmological story . . . relates the interplay of the static vision and the dynamic history.' (*Process and Reality,* Cambridge, 1929, pp. 64, 235; concerning the problem of 'Causation in Historical Events,' cf. the contributions of F. J. Teggart, Morris R. Cohen, and M. Mandelbaum in the *Journal of the History of Ideas,* 1942, pp. 3 ff.) In such statements the term history is used metaphorically for the general temporal character of the world and its events. But in a literal sense the word 'historicity' can be applied only to man. Cf. R. G. Collingwood's important paper 'Human Nature and Human History' (*Proceedings of the British Academy,* vol. XXII, 1936, esp. pp. 8 ff.). It is the distinctive character of man not only to be, but to know that he is, and to actualize this knowledge. In being, thinking, and acting, he is always confronted, therefore, with what he himself and others before him have been, done, and thought. This is what I call his historicity. In this sense the term is used also by Collingwood and by contemporary German philosophers such as Jaspers and Heidegger.

2. In the field of science we have to do with an object which is essentially different from ourselves: we think, but nature does not. The object of historical knowledge is man himself in his subjective nature. In this sphere an ultimate distinction between the knower and his object cannot be maintained. It is not by chance that the word 'history' signifies two different things: the events themselves, and the record or the interpretation of these events. If we consider, for instance, the conflict between a religious and a humanitarian or a naturalistic interpretation we must realize that this con-

flict is not only one of opposite theories. The revolt against the religious interpretation of history is one of the most important events of modern history itself. In the realm of history the object of my self-consciousness is always another self-consciousness, a thinking Ego whom I cannot understand except in terms of myself. I can comprehend another man's speech only so far as I am able to speak his language myself. Hearing corresponds to speaking. It is our own possibilities which we discover in the objects of our historical knowledge. Or as Collingwood (op. cit. p. 18) puts it: 'Historical knowledge is the knowledge of what mind has done in the past, and at the same time it is the redoing of this, the perpetuation of past facts in the present. Its object is therefore not a mere object, something outside the mind which knows it . . . The so-called science of human nature or of the human mind resolves itself into history.' (Cf. the same, *Religion and Philosophy*, London, 1916, pp. 51 ff.)

3. Cf. e.g. Kant's formulation of the latter view: 'Civilization alone can be the ultimate purpose which we have cause for ascribing to nature in respect to the human race.' History must, therefore, be written 'upon a plan tending to unfold this purpose of nature in a perfect civil union of the human species' (*Critique of Judgment*, #83, and *Idea of a Universal History on a Cosmo-political Plan*, Props. 3 and 9). Concerning the present-day concept of history, see C. A. and M. R. Beard, *The American Spirit*, New York, 1942, p. 672 f.: 'The idea of civilization was . . . integrated with a theory of history and it offered to the reflective spirit such a degree of unity and coherence that it became an ultimate construct of values for countless Americans . . . To all pessimism or nihilism it [this idea of civilization] opposes a world-view as optimistic as the need and the will to live.'

4. Karl Marx and F. Engels, *The Holy Family* (*Gesamtausgabe*, Berlin, 1932, p. 265): 'History is simply the activity of man pursuing his ends.' Sidney Hook, *The Hero in History*, New York, 1943, p. xi: 'That History is made by men and women is no longer denied except by some theologians and mystical metaphysicians.' J. B. Bury, *Selected Essays*, Cambridge, 1930, p. 33; 'Historians have for the most part desisted from invoking the naïve conception of a god in history to explain historical movements.' George La Piana, 'Theology of History,' in *The Interpretation of History*, Princeton, 1943, p. 154 f.: 'To the historian these myths [which support the whole structure of the theology of history] are but human interpretations of facts and experiences of life.'

5. Cf. R. G. Collingwood's summarization (*Speculum Mentis*, Oxford, 1924, p. 53): 'Critical history is the child of the eighteenth century. It began in the hands of men like Vico and Hume, Gibbon and Lessing, and Herder and Niebuhr, and ripened into the nine-

teenth century when history stood forth the unmistakable queen of the sciences; biologists like Darwin and Huxley, philosophers like Hegel, theologians like Baur and Newman, and economists like Marx explicitly resolved the problems of their special sciences into historical problems . . . So gigantic has been the effect of this revolution that as yet people hardly appreciate it. They talk of Evolution, of Progress, of the metaphysical reality of Time, as if they were notions of the first importance and grand discoveries of modern science.' J. B. Bury, 'Darwinism and History' (op. cit. p. 23): 'Evolution, and the principles associated with the Darwinian theory, [influenced] the studies connected with the history of civilized man. The "historical" conception of nature . . . belongs to the same order of thought as the conception of human history as a *continuous genetic causal process*—a conception which has revolutionized historical research and made it scientific.' (My italics.) S. Alexander (op. cit. p. 11): 'The thoroughgoing conception of history in its application, not only to the affairs of man but to nature itself, is due as I suppose chiefly to Darwin.' Concerning the history of historiography, see J. W. Thompson and B. J. Holm, *A History of Historical Writing*, New York, 2 vols., 1942; R. Flint, *The Philosophy of History in Europe*, 1874; G. P. Gooch, *History and Historians in the 19th Century*, London, 1912; H. Holborn, 'The Science of History' (in *The Interpretation of History*, Princeton, 1943, pp. 87 ff.).

6. See the dictum of D. Ricardo, *Principles of Political Economy*, ch. v (quoted by J. H. Randall, Jr., *The Making of the Modern Mind*, Boston, etc., 1940, p. 330): 'There is no means of improving the lot of the worker by limiting the number of his children. His destiny is in his own hands.' H. Miller, *The Wisdom of the Heart*, 1941, p. 68: 'The destiny of the race will be determined by man himself.' Cf. the title quoted by H. Spencer (*Study of Sociology*, New York, 1883, p. 425): 'La main de l'homme et le doigt de Dieu dans les malheurs de la France (by J. C. Paris, 1871).'

7. C. A. and M. R. Beard, *The American Spirit*, New York, 1942, p. 672: 'This idea of civilization, in a composite formulation, embraces a conception of history as a struggle of human beings in the world for individual and social perfection—for the good, the true, the beautiful—against ignorance, disease, the harshness of physical nature, the forces of barbarism in individuals and in society.' A. J. Toynbee in his *Study of History* (vols. I-VI, London, 1933-9) restricts himself to analysing the various principles which bear on the genesis and growth of civilizations. Cf. also P. A. Sorokin, *Social and Cultural Dynamics*, New York, 1937-41, and other similar attempts in our days.

8. Cf. the penetrating analysis of this process by W. Dilthey (in his *Collected Works*, vol. III, Leipzig, 1927, pp. 218-47).

9. St. Augustine in his *City of God* was the first to develop that Christian concept of history according to which mankind as a whole is to actualize a purpose in the world throughout the succession of generations. Thus history has a teleological structure: every nation may hope to fulfil its own mission through the development of its particular religious, political, or scientific faculties. In modern thought this teleological idea has been secularized as the idea of rational progress and is considered to be proved by the facts of nature. Kant clearly discerned the contradiction which is implied in the concept of such a 'natural purpose' (cf. note 22 to ch. IV). And yet the rational justification of this modern teleological conception of history is the final aim of his *Critique of Judgment*. (Cf. #83 and note 3 to this chapter.) Concerning the history of 'the idea of progress,' see J. B. Bury's book on this subject (London, 1924). Cf. also George Sorel, *Les Illusions du Progrès*, 2nd ed., Paris, 1911.

10. This idea was first clearly expressed by Hobbes (*Opera Philosophica*, vol. II, p. 137) and was later developed by Comte (*Cours de Philosophie Positive*, 2nd ed., Paris, 1864, vol. V, pp. 179 ff.). Cf. F. J. Teggart, *Theory of History*, New Haven, 1925, pp. 94 ff.

11. Cf. Condorcet, *Outlines of an Historical View of the Progress of the Human Mind* (Engl. transl. Baltimore, 1802, p. 233): 'Do not all the observations . . . prove that the *moral goodness of man,* the necessary consequences of his organization, is like all his other faculties susceptible of an *indefinite improvement?* and that nature has connected by a chain which cannot be broken *truth, happiness, and virtue?*' (My italics.) Cf. ibid. p. 211, and J. B. Bury, *Selected Essays,* pp. 27 ff., who points to Turgot's *Discours sur l'histoire* (1750), where history is presented as a process in which 'the total mass of the human race marches continually though sometimes slowly to an ever increasing perfection.' Cf. Bury, *Idea of Progress,* London, 1924, p. 335 f., and F. J. Teggart, *Theory of History*, p. 91; R. Flint, *History of ·the Philosophy of History (Historical Philosophy in France)*, London, 1893, pp. 280 ff.

12. Condorcet, op. cit. p. 216: 'Then will arrive the moment in which the sun will observe in its course free nations only, acknowledging no other master than their reason, in which *tyrants and slaves, priests* and their stupid or hypocritical instruments *will no longer exist* but in history or upon the stage' (my italics); p. 234: 'The people will learn to regard war as the most dreadful of all calamities, the most terrible of all crimes.'

13. Cf. R. Niebuhr, *The Nature and Destiny of Man*, New York, vol. I, 1940, ch. II.

14. It is a well-known fact that in history the results of our willed actions reach beyond the mark of their intended goal, thus revealing an inner logic of things which overrules the will of man. The leaders of the French Revolution, for instance, intended a liberal constitution for their people and a federation of free nations. The revolutionary movement, however, which they unleashed, led to a military dictatorship and to imperialism. The French revolutionaries sought peace, while the historical forces made for war. Everywhere we see the divergence of accomplishment from aim, a phenomenon for which W. Wundt coined the term 'heterogeneity of ends' (*Völkerpsychologie*, vol. x, 1920, pp. 159 ff., 325 ff.) and which Hegel had called the 'Cunning of Reason' (*Philosophy of History*, p. 33). The Marxists adopted the Hegelian idea and formulated it in the following way: 'In nature . . . there are only blind unconscious agencies acting upon one another out of whose interplay the general law comes into operation. Nothing of all that happens . . . is attained as a consciously desired aim. In the history of society, on the other hand, the actors are all endowed with consciousness, are men acting with deliberation or passion, working towards definite goals. But . . . that which is willed happens rarely; in the majority of instances the numerous desired ends cross and conflict with one another . . . The ends of the actions are intended, but the results which actually follow from these actions are not intended; or when they do seem to correspond to the end intended, they ultimately have consequences quite other than those intended. Historical events thus appear on the whole to be likewise governed by chance. But where on the surface accident holds sway, there actually it is always governed by inner hidden laws.' (Engels, *L. Feuerbach*, transl. by L. Rudas, New York, 1935, pp. 58 ff.)

15. Cf. Aristotle (*Physics*, II, 5, 197a5): 'Chance [luck] is an incidental cause which interferes with our willed actions.' Cf. ibid. 197b3: 'Chance must always be connected with our doings.' In the Hellenistic age the Greek word for chance (luck, Fortune) *Tyche*, signified the 'Power of Destiny' which determines the course of history. Thus the historian Polybius (I, 4, 1) says: 'Tyche has guided almost all the affairs of the world . . . Though she is ever producing something new and ever playing a part in the lives of man, she has not in a single instance ever accomplished such a work, ever achieved such a triumph, as in our own times [namely the growth of Rome].' Cf. W. Warde Fowler, *Classical Review*, 1903, pp. 445 ff.; E. Täubler, *Tyche*, Leipzig, 1926, pp. 2 ff.; W. H. Roscher, *Mytholog. Lexikon*, vol. v, 1922, pp. 1309 ff. Pascal's famous dictum that the course of the world's history depends on accidents such as the

138       NOTES TO CHAPTER V

shape of 'Cleopatra's nose' (*Pensées* no. 162: 'Had it been shorter, the whole aspect of the world would have been altered') gives the title to an interesting paper of J. B. Bury (cf. *Selected Essays*, Cambridge, 1930, pp. 60 ff.).

16. Comte says that obedience to each natural law has its peculiar reward (cf. Lord Acton, *Historical Essays and Studies*, London, 1907, p. 86). Marx's dictum—that it is not the consciousness of men which determines their existence but their social existence which determines their consciousness—is well known. Cf. Marx, *Capital* (transl. by S. Moore and E. Aveling, New York, vol. I, 1890, p. xvii): 'To Hegel, the life-process of the human brain, *i.e.*, the process of thinking (the "Idea") . . . is the *demiurgos* of the real world . . . With me, on the contrary, the ideal is nothing else than the material world reflected by the human mind, and translated into forms of thought.' See also Engels, *Anti-Dühring*, V. 1; Lenin, *The Teachings of K. Marx* (in *A Handbook of Marxism*, New York, 1935, pp. 219, 233, and 538 ff., etc.) On the other hand, M. Weber deals with 'the manner in which ideas become effective forces in history' (*The Protestant Ethic and the Spirit of Capitalism*, transl. by T. Parsons, New York, 1930, esp. pp. 90 ff.). Weber's method is used by E. Troeltsch in his work: *Social Teachings of the Christian Churches*, New York, 1931, esp. vol. II. Cf. also R. H. Tawney, *Religion and the Rise of Capitalism*, London, 1926; J. B. Kraus, S.J., *Scholastik und Kapitalismus*, München, 1930; H. M. Robertson, *Rise of Economic Individualism*, Cambridge, 1935.

17. The term 'ideology,' used by Napoleon to express his contempt of political theories and ideals, has been adopted by Marx and Engels to characterize religious, moral, or political ideas as secondary results of 'the driving forces which—consciously or unconsciously—lie behind the motives of men in their historical actions.' (Engels, *L. Feuerbach*, tr. by E. Rudas, pp. 60, 65; cf. Marx and Engels, 'German Ideology,' in *Handbook of Marxism*, London, 1935, pp. 212 ff. See also K. Mannheim, *Ideology and Utopia*, New York, 1940, pp. 50 ff.) In our day, all ideologies, including that of the Marxists, are approaching a crisis. Cf. the interesting analysis of the present situation given by F. A. Voigt in *Nineteenth Century and After*, 1943, p. 148: 'The First World War began the universal struggle between secular religions—or *ideologies* as they are called (it would be more accurate to call them *demonologies*). The Second World War is bringing that struggle to an end . . . [p. 152] The ultimate origins of the Second World War are to be found in the spiritual crisis of modern man, in his restlessness, and his despair which makes him see refuge in secular religions like socialism (whether it be the National Socialism of Germany, the Guild Socialism of Italy or the Marxian Socialism of Russia) or in the Religion

of Progress (as it has been called) that is so prevalent in England. It seems to us that the end of the modern crisis may not be far off . . . There is little evidence that the Christian Churches' faith is reviving, but it does seem certain that secular religions are losing their hold on the minds and hearts of men. Those outside the Christian churches in Germany no longer believe in anything at all. Even those inside have lost their secular beliefs and are inclined to dismiss everything as propaganda and, therefore, as mendacious, whatever its source may be. In the countries of Eastern and South Eastern Europe patriotism remains . . . but nationalism has declined.'

18. The struggle to actualize the humanitarian ideal led to tragic consequences: Man freed himself from religion and the belief in superhuman forces in order to become independent and to take his destiny into his own hands. But now he again finds himself dependent, and this time on non-human and even sub-human forces against which his will seems powerless.

19. Cf. Nietzsche, note 5 to ch. vi.

20. The most adequate characterization of Caesar is given by Mommsen (*History of Rome,* transl. by W. P. Dickson, New York, 1909, vol. iv, pp. 278 ff.). In this work of his early years, however, Mommsen, ascribed to Caesar many achievements which in his later research he recognized as the work of Augustus. In addition to Mommsen I have consulted the following works: T. R. Holmes, *Caesar's Conquest of Gaul,* Oxford, 1911, pp. 22 ff., and *The Architect of the Roman Empire,* Oxford, 1928-31; E. Meyer, *Caesars Monarchie,* Stuttgart, 1919, pp. 324 ff.; A. von Premerstein in *Abhandlungen der bayr. Akademie der Wissensch,* 1937; John Buchan, *Augustus,* Boston, 1937; R. Syme, *The Roman Revolution,* Oxford, 1939, pp. 121 ff. and *passim.* The relation of Augustus to Caesar is defined by H. Lietzmann (*The Beginnings of the Christian Church,* Engl. transl. New York, 1937, vol. i, p. 218) in the following way: 'Caesar wished to use the stateform of Hellenistic Kingship in order to give graphic expression to the essential meaning of Rome's historical development . . . Octavian Augustus was the heir of Caesar, both of his power and of his conceptions; he became the great monarch who ruled the entire world.'

21. After 38 B.C., the military leader of the Caesarian faction took to calling himself 'Imperator Caesar' (R. Syme, op. cit. p. 113). The word *Imperator* as praenomen of the Caesars clearly expresses the fact that the civil organization of Rome was supplanted by a military one (cf. von Premerstein, op. cit. pp. 132, 247). One need not point to modern analogies.

22. Concerning Caesar's belief in Fortune (*Tyche*) see T. Rice

Holmes, *Caesar's Conquest of Gaul*, pp. 22 ff., and W. Warde Fowler, in *Classical Review*, 1903, pp. 153 ff. Cf. note 15.

23. Shakespeare's psychological analysis of Caesar's character is based on a careful study of the ancient biographies and therefore may be regarded almost an authentic source. The poet represents Caesar as speaking of himself in the third person; so does Caesar in his writings. This feature is characteristic of his whole attitude: he looks at himself with amazement as if he were a higher being, the incarnation of the *Tyche*, of Rome's Destiny (cf. E. Meyer, op. cit. p. 466).

24. Plutarch, *Caesar*, 57: 'When his friends thought it best that he should have a body guard, he would not consent saying that it was better to die once for all than to be always expecting death.' Cf. Appian II, 109, 455 and Aeschylus, *Prometheus*, 750 f.

25. Shakespeare, in his *Julius Caesar*, made this phenomenon perfectly clear. But it was not until the time of Napoleon that poets and philosophers tried to analyse the historical implications of such a genius. Cf. e.g. Goethe (*Truth and Poetry*, last chapter; cf. note 42); Hegel (*Philosophy of History*, Introduction, pp. 29 ff. and 34 ff.), and S. Kierkegaard (*Concept of Dread*, ch. III); cf. also J. Burckhardt (*Force and Freedom*, ed. by T. H. Nichols, New York, 1943, pp. 301 ff.); W. James ('Great Men and Their Environment,' in *Selected Papers on Philosophy*, London, 1918, pp. 165 ff.). Cf. now S. Hook, *The Hero in History*, New York, 1943, pp. 15 ff., 66 ff., 77 ff.

26. Euripides, *The Phoenician Maidens*, v. 541, transl. by R. Potter (*The Tragedies of Euripides*, London, 1781, p. 427): The full significance of the sentence quoted in the text becomes clear in the context of the whole passage:

> 'A kingdom in my grasp, shall I submit
> To live his vassal? No: come fire, come sword,
> Yoke thy proud steeds, fill all the fields with chariots,
> Thou never shalt extort my Kingdom from me.
> If wrong must be, when empire is the prize
> The noble cause gives glory to the wrong:
> In all besides let justice hold her cause.'

In a very similar way Napoleon said: 'My chief maxim has always been, in politics as in war, that all evil—even if within the law—is excusable only in so far as it is necessary; anything beyond this is a crime' (quoted by J. Burckhardt, op. cit. p. 340). But even Cavour, the outstanding representative of nineteenth-century Liberalism, confessed: 'If we did for ourselves what we are doing for Italy we should be thorough scoundrels' (cf. D. A. Binchy, *Church and State in Fascist Italy*, Oxford, 1941, p. 47). It is a strange fact that communities, that nations, consider themselves exempt from the ordinary moral code: 'No power has ever yet been founded without crime . . . The "man after God's heart" then appears . . . his utter ruthlessness is generally condoned for the sake of some service rendered' (Burckhardt, op. cit. p. 339). Cf. Lord Acton, *Historical Essays and Studies*, London, 1907, p. 505: 'The historians, like Froude, Macauley, Carlyle, who praise them [the heroes of history as examples of morality], become teachers of morality . . . Quite frankly, I think there is no greater error . . . If we may debase the currency [the inflexible integrity of the moral code] for the sake of the genius, or success, or rank, or reputation, we may debase it for the sake of a man's influence, of his religion, of his party, of the good cause which prospers by his credit and suffers by his disgrace . . . My dogma is not the special wickedness of my own spiritual superiors, but the general wickedness of men in authority—of Luther and Zwingli, and Calvin . . . of Mary Stuart . . . of Cromwell and Louis XIV, . . . Bossuet and Ken.'

27. Cassius Dio, *Roman History*, 47, 49, transl. by H. B. Foster, Troy, vol. III, 1906, p. 155 (cf. *Fragmenta Tragicorum Graecorum*, ed. Nauck, no. 374, 2nd ed., p. 910). With this impressive passage Dio's report on the Civil War (in the 47th book) ends. Dio who is only a compiler must have taken this effective conclusion from the work of a greater historian. His source may have been Asinius Pollio's history of this period which is supposed to have ended also with the battle of Philippi. Asinius Pollio had been a friend of Caesar and yet a faithful adherent of republican freedom. He 'transmitted the character of Brutus in noble colours' (Tacitus, *The Annals* IV, 34. Cf. R. Syme, *The Roman Revolution*, Oxford, 1939, p. 5). Thus he was the man to understand the tragic fate of Brutus as it is presented by Dio. But the fragments preserved from Pollio's work are too scanty to prove this hypothesis.

28. In 48 B.C., 'the cities, towns and peoples of Asia Minor greeted Caesar as the son of Ares and Aphrodite, God upon earth, and the universal saviour of human life' (W. Dittenberger, *Sylloge Inscriptionum Graecarum*, 2nd ed., Lipsiae, 1917, no. 760). Another inscription (8 B.C.) praises the good fortune of the Augustan period in the following words: 'Is the birthday of the divine Emperor . . . not rightly to be regarded as equal to the beginning of the whole world? . . . For the world this birthday of our God meant the beginning of the *evangelia* [messages of peace] which was conjoined with his person' (W. Dittenberger, *Orientis Graeci Inscriptionis Selectae*, Lipsiae, 1905, no. 458, p. 50 f.) Cf. H. Lietzmann, op. cit. p. 221 f., who in his discussion of these inscriptions says: 'To them [the poets of Rome, cf. Vergil, *Eclogues*, 4] Augustus was a god upon earth, *praesens divus*, the prince of an era similar to paradise').

29. A. J. Toynbee (*A Study of History*, London, vol. III, 1935, p.

232) expresses a different view: 'The individuals who perform the miracle of creation and who therefore bring about the growth of the societies in which they arise are more than mere men.'

30. Cf. R. Syme, op. cit. p. 2: ' "Pax et Princeps." It was the end of a century of anarchy, culminating in twenty years of civil war and military tyranny. If despotism was the price, it was not too high: to a patriotic Roman of Republican sentiments even submission to absolute rule was a lesser evil than war between citizens. Liberty was gone, but only a minority at Rome had ever enjoyed it'; cf. ibid. p. 155: 'The Libertas of the Roman aristocrat meant the rule of a class and the perpetuation of privilege . . . Next to freedom and legitimate government comes peace'; ibid. p. 304, 'To the Roman, . . . the word pax can seldom be divorced from notions of conquest, or at least compulsion.' Cf. Vergil, *The Aeneid*, VI, 851 (transl. by John Dryden, Oxford University Press, 1932, p. 168):

> But, Rome! 'tis thine alone, with awful sway
> To rule mankind, and make the world obey:
> Disposing peace and war thy own majestic way.
> To tame the proud, the fettered slave to free,
> These are imperial arts and worthy thee.

31. Characteristic of the attitude of the modern historian towards this phenomenon is the title of Gibbon's classic work, *History of the Decline and Fall of the Roman Empire*. Cf. esp. the famous fifteenth and sixteenth chapters on the history of the Church under the Roman Empire, which gave rise to a storm of criticism (J. W. Thompson and B. J. Holm, *History of Historical Writing*, New York, vol. II, 1942, p. 84).

32. E.g. A. Harnack, *What is Christianity?*, 2nd ed., New York, 1904, p. 36. With regard to the many writings of a similar nature, Kirsopp Lake (*The Stewardship of Faith*, New York, 1915, p. 51) says: 'It has been called the tragedy of faith, but it really only represents the shipwreck of the hope of liberal criticism in the nineteenth century to find in a critical reconstruction of the historic Jesus a solution for the problem of the present generation . . . Liberal Protestantism in the nineteenth century thought that historical criticism would remove all the misrepresentations of later tradition and reveal the figure of the historic Jesus as infallible. Is that hope also to go? Yes, I fear so.' Concerning E. Meyer's book, *Origin and Beginnings of Christianity* (3 vols., Berlin, 1921 ff.), see J. W. Thompson's (op. cit. vol. II, p. 485) statement: 'Finally he attempted what no secular historian had ventured to do: to write a work on the origins of Christianity.'

33. Cf. Kierkegaard's penetrating discussion of this problem in *Philosophical Fragments*, ch. IV, and *The Journals*, no. 417.

34. John 16. 7: 'I tell you the truth; it is expedient for you that I go away: for if I go not away the Comforter will not come unto you; but if I depart, I will send him unto you . . . [13] Howbeit when he, the Spirit of truth, is come, he will guide you into all truth.' Cf. Hegel's interpretation of this passage in his *Philosophy of History*, pp. 325 ff. Hegel, however, identifies Christ with an abstract principle, the 'Speculative Idea,' which he calls the 'Absolute Truth.'

35. Cf. *Augustine and Greek Thought* (The Augustinian Society), Cambridge, Mass., 1942, pp. 5 ff., where I tried to sketch this process.

36. St. Luke 9. 23: 'And he said to them all, 'If any man will come after me let him deny himself, and take up his cross daily, and follow me.' Matthew 16. 26: 'For what is a man profited if he shall gain the whole world, and lose his own soul?' 22. 21: 'Render therefore unto Caesar the things which are Caesar's; and unto God the things that are God's.' Cf. Luke 23. 2; John 19. 12 f.

37. St. Augustine in his *City of God* (v, 12) gives the following analysis of this process: '[Rome] first earnestly desired to be free and then to be mistress . . . the state grew with amazing rapidity after it had obtained liberty, so great a desire of glory had taken possession of it . . . But it was other things than these that made them great . . . industry at home, just government without, a mind free in deliberation, addicted neither to crime nor to lust.' Cf. III. 21: 'But when the last Punic war had terminated in the utter destruction of Rome's rival [Carthage] . . . then the Roman republic was overwhelmed with a host of ills, which sprang from the corrupt manners induced by prosperity and security . . . During the whole subsequent period down to the time of Caesar Augustus, who seems to have entirely deprived the Romans of liberty,—a liberty, indeed, which in their own judgment was no longer glorious, but full of broils and dangers and which now was quite enervated and languishing—the Romans submitted all things again to the will of a monarch, and infused as it were a new life into the sickly old age of the republic, and inaugurated a fresh régime.'

38. In Latin the word *sacrament* means oath, esp. the military oath of allegiance. In the ancient mystery religions, the word denotes the oath of initiation (cf. Apulejus, *Metamorphoses* XI, 6 and 15; Livy XXXIX, 15,13). Thus the Latin word *sacramentum* gained a meaning similar to the Greek term *mysterion* (secret, mystery). It is the vow for lifelong obedience in the service of God (cf. R. Reitzenstein, *Hellenistische Mysterien Religionen*, Leipzig, 3rd ed., 1927, pp. 20, 192 f., 242). Both armies, that of Caesar and that of Christ, are held together through the same spiritual power of an oath of allegiance.

39. The fatality of this circular process is strongly emphasized in Plato's interpretation of history (cf. my paper 'Plato's View of the State' in the *Harvard Educational Review*, 1941, p. 492). The belief in historical cycles is closely connected with the Greek conception of time (cf. note 41 to ch. III) and is to be found also in ancient historians such as Polybius. In modern times this Greek theory was revived by Machiavelli, Vico, Hegel, Schelling, Spengler, and other philosophers. Following Plato, Hegel distinguishes two phases of royalty—a primary, the patriarchal monarchy, and a secondary, the dictatorship, which of necessity develops out of the dissolution of democracy (*Philosophy of History*, pp. 46 ff.). Among present-day historians A. J. Toynbee is a representative of the theory of life-cycles ('History' in *The Legacy of Greece*, ed. by R. W. Livingstone, Oxford, 1928, p. 303, and *A Study of History*, vol. I, pp. 147 ff., 178 f., etc., IV, 23 ff., V, 27, etc.). Cf. also P. A. Sorokin, *The Crisis of Our Age*, New York, 1941, and *Social and Cultural Dynamics*, New York, 1937-41.

40. Thus Hegel considered the social order a visible God: 'In thinking of freedom we must not take our departure from the individual's self-consciousness, but from the essence of self-consciousness. Let man be aware of it or not, this essence realizes itself as an independent power, in which particular persons are only phases. It [this power of freedom] is the march of God in the world. When thinking of the Idea of the state, we must not have in our mind any particular state—but must contemplate the *'Idea,'* this actual God, by itself.' (*Philosophy of Right*, 258, transl. by S. W. Dyde, London, 1896, p. 246 f.) 'The History of the World . . . is the true *Theodicea*, the justification of God in History' (*Philosophy of History*, last page). On the other hand, 'in England and America, we see the vitality and the attractive power of the "social Gospel" in its various forms,' as J. B. Burnaby, *Amor Dei*, London, 1938, pp. 7 ff.) says, who adds: 'There is a pathetic naïveté, perhaps something of the heretic's age-long deficiency in sense of humour, about J. Macmurray's ideal of an "empirically minded" religion, leading the progressive movement with science as its technical adviser. According to Macmurray, the Christian's most urgent duty is to denounce and combat the "pseudo-religion" of other-worldliness. For Jesus says, *The Kingdom of Heaven is within you*, and so sets the temporal process itself in the frame of an eternal reality, which is a reality of the temporal in the temporal.'

41. When Augustine had become a Christian and tried to define the difference between the peculiar nature of his new faith and the ideas of Plato's philosophy, which before his conversion he had regarded as the ultimate form of truth, he found the basic principle of Christianity in history. He says in *De Vera Religione* (7, 13. I

quote from Burnaby, op. cit. p. 25): 'The fundamental principle for the pursuit of this Religion is history and the prediction of the dispensation of divine providence for the salvation of the human race which needs to be formed anew and restored to eternal life. Upon faith in this order, the soul will be cleansed by a life fashioned into the harmony with the divine commands.' In another writing (*De Genesi ad Litteram*, v, 22, 43) Augustine emphasizes that the proper sphere of divine Providence is the moral life of man. It is this Christian concept of Providence which Hegel formulates in the following way: 'Our belief that Providence in its action reaches even to the individual finds its confirmation in the fact that God has become man . . . and it is owing to this that subjectivity has received the absolute moral justification' (*Philosophy of Religion*, vol. II, 1895, pp. 274 ff.). But with this concept of Providence it is irreconcilable to say, as Hegel does in another passage, that 'Divine Providence may be said to stand to the world and its process in the capacity of absolute cunning' (*The Logic of Hegel*, transl. from the *Encyclopaedia* by W. Wallace, § 209, p. 350) and that virtue, vice, and justice remain outside of history (*Philosophy of History*, pp, 33 ff.). Cf. also Lord Acton, *The History of Freedom*, London, 1909, p. 224.

42. Cf. Goethe, *Truth and Poetry* (last chapter): 'I could detect in nature—both animate and inanimate, with soul or without soul—something which manifests itself in contradictions . . . To this principle I gave the name of "Demoniacal" after the example of the ancients . . . This demoniacal element . . . expresses itself most distinctly in animals, yet with man especially has it a most wonderful connection, forming in him a power which, if it be not opposed to the moral order of the world, nevertheless does often so cross it that one may be regarded as the warp and the other as the woof. For the phenomena which it gave rise to there are innumerable names, for all philosophers and religions have tried in prose and poetry to solve this enigma and to read once for all the riddle, an employment which they are welcome to continue. But the most fearful manifestation of the Demoniacal is when it is seen predominating in some individual character. During my lifetime I have observed several instances of this, either more closely or remotely. Such persons [like Napoleon, Cagliostro] are not always the most eminent men, either morally or intellectually; and it is seldom that they recommend themselves to our affection by goodness of heart; a tremendous energy seems to be seated in them . . . All the moral powers combined are of no avail against them; in vain does the more enlightened portion of mankind attempt to draw suspicion upon them as deceived if not deceivers—the mass is still drawn on by them. Seldom if ever do the great men of an age find their equals

among their contemporaries and they are to be overcome by nothing but the universe itself; and it is from the observation of this fact that the strange but striking proverb must have risen: *Nemo contra Deum nisi Deus ipse.*' (Cf. note 25.)

43. Cf. S. Kierkegaard, *Concept of Dread* (ch. III, 2): 'Destiny is nothing in itself. It is the genius who detects its power and the deeper the roots of his mind reach the deeper are the strata of life in which he discovers it. Destiny is nothing but an anticipation foreshadowing Providence.' Cf. above, note 28, to ch. IV.

44. Cf. Lord Acton (*The History of Freedom*, London, 1909, p. 596).

45. F. Engels, 'Anti-Dühring,' in the *Handbook of Marxism*, London, 1935, p. 299: 'Men's own social organization which has hitherto stood in opposition to them as if arbitrarily decreed by *Nature* and *history*, will then become the *voluntary* act of men themselves. It is only from this point that men, with full consciousness, will fashion their own history . . . It is *humanity's leap from the realm of necessity into the realm of freedom.* (My italics.) Cf. Marx, *Capital*, vol. III (Chicago, 1909, p. 954): 'Just as the savage must wrestle with nature, in order to satisfy his wants, in order to maintain his life and reproduce it, so civilized man has to do it . . . With his development the *realm of natural necessity expands,* because his wants increase; but at the same time the forces of production increase; by which these wants are satisfied. The *freedom* in this field cannot consist of anything else but of the fact that socialized men regulate their interchange with nature rationally, bring it under their common control instead of being ruled by it as by some blind power; that they accomplish their task with the least expenditure of energy and under conditions most adequate to their human nature and worthy of it; *but it always remains a realm of necessity.* Beyond it begins that development of human power which is its own end, *the true realm of freedom,* which, however, can flourish only upon that realm of necessity as its basis . . . In fact, the realm of freedom does not commence until the point is passed where labour under the compulsion of necessity and external necessity is required.' (My italics.) N. J. Bukharin, who quotes this passage, interprets it in the following way: 'In other words, the transition from capitalism to socialism is far from implying entry into the realm of pure chance or of pure "*free will*" on a social scale. It is far from implying the liquidation of *necessity,* i.e., *of objective law,* which remains.' (My italics.) 'Marx's Teaching,' in *Marxism and Modern Thought,* transl. by R. Fox, London, 1935, p. 83.

46. Freud, *Collected Papers,* vol. IV, London, 1925, p. 388: 'There are all those unfulfilled but possible futures to which we still like to cling in phantasy and all our suppressed acts of volition which

nourish in us the illusion of Free Will.' Cf. F. Alexander, 'Psychology and the Interpretation of Historical Events' (in *The Cultural Approach to History*, New York, 1920, p. 55): 'From a clinical point of view, the historical theory of . . . a Marx, in spite of much truth, is equivalent to a paranoid delusion. Also the persecutory delusions of the insane contain a kernel of truth. As Freud has formulated it so succinctly, the paranoiac, who sees in every one a persecutor, falsifies reality only insomuch as he sees in others nothing but the repressed unconscious hostility, which unfortunately all people, even friends, harbor against each other in their unconscious.

47. Cf. Kant's formulation of 'freedom under law' in his *Critique of Practical Reason*, § 8, p. 122): 'The autonomy of the will is the sole principle of all moral laws . . . In fact the sole principle of morality consists in the independence on all matter of the law . . . Now this *independence* is *freedom* in the *negative* sense, and this *self-legislation* of the pure, and therefore practical, reason is *freedom* in the *positive* sense. Thus the moral law expresses nothing else than the *autonomy* of the pure practical reason, that is, freedom.'

# VI. Letter and Spirit

THE idea of creative freedom is a religious conception. It is unverifiable by reason, and yet, only on the supposition of such a freedom can man find truth and destiny in history. Throughout these lectures, belief has proved to be the ultimate ground of fundamental philosophical concepts. Our task has been to elucidate philosophy through belief and belief through philosophical reason. In interpreting the true meaning of religious and philosophical ideas we have tried to grasp the spirit which is behind the letter.

Plato described the task of the philosopher as the endeavour to read the script of the world and to understand its true meaning.[1] But is this not precisely the aim of the religious thinker as well? St. Paul, in formulating the ultimate secret of Christianity, uses the metaphor of letter and spirit.[2] Yet, the significance of his expression surpasses all that philosophers before him had ever thought; it indicates an entirely new understanding of truth, which resulted from the religious experience of the Christian. Greek philosophers, and again modern thinkers, have considered religious ideas as mere letters, figurative expressions to be interpreted in terms of a rational understanding of the world.[3] For St. Paul, the relation between letter and spirit is just the opposite: mundane reality is the letter, which must be read in the spirit of a more sublime truth. To him, everything in the world—man, philosophy, and even morality—is without meaning unless it is taken as a symbol.

In Christianity, interpretation therefore acquired an importance that it had never had before. One may even say that the struggle to ascertain true interpretation epitomizes the whole history of Christian faith. To curb the unrestrained freedom of a merely personal and subjective exegesis, the Church was obliged to establish an objective canon and a strict dogma. In support of its letter, it developed a new rational philosophy based on the Christian spirit. The authority of tradition and the independence of thought were in constant opposition, and by this conflict all Church disputes, among Catholics and Protestants alike, were determined.[4]

Out of this striving after truth arose the sense of intellectual integrity and freedom which led eventually to a repudiation of all religion. It was Nietzsche, the most radical antagonist of the faith, the self-styled anti-Christ, who admitted: 'We atheists, we godless foes of metaphysics, we too take our fire from that conflagration which was kindled by a thousand-year-old faith, from that Christian belief . . . the belief that God is the truth, that truth is *divine.*' [5] Indeed, the philosophical ideas which form the natural and unquestioned presuppositions of the modern sceptic originated in Christianity. Augustine was the first to formulate them in trying to express rationally the Christian spirit as he had found it in himself. He established the new concepts of the conscious ego as opposed to the outside world, of personality, of time and of history; he raised the problems of free will and of inward truth; in short he laid the philosophical foundation of modern thought.[6]

No matter how far present-day man may have deviated from Christianity, liberty, will, love—*these* he is not willing to renounce. More than that: it is precisely his insistence on freedom, his feeling of sovereignty, which is the driving force of modern philosophy. This we find with Descartes, in his indubitable *cogito,* which expresses the

basic assumption of the new age, the independence of reason and the supremacy of man over nature; we find it in
Kant's principle of autonomous morality; we find it in
Marx and in Bolshevism, for which social revolution
means the collective liberation of man; we find it in pragmatism; and we find it in modern Democracy, where the
freedom of the individual forms the basis of all political
activity. Even in the most secularized forms of modern
thinking, then, free will and sovereign personality have
remained pre-eminent ideals.[7]

These principles, however, by which the modern philosopher is led, are entirely at variance with that criterion
by which he would test the truth of his ideas. Modern
philosophy has endeavoured in vain to establish the freedom of will through either positivistic or rationalistic
postulates. The Positivist declares that this problem is
merely illusory: We may observe the psychological fact
that we will, but we shall never be able to prove that this
experience has a correlate in reality.[8] Free will transcends
indeed all that we can perceive, and can never be proved
by the evidence of the senses. Modern rationalists, on the
other hand, have argued that man finds his autonomy precisely in reason, in his concurring with his own rational
laws, but this argument obviously is a vicious circle.[9] Freedom of will does not mean only choice between given possibilities, rather it means the very creation of such possibilities. Free will is the power to act in accordance with
one's own thought, that is, the sovereign power to change
given facts, to reshape factual reality, and to control it.
It remains inexplicable to human reason; and yet, without
such freedom of will and thought, truth itself would be
impossible. We cannot renounce these ideas, even if they
are not substantiated by objective facts.

Although modern man regards nature as the only proper object of understanding, and passionately rejects all

other-worldliness, he is no longer able to look at the world as naïvely as the Greek philosopher was wont to do; he no longer feels thoroughly satisfied within its bounds. For the Greek philosopher, the world was not mute, not senseless. If in all the charm of its beauty it seemed to him to be divine, this was possible because he could not conceive of anything beyond it, he did not know of any higher value.[10] Modern man, however, who has passed through the experience of Christianity, knows of something else even though, or rather just because, he may most emphatically deny it. He clings desperately to this world—not because it seems sufficient to him, but rather because he no longer finds satisfaction in religion. He attributes to empirical reality an increased weight, a new dimension, as it were, unknown in former times.

This new enthusiasm for empirical reality finds expression everywhere today, in philosophy, in the fine arts, in poetry, and even in politics. The pictures of Van Gogh have no perspective into any Beyond. And yet, the reality he depicts is not merely factual; it is surcharged with vital forces which, although they do not break through the surface, still seem to be driving towards an unknown goal. In writers like D. H. Lawrence, Rilke, or James Joyce we observe a similar struggling to describe reality, which in its merely empirical presence seems to acquire an almost mythical meaning.[11] Even thinkers like Dostoevski and Kierkegaard, who wish to re-establish the truth of religion, try to substantiate Christian faith by psychological or other objective phenomena.[12] The various political movements of today likewise understand their own ideologies as a mythical expression of the dynamic forces of life; and the political mythus is meant to replace religion.[13] Modern philosophers of all shades, Positivists and Metaphysicians alike, are inspired by the same ardent longing and admiration for this reality.[14]

Every endeavour to reach out past this world, every suggestion of the idea of a Beyond is considered treacherous by modern man. But by this very longing for reality he betrays to what small extent he is actually absorbed in it, how ill-satisfied he is with the world as it is, how badly he suffers from this self-imposed taboo of transcendence. The spirit of freedom which transcends reality is still alive in him; it determines all his actions and his whole existence, although in his theories he does not acknowledge it.

In Positivism modern realism surpasses itself. Since the Positivist regards as true and meaningful those concepts alone which can be verified by observable facts, there remain literally for him only 'letters,' namely the conventional characters of science or the symbols of mathematics.[15] Even those ideas which stand for the modern consciousness of man, such as will, freedom, and personality, become meaningless. Thus the development of modern philosophy has led to the paradoxical result, that in terms of his own philosophy modern man no longer understands himself. This situation seems to attest to the truth of that thought which St. Paul tried to express by his metaphor of spirit and letter: for him who seeks sufficiency in himself, the world and man become mere letter. This is the meaning of the passage in Corinthians: 'Not that we are sufficient of ourselves to think any thing as of ourselves; but our sufficiency is of God; Who also hath made us able ministers of the new testament; not of the letter but of the spirit: for the letter killeth, but the spirit giveth life.' And then St. Paul continues: 'Therefore if any man be in Christ, he is a new creature: old things are passed away; behold, all things are become new.' [16]

With the religious experience of Christianity something actually new came into the world, a new man was created; and the fundamental structure of this 'new creature' who finds his truth in the freedom of spirit and personality has remained evident even in present-day man and his most secularized forms of life. Of St. Paul's religious idea of a new creation Schelling has given a striking rational interpretation. He says: 'Christ returns into the super-sensible world and in place of himself he proclaims the spirit. It is as though he put an end to the past age—he is the last God—after him comes the spirit, the ideal principle, the soul that rules over the new world.'[17] Is it not an historical fact that Christ was the last God? Is it not true that since His time the history of European religion has become the history of the spirit? And yet, Schelling's words are only a secularized version of a medieval thought; Joachim of Floris, the renowned theologian and philosopher of the twelfth century, first had such a vision of the history of mankind. He saw it divided into three periods or dispensations: the age of the Law or the Father (relating to the Old Testament); the age of the Gospel or the Son (relating to the New Testament); and the age of the Spirit. This 'Third Empire,' he thought, would bring all temporal ages to an end and be the sabbath of humanity. The Church of St. Peter would be purified, and the new Church would be an *ecclesia contemplativa*. The Gospel of Christ would be superseded by the Gospel of the Spirit, which would be final and everlasting.[18]

This apocalyptic vision of a third empire, the age of the Spirit, was to be of tremendous influence on later religious as well as political speculations up to the present time.[19] Joachim's idea marks the beginning of that trend of thought which at first led to an ever more rationalized interpretation of Christianity and which later in a secular form brought about an abstract philosophical spiritualism. This idealistic conception of the Spirit finally turned into the plain materialism of today.[20]

In view of the critical situation following from this modern misunderstanding of spirit and freedom, we may ask what the idea of spirit originally meant in the passage quoted from St. Paul. Spirit and freedom, to him, were just the opposite of what they came to mean in modern philosophy; for they could not be found in individual sovereignty, but rather in the consciousness 'that we are not sufficient of ourselves to think anything as of ourselves; but that our sufficiency is of God.' Spirit, as understood by St. Paul, is not the same as soul or mind; it is the true manifestation of God. It diffuses itself throughout man's existence; his inmost heart is full of the transcendent God who gives form to his life, who reshapes his body as well as his soul, who henceforth dwells within him as his true essence. By taking part in this creative spirit, man understands everything anew; he can read the script of his own existence, which is 'written not with ink, but with the spirit of the living God, not in tablets of stone, but in fleshy tablets of the heart.' [21] Thus, he becomes transparent to himself and understands himself in his true significance. Regarded in this new light, man himself and all objects reveal an eternal, a spiritual content behind their outward appearance. This is 'the ministration of the spirit' of which St. Paul speaks in this passage. But as soon as man, bereaved of the spirit, seeks sufficiency in himself, 'and thinks everything as of himself,' his own existence as well as that of all things in the world become mere letter, dead and meaningless. Man and world, if separated from the spirit, mean 'ministration of death and condemnation.' Never in the history of religion have the remoteness from God and the nearness to Him, His transcendence and immanence, been felt simultaneously with as much fervour as in Christianity.

In the tension of this contradictory experience all words and concepts took on a new meaning. First of all 'spirit' itself. For the Greeks, *pneuma* was the gift of the Muses or the Gods which inspired the poet and the seer to perceive the world in all its beauty and its truth, as it really is, and as the Gods themselves saw it.[22] In Judaism, spirit is the true essence of God, as it is revealed in His Creation and His Law; but only in Christianity does man find in his own heart the whole profundity of the spirit. Or, as St. Paul says: 'In the Old Testament the veil is still upon their hearts which veil is done away in Christ.' Spirit manifests itself only in spirit, in the very core of man's personal existence, in that which is peculiarly his own. Although the spirit is divine, although it is universal, still it is not what is common to everything, like the world-soul or the all-being in the philosophical systems of the Pantheists: Spirit is not an external presence but becomes man's inward being, the centre of his personality.

It is precisely for this reason that to St. Paul spirit, *pneuma,* does not mean soul, or mind, or reason, as it has been understood by the Greeks and again by modern philosophers from Descartes to Hegel.[23] To St. Paul, spirit is far above soul and even 'Nous.' [24] What for the Greeks and for the modern rationalists belongs to soul or mind in contrast to body, in St. Paul's view still belongs to the flesh. For flesh, to him, is by no means the same as body, or 'matter,' which is a philosophical abstraction created by the Greeks.[25] Flesh means body *and* soul, the whole human being, so far as he thinks himself 'sufficient of himself,' so far as he is mere letter as opposed to living spirit. But if spirit is neither mind, nor soul, where can we grasp it? Nowhere, except in the experience of freedom. For, as St. Paul says: 'Where the spirit of the Lord is, there is liberty.' These are the memorable words which mark the beginning of a new era.[26]

In his religious experience of Spirit, the Christian then finds a new meaning of freedom. For the Greek, it meant the liberation of the soul and the intellect from their bondage to body and senses. The philosopher's independence of all emotions and passions, ataraxia or impassiveness, was considered the highest moral ideal.[27] The same can be claimed of modern thinkers like Descartes, Spinoza, or Kant, not to mention those more recent, all of whom understand the freedom of man as the sovereignty of his thought and the autonomy of his moral will, in other words, of his conscious ego.[28] For St. Paul, on the contrary, true liberty of the spirit signifies man's liberation from the narrowness of his ego: 'The adoption for which we are waiting is the redemption of our body.' [29]

This new concept of liberty implied an entirely new meaning of free will, the like of which had never been envisaged before. Greek philosophy possessed no such idea of will, since reason was considered to be the ultimate criterion of truth. God as well as man had merely the choice between various given possibilities which were dependent upon the unalterable order of the universe, and it was reason that enabled god as well as man, to recognize the best among them.[30] In the Old Testament, however, the idea of a free moral will is indicated for the first time: if God created the world with all its laws, not because this was the best possible world, but because out of His own unfathomable volition He wanted it thus, He must also have the power through His own free will to break these rational laws; to put it differently, He must be able to work miracles. Man, who is created in the image of God, reflects this miraculous power in his free moral will, which considers itself superior to all other forces in the world. In this sense the concept of free will was first understood, at any rate, when a Jewish philosopher, Philo, tried to grasp and to interpret in rational terms the idea of creation as he found it in Scripture.[31]

This idea of free moral will was far surpassed by St. Paul's conception of freedom. For him, to be truly free means to be able to will what one wants to do, that is, to have the freedom of the spirit: 'For to will is present with me, but how to perform that which is good, I find not. For the good that I would I do not: but the evil which I would not, that I do.'[32] These Pauline words serve to express man's experience of the insufficiency of his moral will; they stress the psychological fact that it is precisely the autonomous will which creates the disparity between intention and accomplishment and thwarts the achievement of true morality.[33] Spirit alone can free man from the meshes of this net in which his sovereign volition gets him forever entangled, proving thereby that even the power of conscious will belongs to the sphere of the letter, of the flesh.[34] St. Paul, in his most exalted state of true spiritual freedom, exclaims: 'Wherefore henceforth I know no man after the flesh; yea, though we have known Christ after the flesh, yet, now henceforth know we Him no more; therefore if any man be in Christ, he is a new creature.'[35] Thus man gains an entirely new understanding of himself and of his true essence. In experiencing this spiritual freedom, he discovers within himself a power which liberates him, which takes him beyond the narrow limits of the world and of his conscious ego to which he was formerly restricted.

This absolutely novel and unprecedented Christian conception of spiritual freedom led to another, that of free personality. In Greek philosophy, this idea was unknown; individuality was expressed mainly in physical appearance, and the Greek word for 'body' frequently occurs where we would expect 'person.' Yet, it was not the individual body, but rather its universal 'form,' the living soul, in which the Greeks saw the true nature of man, just as of all other things in the world.[36] Plato, in order to express the essence of a thing, chose the word 'Idea,' 'eidos,' which means 'form.'[37] To the Greek philosopher, only the universal form had part in eternal truth; the subjective ego, like everything else that was shapeless and indefinite, belonged to the realm of the perishable.

Personality in the Christian sense of the word first occurs in the discussions of the Church Fathers about the true nature of God.[38] For it is through Christ that God reveals Himself in His true nature, that is as personality; God as spirit is essentially this. Man seeks a personal relation to the divinity and on it the whole Christian religion rests. By interpreting his conscious ego in terms of his relation to God, the Christian individual becomes a free personality.[39] Modern Man, on the other hand, understands by personality a distinctive individuality expressing itself in actual deeds or in particular characteristics. This is a merely psychological definition of personality, whereas the true idea of it involves much more, namely the responsibility of the conscious ego towards a higher authority.[40] The adequate conception of personality, therefore, comprises two other ideas, conscience and repentance, which were indeed of fundamental moral importance in the New Testament.

True, it is the Greeks who formed the concept 'conscience' (*syneidesis*), which originally meant awareness of something and only later on came to signify awareness of oneself.[41] For the Stoics, it implied that man is witness or judge of his own actions. But any symptom of divided personality, such as repentance or shame, was considered by them as a sign of moral inferiority.[42] To the Christian, on the other hand, the soul is split in two, and it is precisely in this cleavage and duality that he discovers his true self and becomes a free personality. He liberates himself from everything that constituted his former objective existence. Through repentance he becomes aware of his genuine ego; he envisions a new and higher Self, which he must actualize in his life. The penitent, by trying to rid his inmost personality of guilt, strives to overcome his limited psychological ego and his preoccupation with his subjective self. The ego, which in stubborn defiance held to its empirical individuality, now opens up, as it were, to an ideal existence, and in this way a new self is born.[43]

Modern man does not accept such a concept of repentance. He is prone to say: let us not repent, let us rather amend our wrongs.[44] Thus ancient and modern philosophers alike have failed to understand that true repentance does not concern our various actions only, but is aimed at a complete change in our very essence. Repentance means that process through which man is transformed into his true self by renouncing the stubborn resistance of his merely particular and subjective personality.[45] Through conscience and repentance man acquires a new dimension, that of depth—a new awareness of himself and his own freedom.

Yet it is the essence of personality, as conceived by Christianity, that the individual cannot exist by himself but becomes real only in communication with others. Man as a personality is not isolated, like a Greek statue, is not that harmonious and plastic individuality which was the loftiest ideal of Greek ethics.[46] Quite the opposite; he throws his soul open to others, renouncing his aloofness. By thus imparting himself, he regains a richer being.[47] It is this spiritual community with others which in Christian terms is love. This, which also constitutes the true essence of God, is altogether different from what Greek philosophers, and after them many among the moderns, have understood by love. To the Christian, it is not merely *eros*, the passionate desire of the human soul for God, for the absolute Ideal, the love of the lower being for the higher one; it is, on the contrary, the love of the higher existence for the lower, of God for man.[48]

Through this Christian experience man learns what love really means: To love a person sincerely is not, as Plato thought, to love him for some ideal value which he may represent, but rather to love him for himself, his individual personality. To love the man himself is to love him even when he may appear humiliated or entirely devoid of worth. For in personality lies the highest good and the only truth, compared with which all other goods and ideas are inconsequential. For a Christian, love in this sense becomes the ultimate and exclusive moral precept. 'Love and do as you like,' to Augustine, is the key of all true morality.[49]

Still, the Golden Rule, which says 'do unto others as you would have them do unto you,' has generally been considered the supreme law of rational ethics. It was recognized long before Christ and to this day, indeed, we follow it in all our moral reasoning. But considered as a rational rule it is empty and merely formal, because it does not indicate what we should really strive to do.[50] Christian religion, however, maintains that it is love and nothing but love for which man longs from the bottom of his heart, and that it is love, therefore, which, according to the Golden Rule, I must give to others. This is what St. Paul means by the profound words: 'Owe no man any thing, but to love one another: for he that loveth another hath fulfilled the law.' Love is indeed the solution of all moral problems. So long as we merely abide by the rational law as the ultimate criterion of our moral judgment, we can understand neither man nor God.[51]

In the light of the new experience of love, even rational ethics and moral law itself appear as mere letters whose script becomes understandable through the Spirit alone. Spirit is Love. If the rational philosopher of today objects that man, as we know from experience, is not capable of such a noble idea of morality, nor of its realization in practical life, this is exactly what St. Paul himself maintains. For it is the quintessence of his doctrine that man, as long as his thought is centred in himself, is not capable of this love which consists precisely in overcoming his feeling of self-sufficiency.

In his concept of love, just as in his ideas of freedom, will, and personality, St. Paul gives expression not only to a new interpretation of religion, he also establishes a new view of truth: everything that man can grasp through his own independent thought is merely *letter;* it reveals its spirit only if seen in the light of a more sublime presence.

\*     \*     \*

But what is truth? That is the old question of Aristotle as well as of Pilate. We have seen that all theoretical knowledge, being a mode of human existence, can never quite coincide with its object, from which it knows itself to be different. Thus our theoretical concepts can be true only in an analogical sense.[52] Practical knowledge, on the other hand, in so far as its object is another self-consciousness, may correspond to its object; my own will may agree or disagree with the will of another.[53] Still, I can interpret the volition of others only by analogy to myself. Besides, the problem remains whether this other will, from an objective point of view, is true and has an essential content. Religious truth is concerned with an absolute will and implies that the demand made upon my conscience expresses the will of God—that my existence finds its truth and its destiny in the fulfilment of His command.[54] Yet, even in faith, man knows that the forms in which he experiences God's will cannot pertain to Him in a literal, but only in an analogical, sense. Thus, since all our knowledge —whether theoretical, practical, or religious—always represents a relation to an object different from itself, its truth can be only that of an analogy through which this relation itself may be determined as true.

In Greek mathematics, analogy meant a geometrical

proportion expressing an equality of relationships.[55] In a broader philosophical sense, one may characterize analogy as similarity of relations in general, as a relation of relations.[56] Thus a relation between two terms can be defined through an analogy. We call reason that faculty which enables us to recognize the relation between our cognition and its object.[57] The truth of this relation must be determined by a fundamental principle, which Aristotle finds in the law of contradiction.[58] But even the most abstract form of this axiom—the tautology that A is A and not non-A—still presupposes a third factor, namely the truth of this relation of identity, a *tertium comparationis* in relation to which alone two thoughts or objects can be called identical.[59] Thus it is the principle of analogy rather than that of contradiction which represents the ultimate presupposition of all philosophical truth.

The idea of identity, however, confronts us with a difficult logical problem. What is the basis for our calling two things or thoughts identical, since we could not call them so if they were not also two? In the proposition A = A the two A's—seen merely as letters—actually are different; they are supposedly identical only in their spirit, in their meaning with regard to discourse (*logos*).[60] It is this difficulty which led Plato to consider as 'Ideas' the concepts of identity, equality, and similarity, which are the foundation of all our philosophical and mathematical reasoning. These relations can be apprehended only in thought, since they are not evident in any perceptible object.[61] Even our ego, which for us possesses the highest form of unity and identity with itself, proves to be also dissimilar and internally divided. It can be one and the same only in relation to another.[62] Therefore the unity of our soul is but an 'Idea.' The unity of our own personality and the substantiality of our own existence can be grasped only in an analogical sense.

Analogy, then, is the ultimate foundation upon which logic and philosophy must be built. This is an axiom which modern philosophers seem to have forgotten.[63] It has been their naïve belief that in their strictly rational terms they could conceive literal truths. Now, the only truth which can be taken literally is that of mathematics. For this reason, modern philosophers since Descartes have tried to model their thought after the pattern of mathematics and mathematical logic, as though we could deduce our truths from certain ultimate axioms either in a straight line or circularly. Through this procedure, modern philosophy, even that of the Sceptics and Positivists, has taken on a dogmatic character which was foreign to classical Greek philosophy.[64] Plato and Aristotle were careful to distinguish the truth of philosophy from that of mathematics and understood even their ultimate metaphysical principles as mere analogies of absolute being.[65] Philosophy is not science, nor can it ever attain the exactitude of mathematics. The truth of philosophy is superior and at the same time inferior to that of science. It is inferior in so far as it cannot be proved cogently and always retains the character of a human analogy; it is superior in so far as it is aware of its own analogical nature.

The philosopher must acquire knowledge by penetrating to the ultimate limits of his own thought and existence, by recognizing his own philosophizing as a mere simile, as a letter which stands for some deeper truth. In this genuinely philosophical experience everything turns into a symbol, a cipher of the absolute.[66] Even ourselves, even freedom, personality, volition, must be understood as analogies, as forms of human existence in which the ray of absolute truth may be refracted. This does not mean that our philosophical ideas are merely subjective and arbitrary, poetical metaphors. They are true analogies, that is, they express in terms of human existence the truth through which they are themselves determined.[67] It is through reading in this spirit the script of our own existence that we may understand ourselves. The philosopher who has recognized this fact will hardly be tempted again to replace the concepts of religion by his own rational ideas. He knows that even the ultimate philosophical principles through which he is trying to understand the world and himself do not have their real truth in themselves, but are determined by a higher truth which he can neither grasp nor prove, but only presuppose.

For the Greek philosopher, *Nous* is the faculty by which we apprehend the real nature of the universe; as Aristotle says, man cannot think too highly of the greatness and power of his reason and 'must make himself like God in accordance with this highest principle in him.' [68] But for us, for whom God is not of this world, it is not through reason but through faith that we can have access to the Absolute. Before God, our reason becomes mute and it is in silence that He reveals Himself to us as the Presence by which we are determined in our whole existence.[69]

And yet, faith does not allow us to acquiesce in vague feeling and religious imagination. What we feel, we must try to recognize in fact or else we do not really believe in it. There is no twofold truth.[70] Faith must come to terms even with the opposing truths of scientific and practical reason, in which we trust in our everyday existence; it is the function of philosophy to strive toward the solution of this antinomy. Reason, on the other hand, cannot rest content with truths that are unrelated to the motivating belief of our life and must seek for their ultimate ground. Only by thus wrestling with its own limitations does our reason gain a glimpse of the Absolute as the Present which lies in the Future. In this struggle consists the perennial task of philosophy.

LETTER AND SPIRIT                    165

NOTES

1. Plato's metaphorical use of the word 'letter' has a distinct philosophical meaning: To him the invention of the alphabet is a symbolic example of a logical analysis (*diaeresis*). This discovery proved to man that even the infinite variety of speech sounds can be reduced to a finite number of general constituents. Thus the Greek word for 'letter' (στοιχεῖον, Latin *elementum*) gained the philosophical meaning of 'element.' In this sense already Democritus seems to have called his atoms 'letters,' 'elements.' For as the word (Greek *logos*) which represents reality consists of ever-recurring constituent parts, so the whole universe consists of simple substances and can be represented through a corresponding combination of these 'elements.' (Cf. Aristotle, *Metaphysics*, I, 4, p. 985b4; *Gen. et Corr.* I, 2, p. 315b14; Lucretius I, 196, 912, II, 1013; H. Diels, *Elementum*, Leipzig, 1899, p. 16 f.; O. Lagercrantz, *Elementum*, Uppsala, 1911, pp. 11 ff.; and my book, *Plato und die sogenannten Pythagoreer*, 1923, pp. 169 ff.)

In an analogous way Plato compared his primary principles, the 'Ideas,' with the letters of the alphabet: The philosopher by means of a *diaeresis* divides reality into its logical 'elements' and represents its original unity through a reciprocal synthesis. Thus his method of dialectic is modelled after the art of writing and reading. (Cf. Plato, *Philebus*, pp. 17A ff.; *Sophistes*, pp. 253A ff.; *Theaetetus*, pp. 20E ff.; *Politicus*, pp. 278A ff.; *Cratylus*, p. 423E and in Diog. Laert. III, 19; Aristotle, *Metaphysics*, pp. 1053a12 ff., 1014a26; 1041b12 etc.) This is a concept of logical procedure which was revived by Leibniz in his plans for a 'Characteristica Universalis' and which through him is effective even in our time. In a general sense then the word 'letter' can be regarded as a symbol for any universal concept, gained through logical analysis, and it is in this sense that I use the word 'letter': to denote the opposite of original unity, of the 'spirit,' which gives the letter its proper meaning.

2. Second Epistle to the Corinthians 3. 6: 'Who also hath made us able ministers of the new testament; not of the letter, but of the spirit: for the letter killeth, but the spirit giveth life.' Cf. below notes 16 and 33.

3. The Greek philosophers considered the gods of popular religion as merely mythical expressions of those rational principles which they understood as the 'true elements' of the world (cf. notes 17 ff. to ch. II). But the same method of allegoric interpretation has also been applied by modern philosophers in order to justify the

ideas of their religion. According to Kant and to most modern thinkers the true meaning of Christ's teaching is not different from the moral law of reason. Philosophers like Hegel or Whitehead interpret religion in terms of their metaphysics (cf. note 45 to ch. IV, and note 40 to ch. v). But no such 'allegoric' interpretation can do justice to the particularity and profundity of religious thought. Long ago Plato ridiculed such a naïve procedure (*Phaedrus*, 229 ff.).

4. The modern methods of historical hermeneutic have their origin chiefly in the discussions of the Protestants and Catholics about the correct interpretation of the Bible. The Council of Trent (1545-63) occupied itself with these problems. In 1567 appeared the Protestant standard work, the *Clavis Scripturae Sacrae* by M. Flacius, and in 1581 R. F. Bellarmin formulated the Catholic principles of exegesis in a polemical treatise which was intended to refute Flacius. (W. Dilthey, *Werke*, vol. v, 324 ff.; II, 110 ff.; cf. also J. Wach, *Das Verstehen*, 3 vols., Leipzig, 1926 ff.)

5. Nietzsche, *The Genealogy of Morals*, III, 24, Engl. transl., 1910, p. 197, cf. p. 194: 'These solitaries and deniers of today; these fanatics in one thing, in their claim to intellectual integrity; all these pale atheists, anti-Christians, immoralists, Nihilists; these sceptics . . . these supreme idealists of knowledge—in point of fact they believe themselves as far away as possible from the ascetic ideal [of Christianity] . . . And yet they represent it nowadays and perhaps no one else, they themselves are its most spiritual products.'

6. Cf. my paper, *St. Augustine and Greek Thought*, 1942. To be sure, Greek philosophers such as Stoics, Sceptics and Neo-platonists had prepared the ground for Augustine's subjectivism (cf. note 28). The Jewish philosopher Philo had tried to ascertain the meaning of biblical concepts like that of free will. (Cf. H. A. Wolfson, *Harvard Theological Review*, 1942, pp. 131 ff. and note 31.) The principle of voluntaristic metaphysics had been developed by the Christian Neoplatonist Marius Victorinus, by whom Augustine undoubtedly was influenced (cf. E. Benz, *Marius Victorinus*, Stuttgart, 1932). Nevertheless Augustine must be considered the true originator of all these ideas. (Cf. note 30.)

7. Cf. the notes 45 f. to ch. v.

8. Cf. the formulation of Bertrand Russell, *Mysticism and Logic*, New York, 1929, p. 208.

9. Cf. note 47 to ch. v. Kant was fully aware of the danger of a vicious circle in such a theory of freedom. He says: 'It must be freely admitted that there is a sort of circle here from which it seems impossible to escape . . . There was indeed a latent circle involved in our reasoning from freedom to autonomy: viz. we lay down the idea of freedom because of the moral law only that we

might afterwards in turn infer the latter from freedom . . . Conse- · quently we could present it as a *petitio principii.*' (Cf. *Fundamental Principles of the Metaphysics of Morals*, London, 1926, pp. 83 and 87.) Although he tried to evade the vicious circle through subtle distinctions, one may doubt that he succeeded. St. Augustine and St. Thomas, on the other hand, did not have to face this difficulty, for neither of them considered the idea of free will (*liberum arbitrium*) as a merely rational concept. (Cf. below, note 30.)

10. Cf. note 15 to ch. II and Aristotle's expression: 'Nature and God' (*On the Heaven*, I, 4, p. 271a33, where the latter term may be taken as explaining the former: 'Nature that is God.'

11. Cf. H. Miller's interpretation of D. H. Lawrence's thought in *The Wisdom of the Heart*, 1941, pp. 159 ff., and *The Cosmological Eye*, 1939, pp. 65 ff. James Joyce speaks of 'the *perverted transcendentalism* to which Mr. S. Dedalus' (*Div. Scep.*) contentions would appear to prove him pretty badly addicted' (*Ulysses*, p. 397). R. M. Rilke sings of the mysterious presence of 'things':

> O house, O sloping field, O setting sun . . .
> One space spreads through all creatures equally—
> Inner-world space. O, I that want to grow
> The tree I look outside at's growing in me.

[*Later Poems*, transl. by J. B. Leishman, London, 1932, p. 128]

And Proust: 'Les Choses ont autant de vie que les hommes' (*A Propos du Style de Flaubert*). In similar terms Evelyn Underhill (*Mysticism*, London, 1912, p. 360) describes mystic contemplation: 'The object of our contemplation may be almost everything we please: a picture, a statue, a tree . . . you will become aware of a heightened significance and intensified existence in this thing at which you look . . . seen thus, a thistle has celestial qualities. Our great comrades, the trees, the clouds, the rivers initiate us into mighty secrets.' (Cf. the penetrating analysis of this modern attitude in K. Jaspers's *Philosophie*, vol. III, Berlin, 1932, pp. 133 ff.)

12. Dostoevski (*Letters*, transl. by E. L. Maync, London, 1904, p. 4): 'Balzac is great—not the spirit of the age but whole millenniums have worked toward such development and liberation in the soul of man.' (Cf. p. 93 and note 27 to ch. IV; in regard to Kierkegaard, cf. note 26 to ch 1.)

13. Cf. George Sorel's theory of the political mythus in his *Reflections on Violence* (transl. by T. E. Hulme, London, 1925); his thought is inspired by Bergson's philosophy. The influence of Sorel's ideas on Mussolini and his theory of Fascism is well known. Cf. note 17 f. and *Enciclopedia Italiana*, vol. 32, 1936, p. 159.

14. A. N. Whitehead, *Process and Reality* (Cambridge, 1929, e.g. p. 497): 'In this way, the insistent craving is justified—the

insistent craving, that zest for existence be refreshed by the ever-present unfading importance of our immediate actions which perish and yet live for ever more.' Cf. the similar idea in P. Weiss, *Reality*, Princeton, 1938, *passim*, esp. pp. 17 ff.

15. One may take symbolic logic as a further example.

16. 2 Corinthians 3. 5 ff. and 5. 17. St. Augustine wrote an important treatise 'On the Spirit and the Letter.' Cf. note 33. Concerning the expression 'ministers of the new testament' the modern commentators remark that the Greek word translated here as well as in the Septuagint by 'testament' is intended to render the Hebrew for 'covenant.' See also Theodoret's interpretation of our passage in Migne, *Patrologia Graeca*, vol. 82, Paris, 1859, pp. 392 ff.

17. Schelling, 'Lectures on the Philosophy of Art,' 1804 (in *Werke*, part 1, vol. v, Stuttgart, 1859, p. 432). The same spiritualistic interpretation of Christian faith is characteristic of Hegel (cf. note 34 to ch. v), with whom Schelling at that time was still on friendly terms. In his later years Schelling elaborated on this principle in a *'Philosophy of Revelation,'* in which he envisages a historical scheme of three ages: after a long period of polytheism humanity rises to Jewish monotheism and then to Christianity. Within the history of the church he assumes again three periods: the Apostles Peter, Paul, and John represent the age of Catholicism, the age of Protestantism, and the future age of a universal religion of perfected humanity. In the years 1841 and 1844 Schelling expounded this philosophy of history in his lectures at the University of Berlin. A motley crowd from all European countries filled lecture room no. 6, eager to hear from Schelling the new philosophical revelation which was to overthrow Hegel's system. Among the audience were Engels, Kierkegaard, Bakunin and other representatives of the younger generation (cf. Marx-Engels, *Gesamtausgabe*, 1930, pp. XLII ff., 173 ff.). The lectures, however, greatly disappointed the students, and their disappointment contributed to their turning from idealism to a radical realism: Kierkegaard conceived his idea of an existential philosophy and theology; Bakunin became the founder of Russian Anarchism, and Engels turned from the worship of God to the worship of human society. Marx and Engels now found in the every-day world of human relations the truth which they had looked for in Hegel's 'Idea.' Yet, however far Marxism may have deviated from its Schelling-Hegelian origins, even today Bolshevism draws its propagandistic force and its Messianic aspirations from the vision of a future age of freedom which will bring humanity to perfection. (Cf. note 45 to ch. v.) Thus from Schelling's lecture room philosophical ideas issued, which were to have a tremendous effect on the history of mankind.

It was a still smaller room in which sixty years later the instigators of a very different movement gathered: the editorial office of the 'Cahiers de la Quinzaine,' in the Rue de Sorbonne in Paris, where Charles Péguy received his friends every Thursday. Under the influence of Bergson's philosophy these revolutionary socialists, among them Sorel, initiated the revolt against their contemporaries' dogmatic confidence in progress, democracy, and modern science. Péguy became Nationalist, Traditionalist, Christian: 'It was through a persistent heart-searching, not at all through a development or a movement backwards that I found the way back to Christianity.' In defence of his conviction he died on the battlefield, in September 1914. (Cf. Charles Péguy, *Basic Verities,* transl. by Ann and Julian Green, New York, 1943, pp. 33 ff., 40, 170 ff.; and J. Maritain in his introduction to H. Iswolsky's *Light before Dusk,* New York, 1942, pp. 3 ff.) In Sorel's mind, on the other hand, those ideas took shape which later influenced Mussolini in his political action and thought and through him Hitler. (Cf. G. Sorel, *Les Illusions du Progrès,* Paris, 1908; *La Décomposition du Marxism,* Paris, 1908; *Reflexions sur la Violence,* Paris, 1908; *De l'Utilité du Pragmatism,* Paris, 1921). In the present war all these antagonistic ideologies are locked in a violent struggle to determine the future of the human race.

18. Joachim of Floris lived from 1145 to 1202. When Schelling worked out his doctrine of the three ages, which was so similar to that of Joachim, he did not know of this medieval thinker. It was not until 1841, the time of his Berlin lectures, that he encountered Joachim in his reading of Neander's *History of Christian Religion and Church* (vol. v, 1, 1841, pp. 220 ff.; Engl. transl. Boston, 1871, vol. IV, p. 236). He was greatly surprised and delighted to find that this notion of his had been anticipated and developed 'in the writings of a man so significant and so prominent in the history of the church' ('Lectures on the Philosophy of Revelation' in *Werke,* part II, vol. 4, p. 298, note). Owing to the political development of the last decades, the interest in Joachim has steadily increased, and a great number of books on this thinker have been published in various countries: Henry Bett, *Joachim of Flora,* London, 1931; Rufus M. Jones, *The Eternal Gospel,* New York, 1938; E. Buonaiuti, *G. da Fiori,* Rome, 1931; H. Grundmann, *J. von Floris,* Leipzig, 1927; E. Benz, *Ecclesia Spiritualis,* Stuttgart, 1934, etc.

19. In Joachim's prophecy the religious fervour of his age found its most characteristic expression. It was a time when the Christians became aware of the discrepancy between the existing order of things and the teachings of the Gospel and were longing for a reformation of church and state, for a regeneration of the soul of man. Joachim prophesied that the time was near when the

religion of the 'letter' would be replaced by the Eternal Gospel of the 'Spirit' and when the order of force and justice would be supplanted by the order of love. Soon would come the 'Novus Dux,' the Messianic leader, to introduce the new Third Age, the realm of the Spirit, just as Christ had been the 'Dux' (Matthew 2. 6, Vulgate), whose birth brought into the world the second age, that of the Son. Joachim's later contemporary, St. Francis, (1182-1226), was stirred by a similar spirit: the Franciscan Spirituals saw in the life and work of their saint the fulfilment of Joachim's prophecy of the 'new Dux.' It is Joachim's prophecy which gave to the terrific ecclesiastical, political, and social conflicts of the period an eschatological aspect. Dante (Paradiso, XI, 33) sings the praise of St. Francis and St. Dominic as the 'princes' whom providence ordained to save the church, and he introduces St. Bonaventura and St. Thomas as the philosophical representatives of the Franciscan spirit and that of the Dominicans. But beside them 'shines the Calabrian Abbot Joachim' (Paradiso, XII, 140). Thus for the medieval poet even the philosophical thought of his time reflects this spiritual revival. In another famous passage (Purgatorio, XXXIII, 43) Dante enigmatically prophesies the DVX who, sent by God, would save Empire and Church. A century later Cola di Rienzo styled himself 'soldier and knight of the Holy Spirit,' destined to regenerate Rome, and with Rome the whole of Christendom: As the new DVX he compared himself even with Christ (cf. his letter, no. 57, 507 ff., ed. Burdach and Piur, part III, pp. 250 ff., v, pp. 308 f.) and it was the poet Petrarch who encouraged him in his belief in a millennial mission.

Never before or after had Europe envisaged a higher goal of secular history or struggled to achieve its ideal with greater expectations than in this period of the Middle Ages. Modern scholars are entirely justified in tracing the origin of the ideas of 'Reformation' and 'Renaissance' to this epoch. (K. Burdach, Reformation, Renaissance, Humanismus, Berlin, 1926; cf. M. E. Cosenza, F. Petrarca in the Revolution of C. di Rienzo, Chicago, 1913; P. Piur, Cola di Rienzo, Vienna, 1931, pp. 108 ff., 119 ff.; G. A. Greenway, Arnold of Brescia, Cambridge, 1931.) The vision of a new age of the Spirit which would bring about paradise on earth and perfection for humanity remained the inspiring force of Europe throughout its history, even if this idea later became more and more secularized and trivial. In seventeenth-century England, Joachim's original idea of an Eternal Gospel was revived by the sect of the Philadelphians, who were led by the prophetess Jane Lead (1623-1704). Her writings, translated into many languages, made a great impression on the Continent. In Italy since Cola di Rienzo, the Joachimite tradition has always been closely connected with

the political dream of a new Rome, liberated from her tyrants.
Thus the Italy of the Risorgimento was called 'La Terza Italia'
by Carducci in his ode to Mazzini (1872):

> With Gracchus' heart and Dante's thought expand
> Glimmering in heaven the Third Italy
> He sees . . .

(Transl. by E. A. Tribe, London, 1921, p. 10.)

Later Mussolini dubbed himself 'Duce,' adopting the traditional
idea of a Messianic leader. In our day the most consequential literary revival of Joachim's vision is to be found in the works of the
outstanding Russian author Merezhkovski, who lived in exile in
Paris from 1905 to 1941. In his prophecy of a third Empire of the
Spirit which would bring the final union of *Logos* and *Cosmos*,
of Religion and Culture, he strangely blended the Joachimite idea
with Dostoevski's mystic and political vision of Russia's mission.
(Prince Mirskii, *Contemporary Russian Literature*, New York, 1926,
pp. 156 ff.; Williams, *Russia of the Russians*, pp. 204 ff.; H. Bett,
op. cit. p. 179.) In Paris, A. Moeller van den Bruck, a Russo-
German litterateur, was closely connected with Merezhkovski. Together they edited the German translation of Dostoevski (1906-15),
and Merezhkovski contributed the introduction to Dostoevski's important *Political Writings*. Moeller van den Bruck later returned
to Germany and after the last war wrote his *Germany's Third
Empire* (Engl. transl. by E. O. Lorimer, London, 1934), undoubtedly influenced by the philosophical thought of his friend. It is
from the title of this book that Hitler took the term *Drittes Reich*.

20. The rationalistic spiritualism of modern philosophy reached
its climax in the thought of Hegel, who identified Spirit with
philosophical reason and made this 'Spirit' the fundamental principle of his whole system (cf. note 47). Within the Hegelian school,
especially with Feuerbach and Marx, this abstract spiritualism immediately turned into materialism. The crisis is marked by the year
1841, when Feuerbach's *Essence of Christianity* appeared and
Schelling gave his lectures in Berlin. (Cf. note 17; K. Löwith, *Von
Hegel bis Nietzsche*, Zuerich, 1941; Sidney Hook, *From Hegel to
Marx*, London, 1936.) P. Tillich, *The Interpretation of History*,
New York, 1936; the same, 'Existential Philosophy,' in *History of
Ideas*, 1944. Cf. note 42 to ch. IV.

21. 2 Corinthians 3. 3. By the 'tables of stone' the Law of Sinai
is meant (cf. Exodus 24. 12; 31. 18; and Jeremiah 38 [31]. 33): the
Decalogue, although written by the finger of God, is visibly written
by means of *letters*, whereas the epistle of Christ is an inspiration
of the heart (cf. Pascal in note 39 to ch. II). But this does not

mean that a merely subjective feeling is a sufficient criterion of truth. Therefore St. Paul immediately adds: 'Not that we are sufficient of ourselves to think any thing as of ourselves . . .' (Cf. 2 Corinthians 3. 5, quoted above, p. 152.

22. Concerning the Greek religious concept of spirit see I. G. van der Leeuw, *Religion in Essence and Manifestation*, Engl. transl. 1938, p. 304 etc.; the same, *Schoepfung*, 1927; H. Leisegang, *Hagion Pneuma*, Leipzig, 1932, pp. 32 ff., the same, *Der Heilige Geist*, 1919, pp. 132 ff.; R. Reitzenstein, *Hellenist. Mysterien-Religionen*, 3rd ed. 1927, p. 184 and *passim*. Characteristic of the original Greek notion of spirit are passages like that of Hesiod; 'They [the Muses] gave me a staff of lusty olive, . . . and breathed in me a voice divine, that I might celebrate the things that shall be and the things that were aforetime' (*Theogony*, v. 31, transl. by A. W. Mair, Oxford, 1908, p. 32). In regard to the Jewish notion of spirit, see G. F. Moore, *Judaism* (vol. I, 1927, pp. 237 ff.); *Jewish Encyclopedia*, VI, p. 445; and Leisegang's interpretation of Philo in the treatises quoted above.

23. It is characteristic of the Greek philosophers that they replaced the religious notion of *pneuma* by the philosophical concept of *nous* (reason), thus restricting the meaning of *pneuma* to the animating vital spirit, the breath of life. (Concerning Aristotle, cf. W. Jaeger in *Hermes*, 1913, pp. 29 ff., and in regard to the Stoics, E. Zeller, *The Stoics* etc., Engl. transl. London, 1870, pp. 141 ff.) The Jewish and Christian thinkers of late antiquity already show the tendency to interpret the Spirit of Scripture in terms of rational philosophy, and this tendency has increased in modern times. In regard to Hegel's 'Spirit,' cf. notes 47 and 20.

24. Concerning the Hellenistic background of St. Paul's distinction between *pneuma* and *psyche*, see T. Wilson, *St. Paul and Paganism*, Edinburgh, 1927, p. 79; R. Reitzenstein, op. cit. pp. 70 ff., 175 ff., etc.)

25. The philosophical concept of an abstract body seems first to have been formulated by Democritus (or by Leucippus). The definition of an abstract 'soul' in opposition to such a 'body' can hardly be found before Plato or the Pythagoreans (cf. U. von Wilamowitz-Moellendorf, *Glaube der Hellenen*, Berlin, 1931, vol. I, pp. 370-75). The word 'matter' (*hyle*), however, is still used by Plato in its literal sense of 'wood' or 'raw, unwrought material.' It is Aristotle who coined the abstract concept of 'matter,' which is fundamental for his whole philosophy in opposition to that of Plato (cf. *Physics*, Book I, 6 ff., C. Baeumker, *Materie*, 1890, p. 210). Concerning St. Paul's concept of Flesh, cf. W. Schauf, *Sarx*, 1924; H. Lietzmann, *Commentary on the Epistle to the Romans*, 7. 13, and note 29.

26. 2 Corinthians 3. 17: By 'liberty' St. Paul means spiritual freedom as opposed to the limitation of him who 'has still a veil on the heart.' This 'veil is done away in Christ' (2 Corinthians 3. 14). It is this freedom of the Spirit which alone gives the frankness and 'plainness of speech' (*parrhesia*), the possibility of giving expression to one's whole heart (E. Peterson, *Parrhesia*, 1927; H. Schlier, *Theolog. Woerterbuch*, vol. ii, pp. 484 ff.).

27. This is true of all Greek philosophers, of Socrates and Plato (especially in the *Phaedo*) as well as of the Stoics (cf. E. Zeller, *The Stoics*, etc., Engl. transl. pp. 206 ff.; W. H. S. Jones, *Greek Morality*, London, 1906, pp. 26, 59 ff., etc.; A. Bonhoeffer, *Epiktet und das Neue Testament*, Giessen, 1911, pp. 164 ff.; R. Bultmann, *Z. N. T. Wft.*, 1912, p. 97; R. Hirzel, *Themis, Dike*, etc., 1907, pp. 25 ff.).

28. It is the Stoic attitude which has been revived in modern rational ethics, in Descartes and Spinoza, as well as in Kant and more recent philosophers. That modern thought is greatly indebted to the Stoics also in other fields, especially in epistemology, logic, and psychology, has rightly been emphasized by W. Dilthey (*Werke, passim*, e.g. vol. ii, 1929, pp. 107 ff., 268). Stoic philosophy is much more in keeping with the subjective tendency of modern thinkers than is the thought of Plato and Aristotle. Thus Stoic ideas such as 'criterion of knowledge,' 'the assent given by the mind to its perceptions' (i.e. subjective consciousness), 'fantasy,' 'substance' (i.e. material substance), etc. were infiltrated into modern philosophy, transmitted mainly through Cicero, who up to the nineteenth century was widely read by the educated.

29. Romans 8. 23. According to John Chrysostom (*The Homilies on the Romans*, Engl. transl. Oxford, 1861, p. 248) and other Fathers, the redemption of the body means 'full redemption, the change of the body and along with it the change of the whole world.' Through its redemption the body becomes free of all its defects and shall be glorified and elevated to the incorruptible body similar to the glorified body of Christ (cf. Philippians 3. 21; 1 Corinthians 15. 54; 7. 31; 2 Corinthians 5. 2, and the modern commentators, esp. E. Kaesemann, *Leib Christi*, 1933). Thus Christian faith implies an entirely new conception of the body. Augustine attacked the Greek philosophers, Plato as well as the Gnostics, for their belief that every evil, every suffering of the soul, originates in its union with the body and the senses. The human body and the senses cannot be evil, since they were created by God and restored to their original dignity through the union of divinity with humanity in Christ. Through the Christian doctrine of incarnation, the life of the individual, the principle of personality, gained new importance. (Augustine, e.g. *De Civitate Dei*, xiv, 5;

x, 29; *De Natura Boni,* 18; *Retract.* I, 5, 3; Cf. E. Frank, *St. Augustine and Greek Thought,* p. 9.)

30. Aristotle had not yet a concept of the truly free will, but only that of free choice *(prohairesis)* between given possibilities, which presupposes the activity of reason and intellect (cf. *Nic. Eth.,* book III, 2; *Magna Moralia,* book I, 17 ff., and the passage quoted from Galen above, ch. III, p. 60). It was not until the thirteenth century that the Christian philosophers became acquainted with Aristotle's intellectualistic theory of freedom, but they had been familiar with the Christian notions of free will *(liberum arbitrium)* from the beginning. For this concept had been formulated by the Fathers, above all by Augustine, in their interpretation of Scripture. It is characteristic that Thomas Aquinas in his philosophical Ethics restricts himself to Aristotle's theory. Only in the theological parts of his *Summa* does he deal with the problems of free will *(liberum arbitrium)*—that is, in close connection with Grace and Creation, which he discusses in terms of the old Augustinian tradition. This fact makes it quite clear that our idea of free will is a religious, not a rational, concept, that its origin is to be found in Scripture and in the Fathers, esp. in Augustine; cf. M. Wittmann, *Ethik des heiligen Thomas,* Muenchen, 1933, pp. 109 ff., where the origin of the doctrine of free will is traced. (See also J. Auer, *Willensfreiheit bei Thomas und Duns Scotus,* Muenchen, 1938.) Modern philosophers, who since Descartes have tried to prove the existence of free will in a rationalistic way, are therefore bound to fail.

31. H. A. Wolfson, op. cit. pp. 131 ff. (cf. note 6), makes it evident that Philo was the first philosopher who in his interpretation of the Old Testament formulated the concept of free will.

32. Romans 7. 18 ff. St. Paul continues: 'Now if I do that which I will not, it is no more "I" that do it, but sin that dwelleth in me. I find then a law, that when I have a will to do good, evil is present with me.' Cf. St. Augustine's interpretation of this passage in *Opus Imperfectum Contra Julianum* IV, 103. (Concerning the meaning of 'will' in the New Testament, cf. H. Riesenfeld in the *Publications of the Seminar for the New Testament in Uppsala,* 1936.)

33. St. Augustine, *On the Spirit and the Letter,* ch. 4, 6 (transl. by P. Holmes, p. 161), gives the following interpretation of the Pauline passage: 'When he says "the letter killeth but the spirit gives life," this prescribes not to take in the literal sense any figurative phrase which in the proper meaning would only produce nonsense . . . The Apostle's principle, however, is not to be confined to this limited application but it must also—and indeed mostly—be regarded as equivalent to what he says elsewhere in the

plainest words: "I had not known lust, except the law had said, Thou shalt not covet" [Romans 7. 7]; . . . the Apostle, indeed, purposely selected this general precept in which he embraced everything as if this were the voice of the Law. And the Law which prohibits this is a good and praiseworthy law. Still, when the Holy Spirit withholds his help which diffuses love in our hearts, that law, however good in itself, only augments the evil desire by forbidding it. Just like the rush of water which flows incessantly in a particular direction, it becomes more violent when it meets with any impediment; and when it has overcome the stoppage it falls in a greater bulk, and with increased impetuosity hurries forward in its downward course. I know not how it is, but the very object which we covet becomes all the more pleasant and desired by being forbidden.' Cf. Romans 2. 27 ff. and 7. 6: 'But now we are delivered [Vulgate: *soluti;* loosed, *released*] from the law of death wherein we are detained, that we should serve in newness of spirit and not in the oldness of the letter.'

34. Cf. Kierkegaard's realistic analysis of the psychological phenomenon, which he calls the 'Demoniacal' (cf. *Concept of Dread* and *Sickness to Death*). One may think also of Freud's analysis of the compulsions to which according to him the conscious will easily leads: 'All these things combine to bring about an ever increasing indecisiveness, loss of energy and curtailment of freedom; and that although the obsessional neurotic is originally always a person of a very energetic disposition, often highly opinionated, and as a rule intellectually gifted above the average.' (*Introductory Lectures on Psycho-Analysis,* transl. by J. Rivière, London, 1922, p. 220.) Cf. note 26 to ch. 1.

35. 2 Corinthians 5. 17 ff. With reference to this passage St. Augustine (*Homilies on St. John,* 94. 4, transl. H. Browne, Oxford, 1849, p. 887) says: 'This surely our Good Master would intimate, in saying, "for if I depart not, the Comforter will not come unto you: but if I depart, I will send Him unto you" [St. John 16. 7, see above note 34 to ch. v].' Cf. the similar passages Romans 8, 9 and Galatians 2, 20.

36. The Greek word *soma* originally means the living body, even life and personal freedom, and person, especially in legal language. Body as opposite to soul first appears with Plato (e.g. *Gorgias,* p. 493A, *Phaedo,* 91C, where the Pythagorean origin of this concept seems to be suggested; cf. above note 25). For Aristotle 'the soul of animals is the general form and the essence of a body of a certain kind.' But when we come to the individual, Socrates is composed of ultimate individual matter (*Metaph.* VII, 8, pp. 1035b14 ff. and VII, 11, pp. 1037a5 ff.; cf. *On the Soul,* II, 1, p. 412a19). Thus for Aristotle as well as for Plato the individuality

of a person like Socrates derives from the body rather than from the soul. To both philosophers matter is the very *principium individuationis* (cf. Plato, *Philebus*, p. 24C; *Timaeus*, p. 52A; *Phaedo*, p. 105D).

37. The Greek word for form (*eidos*) specifically means the form of a living body. If a body is dead its form is called no longer *eidos* but *schema* (like that of a geometrical figure). Plato himself uses the terms *eidos* or 'Idea' only rarely for what are called his 'Ideas' (viz. the universal essence [*ousia*] of things). Cf. U. von Wilamowitz-Moellendorff, *Plato*, 1918, vol. II, 248; C. M. Gillespie in *Classical Quart.* 1912, p. 179; A. E. Taylor, *Varia Socratica*, Oxford, 1911, p. 178; C. Ritter, *Neue Untersuchungen*, 1910, and note 8 to ch. III.

38. Concerning the origin and the history of our concept of personality, cf. U. von Wilamowitz-Moellendorff, op. cit.; A. Trendelenburg in *Kantstudien*, 1908, p. 1 ff.; S. Schlossmann, *Persona*, Kiliae, 1906; H. Rheinfelder, *Persona*, Halle, 1928; R. Hirzel, in *SB der Bayer. Akad., der Wiss.*, 1914, p. 28; F. Altheim, *Persona*, *Archiv f. Relig. Wft.*, 1929, pp. 35 ff.

39. To St. Augustine the Latin word *persona* still means primarily human person, so that he tries to avoid the term in his discussion of the dogma of the Trinity (Sermon 232, ed. by Migne, vol. 39, p. 2173). Boethius is the first to give a philosophical definition of *persona*: 'Persona is the indivisible [individual] substance of a rational nature.' This definition was generally accepted by the medieval philosophers. (Cf. St. Thomas, *Summa Theologica*, part I, qu. 39, art. 1.) In modern philosophy the concept of personality again has been confined to man. In English the word personality, as popularly used, means distinction or excellence of individual and social traits. Kant defines personality as the power which 'elevates man above himself and above the mechanism of nature.' According to him it is through his personality that 'man is an end in himself and maintains humanity in its proper dignity in his own person' (*Critique of Practical Reason*, p. 180 ff.).

40. John Laird (*Problems of the Self*, London, 1917, p. 82): 'Personality, in the current acceptation, implies a certain degree of intellectual and moral development. A person is responsible and cannot be responsible without the power of making deliberate and reflective choice. Personality, in short, is a legal and ethical notion which applies only to beings of a complex and developed type of psychical life.' For a psychological interpretation of personality cf. e.g. G. W. Allport, *Personality*, New York, 1937.

41. Concerning the concept of Conscience in Greek philosophy and in the New Testament see: P. Ewald, *De Vocis 'syneideseos' Vi*, Lipsiae, 1883; F. Zucker, *Syneidesis-Conscientia*, Jena, 1928; B. Snell

in *Gnomon*, 1930, p. 21; H. Osborne, *Classical Review*, 1931, p. 8, and the literature quoted in W. Bauer's *Dictionary, s.v.*

42. Concerning the Greek attitude towards repentance and shame, see Aristotle: 'The wicked are always full of repentance' (*Nic. Eth.* IX, 4, p. 1166b24); 'The virtuous man does not feel shame' (ibid. IV, 9, p. 1128b22); the Stoic Chrysippus: 'The sensible man does not repent or regret' (*Fragment* 548, Arn.); Epictetus: 'He [the philosopher] must not reproach himself, not struggle with himself, nor repent' (*Dissert.* II, 22, 35; *Enchir.* 34) etc. See A. H. Dirksen, *Metanoia*, Washington, 1932; E. F. Thompson in *Historical and Lingual Studies relative to the New Testament*, vol. I, Chicago, 1908; A. Bonhoeffer, *Epiktet und das Neue Testament*, Giessen, 1911, pp. 107, 225 ff.; E. Norden, *Agnostos Theos*, Leipzig, 1913, p. 134 f.

43. See Kierkegaard's Analysis of the 'Demoniacal,' especially in his *Concept of Dread*, ch. 3. Cf. notes 25 and 42 to ch. v.

44. E.g. Spinoza, *Ethics*, IV, 54, or Descartes, *The Passions of the Soul*, III, art. 191. Both philosophers are only reproducing formulations of Aristotle and the Stoics (notes 28, 42; cf. H. A. Wolfson, *Spinoza*, Cambridge, Mass., 1934, vol. II, pp. 254 ff.). The same is true of Nietzsche. Cf. e.g. *Human, All-too-Human*, II (The Wanderer and His Shadow) Engl. transl. Edinburgh, 1911, no. 323: 'Never allow repentance free play but say at once to yourself: "That would be adding a second piece of folly to the first." '

45. Cf. Max Scheler's analysis of repentance and rebirth in *Vom Ewigen im Menschen*, Leipzig, 1923, vol. I, pp. 5 ff.

46. It is Aristotle who compares the *ethos* which man attempts to achieve in his life with a statue carved out in stone by a sculptor. A similar idea is expressed in Plato's *Philebus*. Cf. also W. Jaeger, *Paideia*, vol. II, New York, 1943, p. 277, who refers to *Republic*, p. 500E.

47. Cf. Hegel, *Philosophy of Religion* (vol. III, p. 24): 'Morality, love, just mean the giving up of particularity or of the particular personality and its extension to universality, and so, too, is it with the family and friendship . . . In friendship and love I give up my abstract personality and in this way win it back as concrete personality. It is just that winning back of personality by the act of absorption, by the being absorbed into the other which constitutes the true nature of personality . . . If [abstract] personality is not cancelled, then we have evil, for personality which does not yield itself up to the absolute Idea is evil.' One cannot understand Hegel's philosophy, and especially his Dialectic without being aware of the fact that the concept of personality, as defined in this passage, is the ultimate category even of his Logic. So he says in *Science of Logic* (vol. II, p. 483): 'The highest and acutest point

is simple personality, which by virtue alone of the absolute Dialectic which is its nature, equally holds and comprehends everything within itself, because it perfectly liberates itself.' This principle is what he calls 'The Absolute Idea of Spirit.' Cf. note 20. The Hegelian concept of personality remains fundamental for Kierkegaard's interpretation of human existence and through him to contemporary existential philosophers such as Jaspers.

48. Cf. A. Nygren, *Agape and Eros; A Study of the Christian Ideas of Love*, London, 1937 ff.; M. Scheler, Vom Umsturz der Werte, 1919, vol. I, pp. 107 ff.; D. Kenmore, *The Philosophy of Love*, London, 1942, pp. 136 ff.; R. Niebuhr, *An Interpretation of Christian Ethics*, New York, 1935.

49. St. Augustine, *In Epist. Joannis ad Parthos*, Tr. VII, 8: 'Love and do what thou wilt . . . let the root of love be within, of this root can nothing spring what is not good' (transl. by E. Przywara and C. C. Martindale, New York, 1936, p. 341); *Enarr. in Psalms 32*, Sermon 1, 6: 'He who does not love is frigid, is stiff.' Cf. J. Mausbach, *Ethik d. hlg. Augustinus*, 1909, vol. I, pp. 178 ff.

50. Concerning the rational interpretation of the Golden Rule, cf. P. Weiss's article in *Journal of Philosophy*, 1941, p. 421. The precept, at least in its negative form, is to be found in Judaism (Tobias 4. 16; cf. *Jewish Encyclopedia*, VI, 21 ff.), in Greek philosophy (Aristotle, *Nic. Eth.* IX, 8, p. 1168b ff., and in *Diogenes Laërtius*, V, 21; Epictetus, ed. Schenkl, p. 471), in Chinese literature, in Buddhism, etc.

51. St. Paul, Romans 13. 8. Then he continues: 'For this, Thou shalt not commit adultery, Thou shalt not kill . . . Thou shalt not covet, and if there be any other commandment it is comprehended in this saying, namely, Thou shalt love thy neighbour as thyself. Love worketh no ill to his neighbour, therefore love is the fulfilling of the law.' Cf. John Chrysostom on this passage (Eng. transl. Oxford, 1841, p. 400): 'He does not seek love merely, but intense love, for he does not say merely love thy neighbour, but, as thyself. Hence, also Christ said that "the Law and the Prophets hang upon it" [Matthew 22.40].'

52. See ch. IV, p. 44 and note 22 to ch. IV on Aristotle.

53. Cf. Hegel's analysis of this epistemological process in his *Phenomenology of Mind* under the heading 'Self-Consciousness' (Eng. transl., pp. 215-67).

54. This formulation is by no means intended to be a conclusive definition of religious knowledge. Religion implies awareness of God's awe-inspiring presence as well as experience of His will in moral conscience. The first of these two aspects is usually emphasized by those philosophers who are interested in the psychological and irrational elements of religion (cf. e.g. R. Otto, *The Idea of*

*the Holy*, London, 1928), whereas a rationalistic philosopher like Kant defines religion as 'recognition of all moral duties as divine commands.' But no definition whatever can express the whole complexity of what men mean by the word religion.

55. The mathematical definition of geometrical 'analogy' is to be found in Euclid's *Elements* (Book v, Defin. 6, transl. and interpreted by T. L. Heath, Cambridge, 1908, vol. ii, pp. 112 ff.). Cf. also Plato (*Timaeus*, pp. 31C ff.; *Republic*, 509D, 534A; *Gorgias*, 508A f.), and Aristotle (*Nic. Eth.* v, 6, pp. 1131a31 ff.; ii, 5, p. 1106a36; *Physics*, iv, 8, p. 215b29). Both philosophers indicate that they follow an old 'Pythagorean' tradition.

56. The difference between the mathematical and philosophical concept of analogy is defined by Kant in the following traditional terms: 'In philosophy analogies signify something very different from what they represent in mathematics. In the latter they are formulas which express the equality of two quantitative relations . . . But in philosophy the analogy is not the analogy of two *quantitative* but of two *qualitative* relations.' In this philosophical sense the term analogy had been coined by Plato (*Republic*, vi, p. 509), and Aristotle followed Plato in this usage (cf. note 63). The philosophical meaning of analogy, however, must be distinguished from what modern logicians call reasoning by 'analogy' and what Aristotle calls not analogy but 'example' (*paradigm*): 'We have an example when the major term is proved to belong to the middle by means of a term which resembles the third' (*Anal. Priora*, ii, 24, p. 68b38; cf. *Topics*, viii, 1, pp. 156b10 ff. etc.). When modern philosophers speak of 'analogy' they generally do so in a logical, subjective sense. Cf. e.g. Hume: 'All our reasonings concerning matter of fact are founded on a species of *Analogy*, which leads us to expect from any cause the same events which we have observed to result from similar causes' (*An Inquiry concerning Human Understanding*, #9). Here, however, we have in mind not a logical, but an existential analogy, not any relation within logic but the relation of logic itself to reality and existence. And to designate this relation no term seems more appropriate than the old Greek word 'Analogia,' i.e. a relation of a relation.

57. In this connection it may be of interest to recall that Plato already defined knowledge as duality: 'Knowledge is "Two" and comparable with a line; for knowledge [being one point] goes to another point, different from it in one respect only.' (Fragment from his 'Lectures on Philosophy,' quoted by Aristotle, *On the Soul*, i, 2, p. 404b18).

58. See Aristotle's classical demonstration of the law of contradiction in *Metaphysics*, iv, 3 f. The logical formulation of this principle is the following: 'It is impossible to affirm and deny truly

at the same time' (*Metaphysics*, IV, 6, p. 1011b20; cf. 1008a36, *Anal. Post.* p. 77a10, etc.). From this formulation the ontological formulation is to be distinguished: 'A thing cannot at the same time be and not be' (*Metaph.* III, 2, p. 996b29; *Anal. Priora*, II, 2, p. 53b15, etc.). Both formulas are evidently based upon Aristotle's concept of existential truth: ' "Being" is being combined and one and "not being" is being not combined but more than one' (*Metaph.* IX, 10, p. 1051b12; cf. H. Maier, *Die Syllogistik des Aristoteles*, 1896 ff., vol. I, p. 41). According to Aristotle, the One-ness of 'Being' is, however, the unity of analogy, not that of a substance or that of another categorial existence (cf. *Metaph.* IV, 2, 1003a34 ff.).

59. That any knowledge of an object presupposes a third principle had been emphasized by Plato (cf. *Republic*, VI, p. 507C ff.). Starting from this insight, he developed his doctrine of analogy, which in the last analysis is not as different from that of Aristotle as many students think. Also according to Plato, the ultimate principle, that absolute One-ness of the 'Agathon,' can be grasped in the realm of existence only in terms of an analogy (*Republic*, VI, 509B ff.; note 47 to ch. IV).

60. Aristotle tries to prove the law of contradiction in a negative way, namely by refuting the opposite position. His proof thus is 'elenctic' and valid only in regard to 'discourse': 'I say that proof by refutation differs from simple proof in that he who attempts to prove might seem to beg the fundamental question . . . The starting point for all such discussion is not the claim that he [our opponent] should state that something is or is not so . . . but that he should *say* something significant both for himself and for another . . . for otherwise there is no discourse [*logos*] . . .' (*Metaph.*, III, 6, p. 1006a15). Cf. E. Kapp, *Greek Foundations of Traditional Logic*, New York, 1942.

61. For Plato the ultimate principle is the 'Agathon,' which is 'beyond "Being" and "Thinking" ' (*Republic*, p. 509A). What are called his 'Ideas' are specific forms of being; as examples of his 'Ideas' he generally mentions 'Identity,' 'Difference,' 'Equality,' 'Inequality,' 'Similarity,' 'Dissimilarity,' and other similar relations. Cf. *Parmenides*, 129 ff.; *Sophistes*, 254 ff.; *Theaetetus*, 185A ff.; *Timaeus*, 37A ff.; etc.

62. Cf. Hume's classical statement in his *Treatise of Human Nature*, p. 534: 'When I enter most intimately into what I call *myself* I always stumble on some particular perception or other . . . I never can catch *myself* at any time and never can observe anything but the perception. Thus we are indeed nothing but a bundle or collection of different perceptions which succeed each other . . . and are in a perpetual flux and movement.' In quite similar though more objective terms Plato characterizes the existence of the soul

as a perpetual flux, movement, and change: e.g. *Symposium*, pp. 207D ff.; *Phaedrus*, 245C. But in addition to this he says in the *Theaetetus* (p. 184D): 'It would be strange if there were a number of separate senses and sense perceptions put in us as in wooden horses of Troy. It would be strange indeed if all these sense-perceptions did not tend towards a unity, towards one entity ['*idea*'] of some kind—whether this entity be called "soul" or something else.' Analogously Kant defines the unity of our soul as a 'mere Idea,' as an ideal point (*focus imaginarius*) at which all the soul's functions seem to converge but which cannot be grasped as a definite object. Cf. *Critique of Pure Reason:* 'The Paralogisms' and p. 672 (2nd ed.).

63. The fundamental importance which the principle of analogy had for Aristotle has never been questioned. (Cf. *Metaph.* IV, 2, p. 1003a33; III, 3, p. 998b23; VIII, 2, p. 1043a5; IX, 6, pp. 1048a36; *Eth. Nic.* I, 4 pp. 1096a11 ff.; for other passages, see Bonitz, *Index Aristotelicus*, pp. 47b ff.) The fact is often ignored, however, that Plato had already recognized this principle (cf. notes 59 and 56). Aristotle's 'Analogy of Being' was carefully interpreted by St. Thomas and other medieval philosophers. Thomas Cajetanus' treatise on this subject (*De Nominum Analogia*, ed. N. Zammit, O.P., Rome, 1934) is still worth reading. In modern philosophy the problem has been more and more neglected. Descartes no longer understands the full meaning of this concept and can make nothing of it (cf. *Principles*, I, no. 51). With the exception of Kant later philosophers seem to have ignored the problem altogether (cf. note 56). In the past decades, however, a new interest in the principle of analogy has arisen. (Cf. Ramirez, *De Analogia*, Madrid, 1922; G. B. Phelan, *Analogy and St. Thomas*, Milwaukee, 1943. Cf. the discussion of this problem by R. Garrigou-Lagrange, *God*, London, 1936, vol. I, pp. 213 ff., II, p. 217 ff.; and especially M. Heidegger, *Sein und Zeit*, 1927, p. 93.

64. One must not think only of those who philosophized 'more geometrico.' Even philosophers like Kant and Hegel, who recognized that the method of mathematics cannot be applied to philosophical problems devised systems that are reminiscent of the architectonic form of Euclid's Elements.

65. Aristotle (*Physics*, II, 2, p. 193b23) makes a sharp distinction between the method of philosophy and that of mathematics. Cf. Posidonius' interpretation of this doctrine in Simplicius ad loc. (*In Phys.* p. 292), and Geminus, *Elementa Astronomiae* p. 283 f. (Manit.) The classical passage, however, is Plato's *Republic*, pp. 509 ff.

66. This is at least Plato's conviction. When modern philosophers, in order to describe their own efforts, use the word 'philos-

ophy,' which Plato coined, they implicitly acknowledge this conception of philosophy.

67. This is what distinguishes objective analogy from subjective metaphor or a mere 'cipher.' For a different view of metaphysics, cf. K. Jaspers's 'Reading of the Cipher-Writing' in his *Philosophie*, vol. III, Berlin, 1932, pp. 128 ff.

68. Cf. Plato, *Theaetetus*, pp. 176A ff.; Republic, VI, p. 509A; *Timaeus*, 90A ff.; Aristotle, *Eth. Nic.* x, 7, p. 1177b30; *Metaphysics*, I, 2, pp. 983a2 ff. Concerning Aristotle's doctrine of the 'immediate knowledge' cf. E. Zeller, *Aristotle*, Engl. transl. London, 1897, pp. 247 ff.

69. Silence as a necessary preparation for philosophy was first emphasized by the Pythagoreans. (Cf. Hegel's interpretation of this Pythagorean doctrine in his *History of Philosophy*, Engl. transl. vol. I, p. 202.) For Plato and Plotinus, the *silentium mysticum* is the philosopher's genuine expression of the ineffable. (Cf. Plato, *Seventh Epistle*, p. 341C; cf. also the following pages where the epistemological justification of this attitude is given, and *Symposium*, p. 211; cf. p. 174D, 175B, 220B, etc.)

70. Concerning the 'double-truth theory,' cf. T. Verner-Moore in *The Catholic University Bulletin*, 1911, pp. 20 ff.; T. Heitz, *Essai historique sur les rapports entre la Philosophie et la Foi*, Paris, 1909; M. Baumgartner, *Thomist. Wahrheitsbegriff*, 1913, pp. 241 ff.; H. A. Wolfson, 'The Double Faith Theory' in the *Jewish Quarterly Review*, 1942, pp. 213 ff., etc.

# INDEX

Absolute, the, 53 n.45, 58, 98f., 143 n.34, 161, 163f.
 dialectic of, 99
 unknown, 30, 53 n.43
Academy, 82 n.41, 111 n.32
Acton, Lord, 20 n.12, 45 n.3, 138 n.16, 140 n.26, 144 n.41, 146 n.44
Adaptation, 91; see also Adjustment
Adevism, 48 n.19
Adjustment, 4, 19 n.5, 109 n.23
Aeon, 60, 76 n.14
Agape, 7, 159, 178 n.48
Agathon, 50 n.26, 53 n.45, 58, 105 n.16, 114 n.47, 180 nn.59, 61; see also Plato, Idea of Good
Aims of man, 91, 109 n.23, 117
Alexander, F., 146 n.46
Alexander, S., 65f., 74 n.5, 79 n.29, 81 n.38, 104 n.13, 133 n.1
Alexander the Great, 123
Analogy, 44, 54 n.46, 63ff., 91, 107 n.22, 114 n.47, 161-4, 179 n.55f., 181 n.63, 182 n.67
Analysis, logical, 165 n.1
Anaxagoras, 47 n.9, 48 n.19
Anaximander, 73 n.1
Anselm of Canterbury, 34, 43f., 50 nn.25-6, 51 nn.27-31; see also Ontology
Anthropomorphism, 3, 18 n.2, 55 in Aristotle, 107 n.22
 religion, 98f., 101 n.2
Anti-Christ, 19 n.9, 149, 166 n.5

Antinomy, in Reason, 8, 14f., 21 n.18, 38, 53 n.45, 99, 113 n.44; see also Contradictoriness, Dialectic
Apologists, 49 n.21; modern, 42; see also Church Fathers
Apostles, 127, 129, 168 n.17; see also Paul, Peter (SS.)
Appearance, 87; see also Existence
Appian, 140 n.24
Apuleius, 143 n.38
Aquinas, St. Thomas, 169 n.19
 relation to
  Aristotle, 174 n.30
  Augustine (St.), 50 n.24, 53 n.45
  Boethius, 50 n.24, 77 n.16, 176 n.39
  Dionysius Areopagite, 53 n.45, 101 n.2
 views on
  analogy, 181 n.63
  being, 53 n.45
  choice, doubt, assent of the intellect, 53 nn.44f.
  cosmological argument and ontological argument, 46 n.7, 50 n.24, 52 n.34
  creation, 76 n.13
  essence and existence of God, 45 n.5, 50 n.24, 52 n.34, 53 n.45, 76 n.14
  eternity, 76 n.14, 77 nn.16f.
  faith, 45 n.5, 53 n.44
  free will, liberum arbitrium, 166 n.9, 174 n.30
  imagination, 102 n.4
  metaphor, 101 n.2

183